C00 4502636X

D0505961

ES

# SPORTING SCOTS

# John K. V. Eunson

# SPORTING SCOTS

## How Scotland Brought Sport to the World

**(and the World Wouldn't Let Us Win!)**

BLACK & WHITE PUBLISHING

First published 2012
by Black & White Publishing Ltd
29 Ocean Drive, Edinburgh EH6 6JL

1 3 5 7 9 10 8 6 4 2    12 13 14 15

ISBN: 978 1 84502 414 7

A CIP catalogue record for this book is available from the British Library.

Typeset by Ellipsis Digital Ltd, Glasgow
Printed and bound by ScandBook AB, Sweden

# Contents

# Acknowledgements

I would like to thank Black & White Publishing for all their support and encouragement in bringing *Sporting Scots* from a haphazard idea to the hopefully much less haphazard finished article. And in particular I would like to thank Janne Moller and especially Kristen Susienka, for their input, their patience and above all their unfailingly positive good cheer.

And I would also like to take this opportunity to thank all the supporters of Dundee United, Manchester United, the West Indies cricket team, Whalsay FC, Hibernian FC, Balmain Tigers, Leeds United, Manchester City, Chelsea, Tottenham Hotspur, Rayo Vallecano, Sporting Gijon, FC Barcelona, Dynamo Thule and anybody else that I know who have arguably better things to talk about on a Wednesday evening.

For rain or sleet, disappointment or disaster, dodgy calf or basic inability to pass the ball in a straight line, there is always the eternal hope that next week might possibly be slightly better. This one's for you. Salud!

# Introduction

The 1871–72 season was a highly successful and satisfactory campaign for the British Empire. Under the expansionist managerial tenure of Prime Minister Benjamin Disraeli, and with Queen Victoria as the unsmiling and formidable Chairman of the Board, Britain was remorselessly reinforcing her position at the top of the international table and was well on the way to her zenith of ruling one-quarter of the world's land mass and one-quarter of the world's population by the end of the nineteenth century. Furthermore, the 1871–72 season had also seen the humiliating defeat of Britain's perennial rival, France, by the up-and-coming Prussians, and across the Atlantic Britain's former protégé and upstart pretenders to their crown, the USA, were still in the slow process of rebuilding after the painful divisions of the American Civil War.

Yes, it was a good time to be a Brit, and the North British region of Scotland was more than happy to make the most of the opportunities that were presented and take advantage of the power, prosperity and privilege that were on offer from the Empire where the sun never sets, even if, like their not-amused monarch residing amongst them in Balmoral, they were far too Scottish to ever express any enjoyment whilst doing so. Over two million Scots left their homeland in the eighteenth and nineteenth centuries to make new lives in North America, South and Central America, the Indian sub-continent, the Far East, Africa, Australia, New Zealand and all points in between. And this does not even take into account all the unrecorded numbers of Scots who crossed the border for the foreign climes of England and presumably a hardy few who got lost and ended up in Wales.

In 1871–72 the Prime Minister of Canada was John A.

MacDonald from Glasgow; the Prime Minister of Victoria, Australia, was fellow Glaswegian James McCulloch; and the Prime Minister of New Zealand was Edward Stafford from Edinburgh. The Scottish mercantile company of Jardine Matheson was at the forefront of the rise of the colony of Hong Kong and joining all parts of the Empire and the globe together were the great sailing lines of Cunard, P & O, Allan, Castle and the British–Indian Steam Navigation Company, all of which were run by Scots.

And for those that remained, by 1871 Glasgow, Clydeside and the West of Scotland had capitalised on the invention a century before of Greenock-born James Watt and his new-improved steam engine. The steam engine would kick-start the whole Industrial Revolution and with subsequent decades of innovations by Scottish engineers and scientists, the West of Scotland had become the powerhouse of the Empire and at the heart of British coal, steel and heavy industry, with Clydeside building more locomotives than anywhere else in Europe, and at one point manufacturing up to 20 per cent of all the ships in the world. Thousands flooded to the industrial Lowlands from the countryside, the Highlands and Islands, and from Ireland. As a result, the population of Glasgow increased tenfold over the century before finally topping one million in 1912, proudly boasting their Imperial and Unionist credentials as the self-proclaimed 'Second City of the Empire'.

Scotland was being transformed by the speed of change. The Church of Scotland that had dominated the life and work of the nation for 300 years was beginning its slow but inexorable decline and the notion of a Scottish national identity was fragile and contradictory at best. In 1871–72 there was no Scottish Parliament and not even a Scottish Secretary of State in the government. Talk of Home Rule was still a couple of decades away; the Scottish National Party would not be founded for another sixty-three years and it would be sixty-five years before

Oor Wullie was first introduced to his bucket. Yes, life before Oor Wullie was a very different time.

And amidst all this social and economic upheaval for the Scots at home and the Scots abroad, from all backgrounds and all classes making their way in their new homes and circumstances, the idea of sport as an outlet for those precious few hours and days when you were not in the factory, in the office or down the pit became increasingly prevalent. Of course, sport had been around for centuries; golf, that most Scottish of games, dates back to the fifteenth century; and the first Open Championship had been held in Prestwick in 1860; and early and often rudimentary forms of boxing, athletics, horse racing, football, shinty, curling, cricket, bowls and numerous other games and pastimes have been around, some say, since Menzies Campbell was a lad. But it was the second half of the nineteenth century with its Victorian obsession for rules and regulations, combined with the masses in need of something to keep them out of the pub and/or the Kirk on their day off that saw the rise of organised sport as we know it, both for participants and spectators.

And so it came to pass that in 1871–72, through accident rather than design and several twists of fate, Partick in Glasgow and Stockbridge in Edinburgh were the unknowing witnesses to two of the most historic and important occasions in sporting history when they became the venues of the first internationals in the world in the sports of association football and rugby, respectively. It was the beginning of international sport as we know it, and the world would never be the same again.

And it was Scotland, that non-country country that had exported people and ideas and the fruits of their labour even before the Act of Union, that would now export sport to the rest of the world in the same way as trains and ships, whisky and tartan.

For the next 140 years Scottish sportsmen and sportswomen

would find fame and fortune around the globe, and in the process would magnanimously inspire, coach and train the world to take sport to new levels of excellence and achievement. Eventually, the world would catch up and surpass their Scottish sporting teachers, but Scotland was not bitter, although perhaps a little twisted, as sport had entered the Scottish DNA and had become an integral part of a new Scottish national identity that, for good or for ill (and there have been many of both over the years), represents itself on the football and rugby pitch, on the golf course and the racetrack.

And no matter what trials and tribulations befall Scotland and its sportsmen and sportswomen, what new Hell is discovered of turning expectant anticipation into crushing disappointment or the alternative fleeting but ultimately futile exhilaration of yet another against-the-odds glorious failure, Scots will always have the bittersweet satisfaction that while we may no longer, and may never again, be the greatest sporting nation in the world, no one can doubt our claim to be one of the first, if not the first, sporting nations in the world. And even more importantly, they can take away our oil, they can take away our financial institutions, they can even take away our freedom, but they can never, ever take away our national right to get knocked out in World Cup qualifying rounds every four years.

# 1
## *The Americans*

Bobby Thomson

There are tens of millions of people residing in the continents of America who claim, or for that matter deny, an ancestral link to Scotland, and despite the exact number remaining statistically imprecise, we can safely say that the final figure will be several times greater than the population of the country from which they originated. For two centuries and more, Scots sailed westwards in their tens of thousands, year after year and decade after decade, in search of a new life, new opportunities and a new world, from the Arctic tundra of the Canadian north to the slave plantations of the Caribbean, down to the mines and cattle stations of Patagonia in the south. Many of these Scots left through economic necessity, as an escape route from the Highland Clearances and the social deprivation of the industrialised Lowlands, but many also departed through choice for fame and fortune and a more temperate climate – even if those who were decamped into a Canadian winter discovered that they had been somewhat misinformed.

Scots would play a prominent role in the history of the Americas. The American War of Independence, the foundation of a Federal Canada, the westwards push to the Pacific, the independence movements in South America – all featured Scots in positions of power and influence, not forgetting industrialist Andrew Carnegie, the world's richest man, and inventor and entrepreneur Alexander Graham Bell, the inventor of the telephone, who hailed from Dunfermline and Edinburgh, respectively. And alongside the plethora of Scottish politicians, businessmen, soldiers, inventors, writers, doctors, clerks, labourers, fathers, mothers and children who made up the Scottish Diaspora from Vancouver to Valparaiso, there were Scottish sportsmen and sports fans who were not going to allow a few thousand miles, a language barrier or two and a different set of rules and sensibilities deflect them from pursuing their sporting passion. Some, like the Scottish football pioneers of South America, would turn a British pastime into a national obsession, while other Scots in Canada and the USA would embrace the games the locals played and in the process become revered and iconic national figures, and in one case the purveyor of perhaps the most legendary sporting occasion in American sporting history, but all the while remaining little known in the land of their birth.

For the first golden rule of Sporting Scots, as with all Scots who left the croft and the tenement for a better life overseas, was that while in principle the Scots that remained behind were proud of the achievements of their kith and kin abroad, in truth domestic life, and sport, would always take precedence, and these great Scottish sporting pioneers were mostly forgotten by the time they reached the mid-Atlantic.

## *Flying Down to Belo Horizonte*

If there is one running scar on the sporting psyche of Scottish sport it is the football World Cup. Granted Scotland has qualified for the World Cup Finals a not-unrespectable eight times to date, remained undefeated in the 1974 Finals held in West Germany, and four years later Archie Gemmill from Paisley managed to weave his way through the entire Dutch defence for one of the most famous goals in Scottish sporting history, but otherwise the World Cup has been, as far as Scotland is concerned, a litany of dashed hopes, incompetence, bad luck and coruscating misery. Disaster for Scotland and a lament with no end that has been covered by others in forensic detail and requires little repetition here other than to reiterate the painful facts that Scotland, the country that, as we will discover, was at one point the greatest football nation in the world and brought the game to many parts of the globe, have never managed to get past the first round of the World Cup Finals and have not won a single game in the World Cup Finals since 1990. But fear not, we are here to celebrate and understand Scottish sport and even in the graveyard of the World Cup Finals there are still stories to be told of Scottish glory and success that are honoured and revered through the decades – reflected glory unquestionably, but glory all the same.

The 1950 World Cup Finals were held in Brazil. It was the fourth World Cup Finals and for the first time Scotland as well as England had deigned to play with Johnny Foreigner after having refused to have anything to do with the first three World Cups between 1930–38. The stage would be set for the two countries that had invented the game to take on the best the planet had to offer and no doubt give them a jolly good thrashing and a magnanimous FIFA-allocated two Finals places for the top two of the 1950 Home Nations Championships between England, Scotland, Wales and Northern Ireland. By the time of the last game between Scotland and England at Hampden, Scotland had already done enough to know whatever happened they would be in the top two. However, mere qualification would not be sufficient for those former masters of the universe. After a 1–0 reverse to the auld enemy, the Scottish FA decided if they weren't going as British champions they weren't going at all, and in a giant sulk took their ball away with them, leaving the unfortunate Scottish players to summer in Largs and Blackpool rather than Rio. Less Copacabana, more Co-ops with no bananas – we were still in the era of rationing, after all.

Oblivious to all this self-inflicted Scottish angst, the English set out for South America to make their World Cup debut. The team included such greats as Stanley Matthews, Tom Finney, Billy Wright and a certain future England manager by the name of Alf Ramsey. England comfortably won their first group game against Chile 2–0, and with their next game against the rank outsiders the United States, qualification to the next stage seemed a formality.

The game was played in the city of Belo Horizonte – Portuguese for 'beautiful horizon' – and the last thing that the English were expecting were troublesome Scots spoiling the view. However, the head coach of the USA was a Bill Jeffrey from Edinburgh, who had immigrated to America as a young man and had become coach of the Pennsylvania State University soccer team; and their captain was Ed McIlvenny, a twenty-five-year-old from Greenock who had immigrated the year before and played his football in Philadelphia. Technically, McIlvenny should not have been allowed to play for the USA, as he had not been there long enough to take out US citizenship, and he also wasn't technically the team captain, but head coach Jeffrey had decided that McIlvenny should be captain for the England game, presumably in a not particularly subtle attempt to wind the English up, but even taking these factors into account nobody expected anything other than a comfortable English victory. Jeffrey himself said prior to the game that his team had 'nae chance', either an early example of Scottish managers using psychological mind games or an accurate summary of the realities of the situation.

What happened in Belo Horizonte has remained the subject of much speculation and conjecture to this day. There was no television or even radio coverage, and no English journalists had travelled to the game that was more than 200 miles from Rio. England felt comfortable enough not to select their most famous player, Matthews, but all the same they dominated the game from start to finish, hitting the woodwork several times and missing a hatful of chances, but in the thirty-eighth minute, totally against the run of play, Joe Gaetjens from Haiti, who like McIlvenny should never have been playing for the USA in the first place, scored the only goal with what was either a brilliant diving header or a lucky deflection from a miss-hit shot, depending on whether you were American, Haitian or English.

The only English-speaking journalist at the game was an American, and when he wired through the final extraordinary score of 1–0 to the USA, the English newspapers at first thought that it was a misprint and reported a 10–1 victory to England, so inconceivable was it that the Americans of all people could defeat what they still thought was the greatest football nation in the world.

The Americans lost their final group game to go out of the tournament, but they had already far surpassed all of their expectations. Jeffrey returned to Pennsylvania to continue his coaching career, and McIlvenny returned to Britain where he briefly played for Manchester United before drifting into non-league football, having never actually gained the citizenship of the country that he had captained. A traumatised England also lost their final group game against Spain and were knocked out of the tournament, a painful realisation that, in their self-imposed exile, the world had overtaken them. Which was at least more than the stay-at-home Scots had learned, but at the time they were laughing too much to notice.

The game has become known as 'the miracle of Belo Horizonte' and one of the greatest upsets in World Cup history, but if you look at World Cup history then perhaps we should not be too surprised by American success. For the USA has in fact reached the second stages of the World Cup Finals four times, which is of course four more than Scotland have achieved.

But even considering Ed McIlvenny's captaincy in 1950 and the reflected glory of the appearance of Aberdeen-born Bolton Wanderers midfielder Stuart Holden as a substitute for the USA in the 1–1 draw with England in their group game at Rustenberg, South Africa, it is the team of 1930 where we see Scotland's greatest influence on football's ultimate showcase.

Little was expected of the USA team that travelled to Uruguay in 1930, but at least they had turned up. Only four European nations had made the journey, and unsurprisingly, Scotland was not one of them, having begun their isolation from international football by resigning from FIFA two years earlier in 1928, the same year as the 'Wembley Wizards', including the legendary Hughie Gallacher and Alex James, had destroyed England 5–1 in what was arguably Scotland's greatest-ever team. The world was therefore denied the opportunity of seeing the likes of Gallacher and James up against the best of South America, but there were still a healthy smattering of Scots ready to make their name in Montevideo.

The USA were drawn in Group 4 with Belgium and Paraguay, and on 13th July 1930 in Montevideo, they defeated Belgium 3–0 on the very first day of the very first World Cup. Their opening goal was scored by forward Bart McGhee, which would have been the very first goal in World Cup history, if it had not been for the fact that across town France were playing Mexico at exactly the same time and had scored a goal nineteen minutes earlier.

McGhee was born in Edinburgh, where his father, James McGhee, had both been a star player for Hibs and then manager of Hearts, a combination that even back then was only ever going to end in tears, and after resigning the manager's position, McGhee emigrated with his family to America.

Bart McGhee played his football in New York and Philadelphia before being selected for the 1930 World Cup. He was joined in the team by winger Jim Brown from Kilmarnock (who would later briefly return to Britain to play for Manchester United and was the uncle of Scottish rugby legends Peter and Gordon 'Broon fae Troon' Brown), midfielder Jimmy Gallagher from Kirkintilloch, defender Alec Wood from Lochgelly in Fife and wing-half Andy Auld from Stevenston in Ayrshire. McGhee, Brown, Gallagher, Wood and Auld had all immigrated to the USA, all played football in the American Soccer League that was based around the cities of the eastern seaboard and all played in all of the USA's games in the 1930 Finals, which may or may not have had something to do with the fact that the coach of the USA team was Bob Millar, who came from Paisley and had played for St Mirren before heading westwards.

After defeating Belgium, the USA continued their good form by brushing the highly fancied Paraguay aside 3–0 to qualify straight into the semi-finals without having even conceded a goal. Their strong performances were based on the very modern tactics of a strong and physical packed defence allied to counter-attacking down the wings. The established European and South American nations were not too impressed; the French sneeringly called them 'a team of shot-putters', and the French didn't even have to play them. However, the Scottish–American fairytale finally came to an end when a superior Argentina side outplayed them 6–1 in the semi-final, but at least Jim Brown from Ayrshire had the consolation of scoring USA's goal, a fitting end to the only time that Scots have been in one of the four top teams in the World Cup. Or should I say the only time so far that Scots have been in one of the four top teams in the World Cup, as despite everything and all current and historical evidence to the contrary, we still can't completely let it go. For it is one thing Scots accepting deep down that they will never reach the semi-finals of the World Cup, but it is quite another admitting it to anyone else.

## Ice Cold in Halifax

Of all the countries in the world, it is Canada where the Scottish influence is arguably the most pronounced, for the history of Canada has been intertwined with Scotland ever since the first adventurous Scots headed west in pursuit of beaver – and other furry animals. Canada's first two prime ministers, John A. MacDonald and Alexander Mackenzie, were both Scots; Canada's longest river, the Mackenzie, was named after another Alexander Mackenzie, this time from Stornoway. Canada's most prestigious seat of higher learning, McGill University in Montreal, was named after Glasgow-born James McGill; and the Canadian Pacific Railway that brought Canada together and was the principal factor behind political union was built and financed by a consortium of Canada's wealthiest businessmen, all of whom were born in Scotland and all of whom looked forward to travelling across a country from east to west without ever having to stop at Polmont.

Perhaps the best-known example of the Scottish connection is the province of Nova Scotia, which is Latin for 'New Scotland',

and is the only place in the world outside of Scotland where Scottish Gaelic is still spoken. In fact, at the beginning of the twentieth century, there was thought to be as many Scottish Gaelic speakers in Canada as there was in Scotland. Today numbers of Gaelic speakers in Nova Scotia have fallen to less than 1,000, a sad decline, but granted still a potential doubling of BBC Alba viewing figures.

It was James Creighton, a native of Halifax, the capital of Nova Scotia, who at the indoor Victoria Skating Rink in Montreal in March 1875 organised and participated in the first-ever formal example of a brand-new sport that consisted of two teams of nine players each (soon to be reduced to seven) on skates with sticks, playing a game that featured goals at either end of the rink and a small circular disc. The game proved immediately popular and would become known as ice hockey, but Creighton's inspiration was not the English game of field hockey that was played on grass, but the game of 'shinny' or 'shinney' that for many years had been played on ice throughout Nova Scotia and Ontario. Creighton would have been familiar with shinny from his childhood in his native Halifax and the game was long associated with Scottish immigrants looking for something more energetic than curling in the long winter months.

The game of shinny is most often compared to Scottish shinty, or to give shinty its formal Gaelic name *camanachd*, and is recorded being played in Nova Scotia as far back as the 1800s. Shinny games had no formal rules, no limit on the number of players, and no recognised scoring system, but basically groups of men with sticks chasing a puck or each other around the ice, so intrinsically not too dissimilar to ice hockey today.

However, it would be wrong to say that 'shinny' is the only game to claim to be the predecessor of ice hockey. As well as being home to an overwhelming number of Scots, Nova Scotia was also home to an equivalent number of Irish immigrants. There are numerous references to the game of 'hurley' deriving from shinty's Irish cousin of 'hurling' being played in pre-1875 Nova Scotia, and while the word 'puck' could originate from the Scottish Gaelic *puc*, the same could be said for the word deriving from the Irish *poc*, with both meaning 'to poke' or 'to strike'. And lest we forget, long before the arrival of either the Scots or the Irish, the Native Canadian population had been playing various stick-based games on the ice for centuries. So perhaps, in conclusion, it would be magnanimous to say that, rather than claiming ice hockey as a Scottish or an Irish game, ice hockey is intrinsically a Canadian game.

Yet, as with Scotland's historic influence on so much of what we associate with Canada, Scots would continue to play a role in the history of Canada's national sport. When ice hockey was included in 1924 at the first Winter Olympics at Chamonix, France (after having curiously first appeared in the 1920 Summer Olympics at Antwerp), the captain of the victorious Canadian team was one Duncan Munro from Moray, who had immigrated to Canada as a child. After Olympic glory Munro would turn professional, and in 1926 was captain of the now-defunct Montreal Maroons who won the Stanley Cup, the most prestigious trophy in the world of ice hockey.

However, Munro is not the only Scot to have achieved that feat. Alex Gray from Glasgow played in the New York Rangers' first Stanley Cup victory of 1928; and goaltender Andy Aitkenhead was a member of the New York Rangers' second victory in 1933; Adam Brown from Johnstone was a member of the Detroit Red Wings team that won in 1943; but perhaps the greatest of all the Scottish ice hockey players was Charlie Gardiner from Edinburgh.

Gardiner immigrated to Winnipeg as a child where he began his career as a goaltender. In 1927, Gardiner joined the NHL when he signed for the Chicago Black Hawks and soon made his reputation as the top goaltender in the League. In 1934 Gardiner was the captain and star player of the Black Hawks team that won their first Stanley Cup, the only goaltender to have ever done so. He was at the peak of his profession and fame, but had been playing all season whilst suffering from a persistent tonsil infection that left him exhausted and experiencing increasing problems with his vision. By the time of the play-offs against the Detroit Red Wings he was often in excruciating pain. In June 1934, only two months after he had held aloft the Stanley Cup, Gardiner died of a sudden brain haemorrhage at the age of only twenty-nine.

Charlie 'Chuck' Gardiner is to date the only Scots-born player to have been elected to the Hockey Hall of Fame, but such was his legacy that when the Hall of Fame was founded in 1945 he was one of only twelve players to achieve that honour, unheard of in his native Scotland, but a legend in Canada and Chicago.

## *Where Fields of Dreams are Made*

The more time you spend investigating and researching the rich and idiosyncratic sporting history of America, the more you begin to realise how extraordinary it is that America is so obsessed with golf. Perhaps the game appeals to the Presbyterian spirit of the descendants of the Scots and Scots–Irish who, in the eighteenth century, left their homelands to forge new lives in a new land and refused to be in any way beholden or bending the knee (except when playing a tricky bunker shot) to their imperial Anglican masters, or perhaps, in an admittedly rather tenuous allegory, Americans just like hitting very small objects with big sticks. But what is most unusual about golf in the USA is that it is a British sport – in this case Scottish – that became even more popular over there than here. For when it comes to sport, as with most things, the Americans like to do things their own way, and to hell with the consequences or the mangling of the English language.

If you exclude golf, the top four sports in the USA are and have been for almost all of the past century: baseball, American football, basketball and ice hockey, all of which were born and nurtured in North America and are revered as an article of faith and the pinnacle of sporting achievement by their millions of fans, in spite of, or possibly even because of, the bemusement these sports often engender in the rest of the world.

However, even in these bastions of Americana, Scots have made an impact. Granted, in basketball where – as everyone knows – Scots guys can't jump, this influence can be said to be one bounce removed, as it was the Canadian-born son of Scottish immigrants, James A. Naismith, who in 1891 invented the game in Springfield, Massachusetts.

However, in both of the sports that can historically compete for the honour of being the USA's national game, American football and baseball, there have been Scots who have become famous American sporting heroes. And one Scot in particular would go down in history as playing the lead role in arguably the most iconic moment in American sport.

On 3rd February 2008 at the University of Phoenix Stadium in Arizona, the New York Giants made American football history by becoming the first wildcard team ever to win Super Bowl XLII. The Giants defeated the overwhelming favourites, the previously undefeated New England Patriots 17–14 and contributing five points to one of the greatest upsets in Super Bowl history was the Giants' place-kicker Lawrence Tynes, who through his American father's military posting thirty years previously had the great fortune to have been born in Greenock and became the first and so far only player born in Scotland to have won two Super Bowl rings, in 2008 and again in 2012. Yet if this achievement was not momentous enough, in the game that saw the Giants progress to the 2008 Super Bowl – the NFC Championship Game – the Giants had defeated the Green Bay Packers, led by the legendary Brett Favre, in sub-zero temperatures in the Packers' forbidding home stadium by 23–20 in overtime.

Tynes had missed two opportunities to win the game with field goals in regular play before in overtime landing a mighty forty-seven-yard effort, one of the longest field goals in post-season history. His kick became known as 'the Tynes Redeemer' and immediately went down in American football folklore and just went to show that all those years in Greenock of avoiding angry 300lb men wearing crash helmets had not gone to waste.

One hundred and twenty years before Tynes became a laird of the Super Bowl ring, the first Scot to make his name in American sport was Glasgow-born Jim McCormick, one of baseball's top pitchers in the early years of the sport in the 1880s, when the game was still in its glorified rounders stage as the pitcher was still only allowed to throw underhand. McCormick played and managed several teams in his career, but had his greatest success as pitcher for the Chicago White Stockings (later the Chicago Cubs) winning National League pennants in 1885 and 1886.

Sixty-five years later, in 1951 the race to win the National League was one of the most thrilling in the sport's history. At one stage the Brooklyn Dodgers, including the legendary Jackie Robinson, had a thirteen-game lead over the second-place New York Giants, but the Giants then proceeded to go on one of the most remarkable winning streaks in baseball history, winning thirty-seven out of their last forty-four games (they play a lot of games in baseball) to end up dead equal with the Dodgers at the end of the season.

In 1951 there were no automatic play-offs. The winners over the regular season won the pennant and went on to meet the winners of the American League in the World Series, so there was added excitement to a best of three game series to decide the winners. The Giants won the first game by 3–1, but the Dodgers fought back to comfortably win the second by 10–0, going into the third game, played at the Polo Grounds in Manhattan on 3ʳᵈ October, as favourites. The Dodgers went into a 1–0 lead after the first inning, but the Giants drew level in the fourth. However, in the eighth and penultimate inning, the Dodgers gained what looked like a decisive 4–1 lead, although the Giants then reduced the deficit by 1. By the bottom of the ninth inning, with the Dodgers still winning by 4–2, all looked lost for the Giants. And then who should walk to the plate, but a young man from Townhead in Glasgow, and sporting immortality beckoned.

Bobby Thomson had left Glasgow at the age of two to settle with his family in Staten Island, New York. He had begun a highly successful major league baseball career in 1946 when he made his debut for the New York Giants, and would remain in the major leagues until his retirement in 1960. Thomson would score 264 homeruns in his career, would be selected for the annual All-Star game on three occasions and inadvertently would pave the way for future homerun king and baseball legend, Hank Aaron, for when in 1954 Thomson broke his ankle training for his new team, the Milwaukee Braves, it was Aaron who made his major league debut in his place.

1951 had already been a great season for Thomson. He had achieved a career-best number of homeruns, and in the first play-off game against the Dodgers had scored the decisive homerun (his thirty-first) that had given the Giants a 3–1 victory. The Dodgers pitcher in the first game had been All-Star Ralph Branca, but in the decisive third game it had been their other pitcher Don Newcombe who had stood on the pitcher's mound and had thrown the Dodgers to the brink of victory. However, by the ninth inning Newcombe had grown increasingly weary and when Thomson stepped up to the plate for the final time, it was to find that it was not Newcombe that he would face, but his replacement Ralph Branca.

The Giants had two men on bases when Branca threw his first ball. It was a strike. Branca's second ball was a fastball and Thomson connected. It was a low drive that went down the left field, but stayed in play, and as Thomson, the Dodgers and the Polo Grounds crowd watched and waited for it to drop, it never did, surpassing the 279 feet required to pass the fence before dropping into the lower deck. With the two men out, Thomson's thirty-second homer of the season gave the Giants three runs and meant that, against all the odds, the Giants had achieved an unassailable 5–4 lead and had won the game, the play-off series and the League.

'The Giants have won the Pennant! The Giants Have Won the Pennant!' was the famous cry from American radio commentator Russ Hodges that was broadcast across America. 1951 was also the first year of the Korean War between North and South Korea and the game was broadcast across the Pacific to American troops serving in Korea far away from home. Thomson's homerun became known as 'the shot heard around the world', and even though the Giants would lose the World Series final 4–2 to their great rivals the New York Yankees and uproot themselves from New York in 1958 to head west to become the San Francisco Giants, it has remained one of sport's most iconic moments, when time and a nation stood still, and has been referenced in countless novels and films. Most notably in *The Godfather* where James Caan as Sonny Corleone is listening to the radio commentary of the game, just seconds before its conclusion, as he drives to the tollbooth where not only will he be gunned down and murdered but he doesn't even get to hear Thomson's famous homerun.

In his native Scotland most people have remained oblivious to the enduring fame that Thomson achieved across the Atlantic in 1951 and even in the USA, Bobby Thomson, a modest and unassuming man, was perhaps never as famous as his most important sporting moment. However, Thomson remains a legendary name in the history of American sport, and is possibly the most famous Scottish sportsman there has ever been across the pond, even if as far as most Scots are concerned the phrase 'the shot heard around the world' is one they have probably never heard, but to be fair they might not be too surprised to discover that a Glaswegian was involved.

## *Buenos Días, Señor Hutton*

When Bart McGhee and the other four Scots playing for the USA in the inaugural 1930 World Cup in Uruguay finally saw their fairytale come to an end it was thanks to a crushing 6–1 defeat by Argentina who went on to meet the hosts Uruguay in the final in Montevideo. Granted, neither Scotland nor England nor for that matter Italy, Spain or Germany had deigned to enter the first FIFA World Cup, but even if the leading nations in Europe had made the trip there was no reason to think that in 1930 the finalists would have been any different.

Before the first World Cup, the Olympic Games had become the pinnacle of international football and it had been Uruguay who had won gold in both 1924 and 1928. In the latter tournament it had been Argentina who had been the unlucky silver medallists, and it was Argentina again who were the most recent winners in 1929 of the Copa América, the major international tournament in South America. In the insular British Isles of 1930 precious few were aware that power in international football had shifted across the Atlantic, but it would have been less of a surprise to the pioneering Scots who had played an integral part in the development of fútbol in South America.

When one thinks of the Scottish Diaspora it is the Scottish descendants of North America, Australia, New Zealand, Southern Africa and the other outposts of the former British Empire from Malaysia to Montego Bay that come to mind, with their proud Scottish heritage of kilts, tartan and bagpipes, even if those very same kilts, tartan and bagpipes played a minimal to no part in the lives of most of those who left in the first place. Far less known are the substantial numbers of Scots farmers, engineers, teachers, doctors and labourers who moved to South America in the nineteenth century and proved themselves the exception to the rule by learning a foreign language. 'Al fin y al cabo somos hijos de Jock Tamson' after all, or as they say in the Auld Country, 'We're a' Jock Tamson's bairns.'

The most notable Scot in the history of South America was Thomas 'El Diablo' Cochrane from Hamilton. He was the buccaneering naval officer from the Napoleonic Wars, who between 1817 and 1825 commanded the revolutionary navies of both Chile and Brazil and played a crucial part in both countries' successful fights for independence from Spanish and Portuguese rule and lived to tell the tale with all limbs and eyes intact. But running Cochrane a close second was a man from the Gorbals who changed South American sporting history, Alexander Watson Hutton.

Alexander Watson Hutton was a teacher from Glasgow who immigrated to Buenos Aires in 1882 to work at the St Andrew's Scots School, a school that had been established in 1838 to provide a suitable Scottish education for the growing number of Scottish settlers. Watson Hutton was a firm believer in the benefit of sport, and when he founded his own school, the Buenos Aires

English High School, in 1884 he ensured that football was part of the curriculum.

British immigrants in Argentina had played football of varying forms since the late 1860s, but it was Watson Hutton's promotion, along with others of the association rules that saw the game begin to flourish in the expatriate community of Buenos Aires. And the Scottish influence can clearly be seen, for in an inaugural league that was played in 1891 the two leading sides were Old Caledonians and Watson Hutton's former school of St Andrew's.

However, the decisive moment in the establishment of organised football in Argentina was to take place on 21$^{st}$ February 1893 in Buenos Aires, when Alexander Watson Hutton founded the Argentine Association Football League, which would later become La Asociación del Fútbol Argentino, the oldest football association in South America.

Watson Hutton remained President of the League until 1896 when he retired to concentrate on his day job of teaching students the offside rule. He would then have the satisfaction of seeing his school's team, Alumni, dominate the early years of the Argentine league, winning ten titles between 1900 and 1911, before inevitably the local teams and local players superseded the British-based teams. Argentina would go on to become one of the leading nations in world football, winning two World Cups and giving us such legendary names as Alfredo di Stefano, Lionel Messi and Diego Maradona, whose accomplishments in the 1960 European Cup Final at Hampden Park, the Champions League Finals of 2009 and 2011 and of course the 1986 World Cup Quarter Final, were sportingly appreciated throughout Scotland, no doubt in recognition of the role that a Glaswegian had played in teaching diminutive Argentinians how to compete for headers against significantly taller opponents.

## Size Isn't Everything

In the year 2012 when the leading players in the SPL are far more likely to hail from Bosnia, Romania, Nigeria, Honduras, Kenya, South Korea and Israel than from Glasgow, Edinburgh or Dundee, can you tell me who are the only two players to have played in World Cup Final-winning teams and also appeared in the SPL? The answer is 1998 French striker Stéphane Guivarc'h and 2006 Italian midfielder Gennaro Gattuso, who both played for Rangers in the 1998–99 season, although never at the same time, and as far as Guivarc'h was concerned, so forgettable were his performances there was some debate about whether he actually ever played at all. Gattuso, of course, would take the skills he developed in Scottish football and go on to a combative if highly successful career with Milan and Italy. However, even less known than Guivarc'h and Gattuso's Scottish connections is the career of the Italian international who, rather than playing in Scotland, was actually born there.

Giovanni 'Johnny' Moscadini was born in Falkirk in 1897. His family had come to Scotland from the town of Barga in Tuscany, a hillside Tuscan enclave that saw a large number of its inhabitants immigrate to Scotland from the nineteenth century onwards and still celebrates its longstanding Scottish connections today. Moscadini may have been born in Scotland, but he enlisted in the Italian army in the First World War and then afterwards settled in the family home of Barga where he began a football career that would take him to the top Italian teams, Pisa and Genoa. Moscadini was a goal-scoring forward and made his debut for the Azzurri (the Italian national team) in 1921, winning nine caps in total and scoring seven goals through to 1925. Johnny Moscadini may well have gone on to further success for club and country, but instead returned to Scotland, undoubtedly the only example to date of an Italian football international giving up his career to run a café in Campbeltown. Moscadini remained in Scotland for the rest of his life, retiring to Prestwick where he died in 1985, but is still remembered in Barga, where the football stadium is named after him.

Giovanni Moscadini was one of the first examples of the Italian football tradition of 'Oriundi', players with Italian heritage who were born outside Italy but were nevertheless chosen for the Italian national team. When Italy hosted the second FIFA World Cup in 1934 Moscadini may have long since departed for deepest Argyll, but there were still three non-Italians in Italy's first team, and with home advantage and with Mussolini himself looking imperiously on, it was no great surprise that the Italians became the second nation to become world champions. It was a close-run thing though, as with only nine minutes of normal time to go they were trailing 1–0 to a talented Czechoslovakia team, before eventually winning 2–1 in extra-time.

The nation of Czechoslovakia had only come into existence in 1918 at the end of the First World War and the break-up of the Austro-Hungarian Empire and played their first international in 1920, but had quickly become a major force in European football. Czechoslovakia specialised in the short passing game that had long been associated with the Scottish style of football, and as you may already have suspected, it was indeed two ex-pat Scots who played an integral role in this Bohemian rhapsody.

John Madden was born in Dumbarton and had the honour of being centre forward in the very first game played by Celtic in 1888. He did not score on that occasion, but would win three League titles for Celtic between 1893 and 1896 and score four goals on his debut for Scotland against Wales in 1893, although incredibly he would only win one more cap. In 1905, as a retired forty-year-old ex-footballer, Madden was surprisingly offered the position of manager of Slavia Prague and left Scotland for a new life in Central Europe.

Life in Prague must clearly have agreed with him as Madden remained there through two World Wars, the creation of a new country and first German and then Soviet occupation until his death in 1948. Madden remained manager of Slavia Prague until 1930, instilling the Scottish style of play and a strong disciplinary ethic that, remarkably considering the city that he found himself in, included the prohibition of alcohol before matches.

In 1919 Madden was joined in Prague by fellow Scot John Dick from Renfrewshire, who had played over 250 times for Woolwich Arsenal (before they became just Arsenal) between 1898 and 1912, as a no-nonsense centre-half and one-time captain. Dick was appointed manager of Sparta Prague, and when the Czechoslovakia League was founded in 1925, the two Scots led their respective sides to a series of titles with Slavia winning in 1925, 1929 and 1930 and Sparta in 1926, 1927 and 1932. Madden would retire from Slavia in 1930 and Dick from Sparta three years later in 1933, but between them they had established the most successful clubs in Czech football history.

And in 1927 Dick led his Sparta Prague to victory in the first-ever Mitropa Cup, an early incarnation of the European Cup and Champions League, that was contested by the best teams in Central Europe, and before the advent of the European Cup in 1956 it was the premier club tournament on the European continent.

This was a golden age of football in Czechoslovakia. At the 1934 World Cup Finals held in Mussolini's Italy, Czechoslovakia made it through to the final playing the same Scottish short-passing game that Madden and Dick had introduced. Remarkably, the entire Czechoslovak side, including such legendary figures as goalkeeper and captain Frantisek Planicka and forwards

Antonin Puc and Oldrich Nejedly, were all selected from either Slavia or Sparta Prague, and therefore had all been coached and unquestionably lectured on their Staropramen intake by the two men who can lay claim to having been Scotland's most successful overseas managers in history.

Czechoslovakia remained a consistently strong force in world football, reaching the World Cup Final again in 1962 and earning the title of European Champions in 1976, until the Velvet Divorce of 1993, when the nation was divided into the new independent nations of the Czech Republic and Slovakia, a peaceful and remarkably harmonious separation that curiously appeared to proceed without any requirement for a national referendum in either country.

Still, the 1934 defeat in Rome remains the closest that Czechoslovakia ever came to joining the elite group who have won the ultimate prize of the World Cup. Spain's victory in 2010 brought the number of countries that have lifted the World Cup to eight, and the 2010 finals would also see the unexpected return to the top table of world football of the nation that first lifted the Jules Rimet trophy.

For forty years up until 2010, as far as the rest of the world was concerned, South American football consisted solely of Argentina and Brazil. True, the Colombian Carlos Valderrama had great hair and in Scotland the less we remembered of Peru the better, but when it came to potential world champions and world footballers of the year, there were only two nations from the southern hemisphere to be considered. And then at South Africa, after the highly fancied Argentina and Brazil both crashed and burned, it was little old forgotten Uruguay who, to the consternation of most of Africa, somehow sneaked past Ghana on penalties to reach the semi-finals. It was the first time since 1970 that Uruguay had reached the last four of the World Cup, and while for some it was a shock that a country of only three million could gate-crash the greatest football show on earth, for those who know their sporting history it was simply one more achievement of a nation who have been upsetting the odds for the last 100 years.

Uruguay have been Champions of South America's Copa América on fourteen occasions (equal first with Argentina and well ahead of Brazil); have won the Olympic Games twice in 1924 and 1928, which in those pre-World Cup days was the only international tournament where Europe played South America; have been World Cup semi-finalists three times in 1954, 1970 and 2010; and of course were World Cup winners twice in 1930 and 1950, which considering that they did not take part in either 1934 or 1938, meant that, in fact, they were undefeated for an extraordinary twenty-four years, until losing to the Magnificent Magyars of Hungary in 1954.

It is not for nothing that it is said of Uruguay that 'while other countries have history, Uruguay has football', and if you think the task of naming five Belgians is difficult, try naming a single Uruguayan who does not wear their sky-blue shirt.

But where does this incredible football heritage come from? Well, the origins of Uruguayan football have much to do with their geographical proximity to Argentina, their much larger neighbour across the River Plate, where the Glaswegian schoolmaster Alexander Watson Hutton had established the Argentine Football Association in 1893, and as with Argentina, football was introduced by British workers residing in the country.

The Uruguay Football Association and the Uruguay Football League were founded in 1900 and they played their first international against Argentina in 1902. In 1905 Glasgow tea magnate Thomas Lipton gave his name to the Copa de Caridad

Lipton, a trophy to be played between Argentina and Uruguay on an annual basis and was competed for regularly until 1929 and was last played for in 1992. Lipton would also give his name six years later to the Sir Thomas Lipton Trophy, a prototype European Cup that featured the leading clubs of Europe, plus the unlikely English winner West Auckland, and either showed Lipton's largesse in promoting his sporting enthusiasms or a clever attempt to make sure that every Cup around the world would be associated with his own brand of tea. Yet Lipton was not the Scot who would have the greatest influence of Uruguay to the pinnacle of world football.

In 1906, a young twenty-year-old by the name of John Harley moved from Springburn in Glasgow to take up a job in Argentina working on the new railway system that was being built along and from the River Plate or Rio de la Plata. Harley was a railway engineer, and in the nineteenth century Springburn was a world centre of locomotive production and Scotland was at the forefront of railway engineering around the world.

On his arrival in Argentina, Harley began playing for a Buenos Aires Railways football team, but when he moved across the border to work for the Central Uruguay Railways in 1909 he also switched to play for their works team, the Central Uruguay Railways Cricket Club, who despite their name, played football as well and would eventually become known by their local name of Peñarol.

As with Argentina, football in Uruguay had initially been the preserve of the British who lived and worked there, but as with Argentina the local population had taken up the game and then taken over. However, this did not prevent Harley from quickly becoming a tough-tackling centre-half and captain of the Peñarol team and furthermore making his debut for the Uruguay national team in September 1909.

Juan Harley, as he was known, made a huge impact on Uruguayan football. As with John Madden and John Dick in Prague he preached the virtues of hard work, a team ethic and the short passing game that he knew from Scotland, rather than the English kick and rush style that he encountered on arriving in South America. As well as playing for Uruguay he was also appointed trainer and was effectively player-manager of the national side and made seventeen appearances in total between 1909 and 1916. Although he did not play in the inaugural Copa América tournament of 1916, his methods were clearly bearing fruit, as Uruguay were crowned the first official champions of South America.

Harley remained an amateur player throughout, and his football commitments had always to be reconciled with his work on the Uruguayan railways. When he finally gave up playing for Peñarol in 1920 he remained working in Uruguay until the 1940s and in his retirement continued to reside in Montevideo.

Peñarol would go on to become the most successful football club in Uruguay history with a record number of League Championships and five times lifting the Copa Libertadores, the premier football tournament in South America, while within twenty-one years of Harley arriving in the country the Uruguayan national team had become the number one football country in the world, with their two victories at the Olympics, followed by success at the 1930 World Cup.

John 'Juan' Harley's role in the rise of the smallest nation by far ever to be crowned champions of the world was not forgotten and he remained a popular and revered figure in Uruguay until his death in 1960. Beyond the River Plate the name of John Harley was far less known and hardly at all in his native country, despite the fact that it had been the Scottish tradition of playing football that Harley had introduced to his adopted home.

In 1954 when after snubbing the whole notion of a World Cup for twenty-four years, Scotland made their belated debut in the Finals in Switzerland they were drawn against Uruguay in the Group stages. One can but imagine the varying emotions that John Harley must have had at the prospect of his adopted nation finally meeting the nation of his birth in the world's most important football tournament. Both Scotland and Uruguay were nations with an incredible football heritage and a reputation that far surpassed the respective sizes of their populations. Both countries had been, at their peak, the leading countries in world football. And in the person of John Harley, both countries had more in common than certainly almost everyone in Scotland actually realised.

It was a battle for the crown of who in fact actually was 'the best small football country in the world' and Uruguay would win by 7–0, which still remains Scotland's worst international defeat. Somewhere in Montevideo a now-elderly Scotsman probably did not know whether to laugh or cry.

## Lairds of the Ring

Of all the regions of Scotland it is arguably the South West and Dumfries and Galloway that is most often overlooked. The rolling hills and bucolic farmland of the Southern Uplands lend themselves to a quieter and slower pace of life, enjoyed and appreciated by their quieter and slower inhabitants, who one suspects lose little sleep (or sheep) over this lack of international profile. However, behind the picturesque tranquillity of Dumfries and Galloway lies a proud and bloody history that has seen the murder of John Comyn by his rival Robert the Bruce in a Dumfries church in 1306, the most hard-core of the Covenanters in the seventeenth century and lest any brave but unsuspecting visitor forget, the setting of *The Wicker Man* in 1973.

\* \* \*

For centuries the Douglas clan were one of the most powerful and fearsome families in the South of Scotland. This was their region, and in 1633 the Douglas clan received, amongst their many titles and many disparate family lines, the title of the Earl of Queensberry, later raised to the Marquess of Queensberry (and briefly the Duke of Queensberry) in honour of Queensberry Hill, in the Lowther Hills that constitute part of the Southern Uplands. In Scotland, the Queensberry name would gain notoriety when James Douglas, the 3rd Marquess and 2nd Duke of Queensberry, played a pivotal role in the Scottish Parliament's acquiescence to the Act of Union of 1707, however would be successfully re-branded in 1867 when the Italian-born 9th Marquess agreed to sponsor a new set of twelve rules proposed by Welsh sportsman John Chambers regarding the sport of boxing.

As was the case with so many pastimes in Victorian Britain, Chambers was determined to codify and regulate the centuries-old activity of two men hitting each other and called for the mandatory use of boxing gloves, the introduction of three-minute rounds, the prohibition of wrestling and throwing an opponent to the floor and above all, the promotion of boxing as a noble art, hence the necessity of an actual noble to be the sponsor.

The Queensberry Rules, as drawn up by Chambers, became accepted internationally as the foundation rules of the sport and an obscure Southern Uplands hill became known throughout the world, despite the fact that even in Scotland nobody actually knew where Queensberry was.

Boxing has been one of the most popular sports in Scotland for well over a century, but it would be 1937 and seventy years after the publication of the Queensberry Rules before Scotland would have an undisputed world boxing champion to call their own. But in the murky alphabet soup of the world of boxing, where even the definition of the word 'undisputed' is disputed, this does not mean that Scotland did not have a 'world champion' before then.

Johnny Hill was a brilliant amateur flyweight from Edinburgh who turned professional in 1926, and by 1928 he had won both the British and European Flyweight titles. He was a boxing prodigy and one of the most popular fighters in Britain, attracting large crowds whenever he fought in London.

In August 1928 at the age of twenty-two, Hill defeated the Russian-born American David 'Newsboy Brown' Montrose on points over fifteen rounds in front of over 30,000 spectators in Clapham, London. A new sporting superstar was acclaimed, and in Britain Hill's victory over Brown was celebrated as the crowning of a new World Champion. However, in America Newsboy Brown had been but one of several claimants to the title of World Champion, and it was only in California and Britain that Hill was so recognised.

In March 1929 Hill lost his only professional fight of his career in Paris to Frenchman Emile Pladner (who he had already twice defeated). Pladner would then almost immediately lose to the best of the American flyweights, former Olympic gold medallist and National Boxing Association (later the World Boxing Association) World Champion, Frankie Genaro.

A resilient Hill had recovered from his unexpected defeat in Paris and had returned to his winning ways throughout the spring and summer of 1929. That same year it was announced that the Scot would meet Genaro in London in September in a world title bout that, this time, would be recognised on both sides of the Atlantic.

Johnny Hill had already shown in his meteoric career that he was a dedicated and incredible boxing talent, and victory over Genaro would be the next step to dominating the world Flyweight division for years to come. However, in training for the biggest fight of his life, Hill caught a chill that quickly developed into pneumonia, and on 27th September 1929 – the very day the contest was due to take place – Johnny Hill died in his home city of Edinburgh. A shocked Genaro, rather than fighting Hill for the World Flyweight title, was one of the pallbearers at his funeral. Johnny Hill was only twenty-three years of age.

Two years after Hill's tragic death, another Scottish flyweight, this time from the Gorbals in Glasgow, turned professional at the age of eighteen. In the 1920s and 1930s the Gorbals was one of the poorest inner city areas in the whole of Europe. To earn his living, Benny Lynch had taken to fighting on the circuit of carnival and fairground boxing competitions that proliferated in the West of Scotland. From the outset it was clear that Lynch, with his immaculate timing, brilliant command of the ring and explosive punching power, was a rare talent, and he embarked on an incredibly punishing schedule that saw him fight twenty-nine bouts in one year.

On 8th September 1935 he travelled to Belle Vue in Manchester to fight the Englishman Jackie Brown for the British, European and NBA World Flyweight titles. This was the second time that Lynch and Brown had fought each other – the first being a non-title bout in March of 1935 in Glasgow that ended in a draw – but at the Belle Vue Stadium in Manchester, the Scot, twenty-two years old, knocked down the champion six times in a two-round demolition to claim all his titles and return to the praise of hundreds of thousands of his fellow Glaswegians who came to honour Glasgow's champion, the people's champion and the greatest flyweight in the world.

However, while as far as Glasgow, Britain, Europe and the NBA were concerned, Lynch was the unquestioned Champion of the World, the NBA's main rival, the New York State Boxing Commission, had other ideas. They insisted that the Filipinoborn American champion Small Montana (real name Benjamin Gans) was the legitimate World Champion.

On 9th January 1937 the two World Champions met at Wembley Arena in London to decide the matter once and for all. The fight was a hard-fought tactical contest between two great boxers that went the full fifteen rounds, but at the end it was clear that Lynch's greater ring-craft and aggression were superior to his opponent's. For the first time in a decade there was an undisputed World Flyweight Champion, and he came from Glasgow.

In October 1937 Benny Lynch knocked out future World Champion Peter Kane from England in the thirteenth round in front of 40,000 home fans at Shawfield Stadium in Rutherglen. The Lynch–Kane fight is one of the most famous fights ever to take place in Britain, and for Lynch, fighting in front of his devoted supporters was arguably the greatest moment of a momentous career.

Benny Lynch was only twenty-four and at the pinnacle of world boxing, but within twelve months his career would be all but over. While his predecessor Johnny Hill had been a teetotaller, Lynch liked a drink. At first his convivial habits were kept in check by his gruelling training and fighting schedule, but as he became more successful and more famous, the temptations became greater. Benny Lynch was a man of the people and the people were more than happy to buy their hero a drink.

As his life became more chaotic it became increasingly difficult to maintain his training regime and even more difficult to remain at his flyweight fighting weight of 112lbs (51kg). A March 1938 re-match versus Kane at Anfield Stadium in Liverpool resulted in a controversial draw, with many proclaiming the Englishman the winner, but it had been declared a non-title bout, as Lynch had failed to make the flyweight limit. Three months later he turned up for the weigh-in for a title defence against American

Jackie Jurich to find he was six pounds over the limit, and he was promptly stripped of his titles.

In October 1938, in his 108th fight in just over seven years, Benny Lynch was knocked out for the first time in his career. He was twenty-five and never fought again. Eight years later, in 1946, Scotland's greatest-ever boxer and first undisputed Champion of the World finally succumbed to the ravages of alcoholism and died of pneumonia at the age of thirty-three.

It was a terribly sad end to a life less ordinary that had burned so brightly for such a brief period of time, but for those who knew what life was truly like in the Gorbals tenements from where Benny Lynch came, his talent and his achievements would be proudly remembered after both the man and the tenements had long gone.

Johnny Hill and Benny Lynch were both flyweights, and it was in this, the lightest of all the divisions where the wee hard men ruled, that Scotland continued to find success. In 1943, at the age of twenty-two, Jackie Paterson, a southpaw from the village of Springside in Ayrshire with a mighty punch and the British Flyweight and Bantamweight Champion for most of the 1940s, knocked out Peter Kane in the first round at Hampden Park and was declared the NBA World Flyweight Champion. Paterson held the title until 1947, but due to the circumstances of wartime that made it impossible for the leading fighters around the world to fight each other, he was only able to defend his crown once in those four years.

Nineteen years later, in the same year that Jackie Paterson was tragically stabbed and killed in his new home of South Africa at the age of forty-six, Walter McGowan from Burnbank in Hamilton defeated defending champion Salvatore Burruni from Italy on points, to be crowned WBC World Flyweight Champion.

McGowan was an extremely talented boxer, renowned for his ring-craft and footwork, and like all three of his illustrious

Scottish predecessors, a precocious talent who became World Champion at the young age of twenty-three. And although his career would be bedevilled by problems with cuts and he would lose his title in his first defence in December 1966, there were further echoes of momentous nights in Scottish boxing history and a continuation of a Caledonian line of legendary champions as it had been in the same Wembley Arena where Benny Lynch had defeated Small Montana in 1937 that McGowan won his title in June 1966.

The last Scottish boxer to lift either a WBA or WBC World Championship belt (the two oldest and most prestigious of the inexplicable four major international sanctioning bodies that currently run world boxing) was Jim Watt from Glasgow. He won the vacant WBC Lightweight Championship in April 1979 in front of a passionate home crowd at Kelvin Hall, and for the next two years and four successful defences, would bring big-time boxing back to Glasgow before eventually losing his title in London in 1981 to the Nicaraguan Alexis Arguello.

The vacant Lightweight title that Jim Watt had claimed in April 1979 had belonged to a certain Roberto Duran from Panama, who regularly heads the list of being the greatest lightweight boxer of all time – as compared to being the greatest lightweight of all time, which is not something one would ever advise calling any professional boxer, never mind a man who was known as 'Hands of Stone'. Duran had been WBC World Champion since 1972, before finally unifying the division in 1978, and in 1979 he departed the division for a decade of brawls and battles at welterweight and middleweight against the likes of Sugar Ray Leonard and Marvelous Marvin Hagler.

Jim Watt had never fought the Panamanian during both of their long careers, but another Scot, who can lay claim to being, along with Benny Lynch, Scotland's greatest-ever boxer, would prove to be less fortunate.

Ken Buchanan, like Johnny Hill, came from Edinburgh. He turned professional in 1965 and won his first thirty-three fights. He became British champion in 1968 and European champion two years later. In September of 1970 Buchanan travelled to Puerto Rico to meet another legendary Panamanian, Ismael Laguna, who had ruled the Lightweight division since 1965.

Few gave the Scot any chance against the champion, especially in the hot and humid conditions of the San Juan open-air stadium, where temperatures edged above 100 degrees. However, Buchanan, a clever, skilful and incredibly brave fighter, managed to counter the conditions and his more experienced opponent by taking the fight to Laguna to win a narrow points decision. Ken Buchanan had, against all the odds, become the WBA World Lightweight Champion and was the first Scot to hold a world title at a weight above flyweight.

In February 1971 Buchanan was awarded the WBC World Lightweight title after a points victory over Mexican Ruben Navarro in Los Angeles, and although he was soon stripped of the WBC belt for failing to meet their designated challenger, Ken Buchanan had become, after Benny Lynch, only the second Scot to be proclaimed undisputed World Champion. Buchanan retained his WBA title with another fifteen-rounds points victory over Laguna at Madison Square Gardens, New York, in September 1971 and Buchanan would return to the Gardens on June 1972 in what would become one of the most famous and contentious fights of all time.

Ken Buchanan fought at Madison Square Gardens, the then-Mecca of world boxing, five times in his career. In 1970 he had been voted Fighter of the Year by the Boxing Writers Association of America for his victory over Laguna in Puerto Rico, and while in his native Britain the authorities were slow to recognise his talent and even initially banned him from boxing at home because of a dispute with the WBA, in America they were quick to appreciate the talent and the guts of the Scot with the fast hands and the trademark tartan shorts.

Buchanan's WBA title was on the line when he agreed to meet Roberto Duran at the Gardens in June 1972. Despite the Scot being the more experienced and the favourite, the undefeated Panamanian was six years his junior and the coming force in the division.

From the very first seconds, Duran came charging out to attempt to take control of the fight and briefly had Buchanan down in the first round, but as the fight went on the clever Scot managed to just about keep the swarming Duran at bay with his trademark jab and combinations. It was the classic contest between a fighter and a boxer, with Duran desperate to get inside Buchanan's defences and prepared to use any part of his anatomy to do so, and Buchanan equally determined to keep Duran at a distance. By the start of the thirteenth round Duran was ahead, but there were still three rounds to go, meaning the Champion, with his undoubted stamina and the proven resilience that he had shown throughout his career, could not be ruled out. At the end of the thirteenth round the bell sounded and what happened next has been disputed for decades.

As both men kept swinging and the referee struggled to separate them, Buchanan fell to the canvas, clutching his groin and claiming a low blow from Duran – although Buchanan's trainer later said it was Duran's knee that did the damage, while others said that Duran's punch had been deflected below the belt when the referee jumped in to try and get Duran back to his corner.

With the Scot in agony but back in his corner, and with pandemonium all around the Gardens, the question was: What would experienced, Italian-born New York referee Johnny LoBianco do next? Would he disqualify Duran for the low blow or for landing a blow after the bell, meaning Buchanan would remain the champion? Or would he allow the Scot, now back on his feet and prepared to carry on, the chance to continue as the time that he had been on the canvas had been after the bell?

However, LoBianco determined that Buchanan was in no fit state to continue and claimed he had not seen any low blow by Duran, reasoning that Buchanan hit the deck because of a culmination of blows, all legal. It was an extraordinary decision, but Duran was given the victory by a technical knockout. Now it was, of course, perfectly possible, and in fact highly probable, that if the low blow had not taken place then Duran would still have been given the verdict (he was ahead on all three judges' cards), but it was a dreadful way for Buchanan's popular and exemplary reign as World Champion to come to an end. For the man himself it was a bitter, bitter blow and one he could never accept the justice of.

For the next three years Ken Buchanan fought on at the highest level, remaining undefeated, and along the way defeating future World Champion and fellow Scot Jim Watt in Glasgow in 1973 and regaining his European Championship in 1974. Finally and belatedly, in February 1975 he got another chance at world glory, this time against the WBC World Lightweight Champion, 'Guts' Ishimatsu from Japan (real name Yuji Suzuki) in Tokyo. But after showing all his old skill and ring-craft to take control of the first half of the fight, he could not stop the local man from coming back strongly to dominate the final rounds and retain his title with a unanimous points decision. For Buchanan it was the end of the road, as despite all the controversy, all Buchanan's popularity in America, and all the public debate that should have made a Buchanan–Duran II – one of the most obvious and presumably commercially-lucrative re-matches of the 1970s – the handlers behind the warrior with 'the Hands of Stone' and one of the greatest fighters of all time whose career at the top would last another two decades after 1972, always refused to allow their fighter to go back in the ring with the man from Edinburgh, an unresolved legacy that remains to this day.

For Scotland's great boxing champions life after the ring has not always been easy – not that this makes Scotland any different from anywhere else in the world. The glory, the adulation and the fame that comes with titles and belts and sold-out stadiums seem rarely to be accompanied by the fortune and security that can be expected in other sports. It is the hardest and toughest of sport stripped down to – depending on your personal views – its purest or basest form, of one man versus another with only a pair of gloves as accessories and where retirement comes not just from a loss of form and a loss of pace, but from a physical beating in a ring. And for all the tragedy, all the corruption, all the unfairness, all the cruel disappointment and all the organisational incoherence, it remains, despite everything, a sport that people return to again and again in search of new heroes to join the legends of the past. And of those legends we honour Benny Lynch and Ken Buchanan, undisputed Champions of the World and the only two Scottish boxers to have been elected to the International Boxing Hall of Fame.

Perhaps as a final postscript to the history of Scottish boxing we should return to the life of James Douglas, the 3rd Marquess of Queensberry. Seven years before he paved the way for the Act of Union in 1707, the Marquess had, with many other Scots, lost a considerable personal fortune in the ill-fated Darien Scheme of 1698–1700. Darien had been Scotland's disastrous attempt to establish a New Caledonia colony in Central America and would end in the abandonment of the colony, the bankruptcy of the Scottish economy and finally the decision by the political elite that Union with England was the only way they would recoup their financial losses. Darien, strategically located as it was on the Isthmus of Panama, was to prove one of the most pivotal and controversial events in Scottish history with ramifications that are still felt to this day, but if you consider the sporting history of Scotland alongside the political for one moment, and as Ken Buchanan would testify to better than most, Panamanians never play by Queensberry Rules.

# 2
## The Golfers

Plaque of The Honourable Company of Edinburgh
Golfers in Leith

Scotland has quite justifiably taken great pride in its historic
reputation as a country of inventors and inventions. James
Watt's steam engine, John Logie Baird's television and Alexander
Fleming's penicillin are but only a few of the long list of discoveries
that changed the world, for good and for ill.

And it was not just in science and medicine and engineering
that Scotland has made its reputation internationally. Bagpipes,
men wearing skirts, monsters in lakes and remote, desolate castles
enveloped in mist are all inventions that could not be said to have
originated in Scotland, but thanks to some ingenious innovation
and astute marketing, they have become so synonymous with
Scotland that no other country is allowed a look in – not that

there is much of an international queue to claim credit for bagpipes, men wearing skirts, monsters in lakes and remote, desolate castles enveloped in mist.

Of course, Scotland can claim with more authenticity the invention of whisky, 'the water of life', and a billion-pounds-a-year industry that can officially only be recognised as 'Scotch' if it is distilled and matured within Scotland's geographic boundaries. And in the world of sport, amongst these many Scottish innovations, there is another international billion-pound industry that can, with some justification, be considered a contender for the title of the world's most popular sport.

There are many similarities between those two great Scottish global inventions of whisky and golf. Both ideas are in essence intrinsically straightforward – one the distilling of barley with water, and the other the hitting of a small object over a large area with a stick. Both date back to medieval times and underwent centuries of evolution before beginning to resemble what we recognise today. Both would be taken by émigré Scots and canny Scottish businessmen to all corners of the globe. And both would retain the inherent and unique qualities that had been ingrained and refined by exposure to centuries of variable Scottish weather and Scottish economics – not forgetting the competing influences of Calvinist work ethic and Calvinist guilt that make Scotland the laidback and devil-may-care society that we know and love.

It was Scots who nurtured the game of golf, built the first golf courses, compiled the first set of rules, held the first and still the greatest 'major' competition in the world, and took their idiosyncratic Caledonian pastime to first the rest of Britain, then the Empire, and finally America and the rest of the planet.

As we will see, there are many other sports and pastimes where Scots and Scotland can legitimately stake a claim as sporting innovators and pioneers, but even if this was not the case in the history of sport, Scotland will always be under-par for introducing the world to the curious game of 'gowff' – even if it took them over 400 years to get around to it.

## *Have Clubs, Will Travel*

Despite all the recent success of European golfers at the top of the world rankings and the European victory under the captaincy of Glasgow-born Colin Montgomerie in the 2010 Ryder Cup, the dominant golfing nation in the world for the past century has unquestionably been the USA. More players than anywhere else, more golf courses, more 'major championships', more prize money and the greatest players – Hagen, Jones, Hogan, Palmer, Nicklaus, Watson and Woods – have all been American. Yet, relatively speaking, golf came surprisingly late to the USA. Still, just as with the rest of the world, it would be Scots who brought the game to them, built the courses, taught them how to play and then grudgingly let them win.

It is unclear exactly when golf was first played in America. There is mention of the game in New York in the second half of the eighteenth century, and there is a record of a golf club in South Carolina in 1786 – both of which were areas associated with considerable Scottish immigration; however, it remains unclear for how long the South Carolina club (or for that matter any other golf club in the USA) actually existed. And while the nineteenth century saw more enduring golf clubs founded in France, India, Australia and South Africa, there was no comparable golf club anywhere in North America until the Royal Montreal Club was established in Canada in 1873, with Scotsman Willie Davis their first professional.

In 1888 John Reid and Robert Lockhart, two men from

Dunfermline living in New York, found themselves with a set of golf clubs but nowhere to play and decided to do something about it. They first created a three-hole golf course in Yonkers on the River Hudson, before designing a six-hole golf course in the middle of an orchard where they would play with friends and acquaintances and were given the soubriquet of 'the Apple Tree Gang', with wayward shots into the foliage always offering the consolation of a delicious addition to your packed lunch.

Buoyed by the popularity of their golfing adventures, Reid founded the St Andrew's Golf Club, named in honour of the Royal and Ancient in Fife, but with an additional apostrophe so as to avoid any confusion between the two. In 1894 it was one of the five founding members of the United States Golf Championship, who, one year later, held its first Open Championship and remains the oldest surviving golf club in the USA.

At first the expansion of golf was restricted to the more exclusive country clubs of the American establishment, but it did not take long for the American middle classes to catch the golfing bug. As the game grew in popularity there was an increasing demand for golfing professionals to teach the locals how to play and golf course designers to build the courses for them to play on. In the 1890s and 1900s, there was only one place in the world where such expertise could be found.

For two decades hundreds of young and not so young Scottish golfers of varying levels of ability packed up their golf clubs and sailed westwards to begin a new life as the first golf professionals of the new golf clubs that were sprouting up throughout the States.

One of these émigrés was James Foulis from St Andrews (as in Fife and not Yonkers). He had been employed as the first golf professional of the Chicago Golf Club, one of the original five clubs and the first in the US to have an eighteen-hole course. In 1896, he won the second US Open to be held, and his victory would usher in a remarkable period of Scottish dominance. Between 1896 and 1910, twelve of the next fifteen US Open champions would all hail from Scotland: Fred Herd, St Andrews (1898); Willie Smith, Carnoustie (1899); Willie Anderson, North Berwick (1901, 1903, 1904, 1905); Laurie Auchterlonie, St Andrews (1902); Alec Smith, Carnoustie (1906, 1910); Alec Ross, Dornoch (1907) and Fred McLeod, North Berwick (1908).

Fred McLeod, the 1908 champion, had immigrated to America in 1903. Seventy years later, he was still a household name in American golf, due to his role as the joint honorary starter of the US Masters at Augusta, along with another legendary Scottish American golfer, Jock Hutchison from St Andrews, who had won the US PGA in 1921. McLeod and Hutchison were first given the honour in 1963 and continued their symbolic East Lothian–Fife rivalry amongst the azaleas until 1973 when Hutchison finally retired, leaving McLeod to soldier on until 1976 when he was ninety-four years of age, the oldest swinger in town.

Both the 1898 champion Fred Herd and the 1902 champion Laurie Auchterlonie came from prominent St Andrews golfing families. Both had brothers, Sandy Herd (1903) and Willie Auchterlonie (1902), who won The Open (as in the original on the other side of the Atlantic) in their distinguished careers. And as we will see, sibling rivalry would prove a recurring theme in the Scots who brought golf to America.

The 1907 champion Alec Ross came from the Highland golfing outpost of Dornoch, but it would be his big brother Donald who would go on to have the greater influence on the world of golf as America's most famous golf designer. Yet as far as the title of first family of American golf went, even the Ross brothers had to concede defeat to the Smith boys from Carnoustie.

Willie Smith, Alex Smith and Macdonald Smith learned their craft on their local course before immigrating en masse to

America. Willie Smith won the 1899 US Open before winding up in Mexico teaching golf in the midst of a revolution, which must have still seemed like a breeze compared to the notoriously difficult links course at Carnoustie. Alex Smith went one better than Willie by winning two US Opens in 1906 and 1910 and younger brother Macdonald Smith was arguably the best of the three, winning twenty-four PGA events and would find himself in the top three six times in 'major' championships between 1910 and 1932, without somehow ever quite managing to find himself in the top one – unless it was the unwanted accolade of being greatest golfer never to win a 'major', an honour that would sound familiar to another Scottish golfer seventy years later.

The greatest of all the pioneering Scottish golfers, however, was Willie Anderson. Like Fred McLeod, Anderson hailed from North Berwick. Both he and McLeod went to school together and Anderson immigrated to America at the age of seventeen. Between 1901 and 1905 Anderson was almost invincible. He won the US Open four times and is the only man in golfing history to win three US Opens in succession between 1903 and 1905 – and all this by the age of twenty-five.

Anderson was a formidable competitor, known for his incredible accuracy and ice-cool temperament when under pressure. On the course he was taciturn and dour and let nothing distract him from the task at hand, but off the course he was said to be more gregarious and was partial to the occasional drink (or three) with his Scottish golfing buddies. He died suddenly in 1910 at the age of only thirty-one, following a period that saw his career recede into relative decline and failure to hold down one golf pro job for any length of time. Following news of his death, rumours circulated that alcohol may have been a contributing factor towards his premature demise, but the official cause was the more prosaic, but no less tragic one of an epileptic seizure.

The death of Anderson brought an end to the golden era of Scottish golfers in America that had begun with John Reid and the St Andrew's Golf Club in 1888. When Reid and his friends began hooking and slicing into the apple trees in Yonkers there was no other golf club anywhere in the USA, but by 1910 there were over 250, with the vast majority of them employing Scots as professionals and course designers. The game had become firmly established with the locals on the cusp of beating their Scottish teachers. And although the great American golfers Bobby Jones, Ben Hogan and Jack Nicklaus would go on to emulate Willie Anderson's record of four US Opens, nobody has yet surpassed it, ensuring that the name of Willie Anderson retains legendary status in the history of golf. Even if in Scotland his name, like so many of the great pioneering Scottish golfers who changed the history of international sport and made golf one of Scotland's greatest exports, is sadly almost completely forgotten.

## The Biggest Golf Course in the World

Over 100,000 young Scottish men died in the fields of France and Flanders in The Great War from 1914–1918, with many thousands more maimed, injured, shell-shocked and traumatised for life, all for the sake of a few miles of mud. All aspects of Scottish life and every part of Scotland from city to country, from Dumfries to Shetland, Lewis to Leuchars, would be disrupted, and sport would be no exception.

Up until 1914 Scotland had been unquestionably the premier nation in golf. Scotland was where the game had been born and raised and it had been Scots who had taken the game to first the rest of Britain, then the Empire, before finally and crucially establishing the game in America, a feat that eluded those other

British sports of football, cricket and rugby, which were, as far as the USA was concerned, minor pastimes at best. However, after 1918 there was unsurprisingly a shortage of up-and-coming Scottish golfers, and Scotland saw their position challenged at home by golfers from the rest of Britain and usurped in the USA by American golfers who were ready and willing to make the game their own. The balance of power had shifted irrevocably, but this does not mean that Scots were no longer playing an integral part in the development of the game.

By 1930 the 250 golf courses that existed in the USA in 1910 had quadrupled to over 1,000 as golf continued to sweep the nation. And in order to keep up with this phenomenal growth, 'golfing architects' were employed to build these new golf courses and ensure that, as some golfing critics would suggest, 'more good walks were spoiled'.

Probably the most prolific of these golfing architects was Tom Bendelow from Aberdeen who, it is said, designed and built over 700 golf courses between 1895 and 1933. In his native Aberdeen, however, his surname remained better known for the popular and longstanding Bendelow Pie Shop run by his parents – because while you may often be disappointed on the golf course, you would never be disappointed by a Bendelow pie.

Bendelow was a printer and keen amateur golfer who had immigrated to New York in 1892 at the age of twenty-four. But before finding his true calling as a golf course designer, he found work for *The New York Herald*, America's biggest-selling newspaper, founded in 1834 by another son of the North East, James Gordon Bennett from Moray.

Bendelow's prodigious output throughout America was marked by working swiftly on one course before moving on to the next. His technique was to follow the traditions of the great Scottish golf courses by utilising the natural features and contours of the land. Bendelow's most famous golf course and most successful example of his naturalistic style would prove to be Medinah Country Club in Illinois. It has hosted, to date, five major championships, is regularly voted one of the most popular golf courses in North America and will be the venue of the 2012 Ryder Cup (although Tom Bendelow would no doubt be choking on his pie at the possibility of no Scottish golfer making the European team).

The greatest of all America's golfing architects, however, was another Scot, Donald Ross from Dornoch, the brother of 1907 US Open winner Alec Ross. Donald Ross had served his apprenticeship at St Andrews in Fife under Old Tom Morris before immigrating to New York in 1899 at the age of twenty-six. His career in golf design lasted until his death in 1948. Like Bendelow, he also followed the natural style of laying out golf courses, allied with incredible attention to detail. Three of the most famous and revered golf courses in the USA, Pinehurst in North Carolina, Oak Hill in New York state and Oakmont in Michigan were built by Ross. Between them, they have played host to seventeen major championships; each have hosted the Ryder Cup; and each of them are curiously named after trees. Donald Ross would eventually settle in Pinehurst where he would have his own world-class golf course on his doorstep if he ever fancied a round, with the only drawback being that if he ended up in a bunker he would have no one other than himself to blame.

By the end of the 1930s USA domination of world golf was all but complete. However, the Scottish legacy on American golf would live on in the form of the golf courses that Bendelow, Ross and others would build from east to west and transform both American sporting culture and the American landscape in the process. A little piece of Scotland transported across the Atlantic, with added local foliage and ever more curious examples of fashion sportswear – and to hell with what the environmentalists might say. Aye, it makes you proud.

## The Royal & Quite Some Time Ago

In 2009, Catriona Matthew from Edinburgh, Scotland's very own six-million-dollar woman, having accumulated earnings of that amount on the LPGA, became the first Scottish woman to win a 'major' when she won the Women's British Open at Royal Lytham & St Anne's in Lancashire, England by three strokes. Two years earlier, in a symbolic and long overdue recognition of the strength and popularity of the women's game, the Women's British Open had been hosted for the first time at St Andrews – 'the home of golf'. Combined with Matthew's victory, there was a very real feeling that women's golf had returned full circle.

The history of women's professional golf is relatively short compared to men's. The first officially recognised women's 'major', the Western Open, was held in Illinois in 1930, and the Ladies Professional Golf Association (LPGA) was established in Florida in 1950. The growth of women's golf and its greatest early exponents such as Mildred 'Babe' Zaharias were all American, and it would not be until 2001 that the Women's British Open, which had first been played as recently as 1976, was classified as a recognised world 'major'. However, if the development of women's golf as a multi-million sport had been nurtured almost exclusively in the USA, its history dates back centuries, and as with most things golfing-related the story not only begins on the sandy links of the east coast of Scotland, but has the added frisson of providing the back-drop of one of the most tumultuous and infamous episodes in Scottish history.

\* \* \*

There is an apocryphal and long-held belief that the word 'golf' is actually an acronym for the popular and highly prejudicial phrase 'gentleman only, ladies forbidden'. It is unclear where and when this urban legend behind the meaning of the word 'golf' originated, but it gained much credence in the early twentieth century as the game's popularity spread throughout first Britain and then America. In no time at all, 'gentlemen only, ladies forbidden' swiftly became the reality of the situation.

Golf was predominantly a male pastime, played by men, against men, in golf clubs where the only women to be seen (and preferably not) were the cleaners and tea-ladies in the clubhouse. As golf moved away from its inherently egalitarian Scottish roots, the golf course became the preserve of the middle-class businessman doing deals, making contacts and demonstrating masculine competitiveness in all its finery.

The term 'golfing widow' was coined for the wives left at home, making the tea and looking after the children, while their husbands went through their ritual of playing a round at the golf course, no doubt followed by the obligatory hour or so at the nineteenth hole, analysing in great depth what had gone wrong on the previous eighteen.

Yet even at its most chauvinist, there were always intrepid female golfers prepared to battle the prejudice and demonstrate that golf was indeed a game for everybody and could be played well by anybody, and that ladies, too, could enjoy a relaxing gin & tonic afterwards.

The Royal and Ancient Golf Club of St Andrews may have taken until 2007 to host the Women's British Open, but appropriately enough it was 'the home of golf' that had the forethought and vision to found the world's first female golfing club in 1867, with the establishment of the St Andrews Ladies' Golf Club. Granted, the Ladies' Club was not the result of any concerted campaign for female emancipation by the radical gentlewomen of Fife. It had been established by the male members of the R & A in an attempt to get their unmarried daughters out of the house and on to the golf course, where not only would they gain the benefit of some bracing fresh air, but would no doubt increase their chances of finding a suitable golf-playing spouse.

Whatever the motives, the Ladies' Club had no shortage of members, even if they were restricted to playing only on the putting holes adjacent to the Old Course known as 'the Himalayas' on account of the varying height levels of the ground – an entirely appropriate name for the Ladies', as it demonstrated the challenges that they would have to overcome before they would be allowed to participate on the same basis as the men.

However, if St Andrews was the venue for the world's first women's golf club, it was another legendary Scottish golf course further south that had been hosting a women's golf tournament at least fifty-six years earlier.

The 'honest toun' of Musselburgh in East Lothian lies only six miles from the city centre of Edinburgh and is the home of the Musselburgh Links golf course, which in the nineteenth century was, alongside St Andrews and Prestwick in Ayrshire, one of the three premier golf courses in Scotland, and by definition, the world.

Musselburgh had gained its reputation in 1836, when the world's oldest surviving golf club, the Honourable Company of Edinburgh Golfers, had finally left their original home of Leith Links in Edinburgh to the dog-walkers and set up in Musselburgh where they stayed until 1891. From Musselburgh they moved even further east into deepest East Lothian and a brand new, eighteen-hole golf course and future Open venue, Muirfield. The abandonment of Musselburgh by the Honourable Company saw Musselburgh disappear from the top rank of Scottish golf courses, but no one could take away their incredible history and legacy to the game.

Musselburgh hosted the Open six times between 1874 and 1889, and such was the golfing strength of the town that five great golfing champions came from the area. Bob Ferguson won at Musselburgh in 1880, the first of a hat trick of consecutive Open victories between 1880 and 1882. David Brown won at his home course in 1886 before immigrating to America where, seventeen years later, he would lose the 1903 US Open in an eighteen-hole play-off to North Berwick-born Willie Anderson. Pride of place in the Musselburgh hall of golfing fame, however, would have to be the Park family. Willie Park Senior was the man who, as we will see, became the inaugural Open champion at Prestwick in 1860 and would win four Opens in total between then and 1875 – although never at his home course. That honour would instead fall to his younger brother, Mungo Park, the namesake of the Scottish explorer from Glasgow who travelled through Western Africa in the late eighteenth century, but sadly without any records stating whether he brought his golf clubs with him.

The Musselburgh-born Mungo Park won the Open at the first playing of the Open at the Links, and he was followed by his nephew and Willie Park Senior's son, Willie Park Junior, who won his second Open (and the last Open to be played at Musselburgh) in 1879.

However, an even greater legacy than these golfing champions would prove to be the Musselburgh golf hole, which was set at a diameter of 4.25 inches and became the standard size of golf holes around the world to this day. There has been much speculation over how the size of 4.25 inches came about, and what the mathematical logic behind this most integral part of the game of golf was. Reassuringly perhaps, there does not appear to have been any Eureka moment of scientific illumination behind the decision. It was simply the case that the world's first hole-cutter, made in 1829 and on display today in the clubhouse of the Royal Musselburgh Golf Club, was for whatever reason 4.25 inches in diameter, so that was the size that golf holes would be, much to the dismay of millions of golfers whose enjoyment of the game would have been greatly improved if the Musselburgh green-keepers had made them just that wee bit bigger.

The Royal Musselburgh Golf Club was originally named the more egalitarian Musselburgh Golf Club and had been founded back in 1774. The original nine-hole Musselburgh Links remains a municipal golf course open to the public, and with records dating back to 1672, lays claim to being the oldest golf course in continuous use anywhere in the world.

Records also state that as far back as 1811 an annual golf tournament was held in January for the fishwives of Musselburgh (as in women who worked in the local fishing industry rather than for any less complimentary connotations). In 1811, the winner of the ladies' competition received the winner's prize of a creel and a small fishing basket known as 'a skull' – a highly practical if somewhat functional reward for the good fishwives of Musselburgh. The runner-up received a prize of two fine-silk handkerchiefs from Barcelona, and it is sadly not recorded how many putts were missed in an attempt not to end up in first place.

A Scottish lady golfer who we can safely assume did not have much cause for gutting fish in her life was Mary Stuart, Queen of Scots from 1542 to 1567, Queen Consort of France from 1559 to 1560, claimant to the throne of England, the most glamorous and controversial figure in Scottish history – and allegedly something of a golf fanatic It is said that Mary began playing the game as a young girl in France, where she spent her childhood in readiness for her short-lived marriage to the future French king. On her return to her homeland as a teenage widow in 1560, Queen Mary continued her golfing obsession and is reputed to have played at St Andrews on several occasions. Mary had been born at Linlithgow Palace in West Lothian, but it was at Musselburgh in East Lothian that she played her most notorious round of golf.

Mary's regular playing partner was her faithful lady-in-waiting, Mary Seton, who returned with Mary from France to Scotland and then on to exile and imprisonment in England where opportunities to play golf became somewhat limited. Mary Seton came from the high-ranking Seton family of East Lothian, whose stately home was to be found near to Musselburgh. Mary Stuart may have been the monarch and Mary Seton the attendant, but this did not appear to prevent the two Marys from taking their games extremely seriously. In an omen of events to come, the Queen, who would go on to lose her crown and then lose her head, would also lose to Mary Seton at golf, but would magnanimously reward the victor with 'the Seton necklace' that today resides in the Royal Collection. It is unclear when exactly this game took place, but it is possible that it might have been the round of golf that Queen Mary played in February 1567, only a few days after the murder of her second husband and father of her only child, Lord Darnley.

Now Darnley is and was at the time considered a fairly loathsome individual, but it was generally considered that actually murdering the Queen's husband was taking things a tad too far. It has historically never been proven to what extent, if at all, Mary was implicated in the death of her husband, but it was her decision to play golf rather than to follow the appropriate mourning period that was used as *prima facie* evidence of her guilt.

Mary's time in Scotland had coincided with the most revolutionary in Scottish history, with the conversion of the country from Catholicism, to which Mary remained devout, to a radical Presbyterian Protestantism, but it was the murder of her husband, her almost immediate third marriage to the dastardly Earl of Bothwell and that infamous round of golf in Musselburgh that would bring events to a head and within six months Mary was forced to abdicate her throne and would never get the opportunity to win 'the Seton necklace' back in a re-match.

If it is not enough that Mary, Queen of Scots was literally the world's first-ever 'golfing widow' and proves conclusively that women have been playing the game for well over 500 years, one other legacy of her sporting career is that, apparently, we can thank Mary for the popularisation of the word 'caddy' as the name of the person who carries a golfer's clubs. 'Caddy' derives from the French word *cadet*, meaning 'servant'.

Sadly, we will never know conclusively whether it is anything other than coincidence that a golfing term with a French origin has any connection to a golf-playing monarch who was brought up in France, but it will no doubt be of some interest to all those who have followed the maxim of 'gentleman only, ladies forbidden' over the years – and all those who have fought against it – that historically not only have women been at the forefront of golf for centuries, but that men were only allowed on the course to carry their bags.

## The First Thirteen Rules of Golf Club

When one thinks of Leith and sporting history, it is most often the mighty Hibernian Football Club that comes to mind. Founded in 1875 as Hibernians by Irish immigrants, they were a leading force in Scottish football in the 1880s, and after winning the Scottish Cup in 1887, defeated their English counterparts, Preston North End, in a friendly match that was billed, rather grandiosely (if more or less accurately) as the Association Football Championship of the World Decider, before moving to their current home of Easter Road in Leith as Hibernian FC in 1893. However, long before Hibs last won the Scottish Cup in 1902, the sun shone down on another group of sportsmen who were to have an even more significant role in the history of sport.

Our knowledge of the origins of golf mostly comes to the game's relationship with the crown and in particular the House of Stewart. We know that James II banned the game of 'gowf' in 1457 through an Act of Parliament because it was causing too much distraction for his nobles when they should have been practicing archery instead – which perhaps explains Scotland's lack of world and Olympic champion archers over the years. This prohibition continued until 1502 and the reign of James IV, although it is unclear how rigidly the ban was enforced, as in that same year there is a record in James's official accounts of the king purchasing a set of golf clubs from 'a bowmaker' in Perth for the cost of fourteen shillings. Furthermore James IV must have either been an extremely enthusiastic golfer or incredibly careless with his equipment, as he is also known to have bought further sets of clubs in Edinburgh and St Andrews. Whatever the truth, these purchases and a game he played against the Earl of Bothwell in 1504 makes James IV, Scotland's very own Renaissance prince, also the first recorded golfer in the world.

After James, we know that his granddaughter Mary played Mary Seton at Musselburgh in 1567, and although there is no record of either James or Mary ever playing at Leith, the first mention of golf in the area dates back to 1552 and the 'gouff ball makers of North Leith', which presumably means that the game was played there considerably before that date. We also know that by the end of the sixteenth century golf had become so popular in Leith that, from at least 1593, the fun-loving Church of Scotland were imposing fines on and condemning in terms of fire, brimstone and eternal double bogies any golfers who dared to play on the Sabbath, so beginning a centuries-old battle between the Kirk and sport for the very soul of Scotland.

There is a story (which may be apocryphal) that in 1641 Charles I, on one of his rare excursions to the country of his birth and with his various kingdoms in imminent revolt, was playing golf at Leith Links when he was informed of a rebellion in Ireland and proceeded to finish his match, which of course he lost – as we are talking about Charles I after all.

Much more verifiable is golf's first international match between England and Scotland that took place at Leith in 1681, with two English nobles taking on a Scottish team of the Duke of York and future king James VII (son of the Dunfermline-born Charles I), who presumably qualified through the parental qualification rule, and local champion golfer John Paterson. Unsurprisingly, what with Paterson in the team and playing on his home course, Scotland were the victors, with Paterson able to buy a house in the Canongate and be set up for life from his share of his winnings – which was considerably better than the fate of James, who was overthrown as king after only three years on the throne.

Leith's greatest gift to the sport of golf, however, took place on 2nd April 1744 when a competition was held by the Gentleman Golfers of Edinburgh (later to be better known as The Honourable Company of Edinburgh Golfers) – the world's first recorded golf tournament. To coincide with this competition, a committee had been formed to draw up the Thirteen Rules of Golf that all players would abide by – which does make you wonder how gentlemanly these Gentleman Golfers actually were.

The club captain of the Gentlemen Golfers was an Edinburgh surgeon by the name of John Rattray. Rattray was born in Blairgowrie and was a champion archer as well as a champion golfer (so proving to the ghost of James II that it was indeed possible to do both). It is John Rattray's signature that can be found on the original Thirteen 'Articles and Laws in Playing Golf, many of which remain untouched to this day. Rule 3 states that you should not change your ball. Rule 4 states that you should not remove stones (or anything else) for the sake of playing your ball. Rule 5 states that if your ball enters water or a hazard (or as Rattray delightfully puts it 'wattery filth') you can remove your ball and play it behind said hazard, but at the cost of one stroke. Rule 8 states that if your ball is lost then you can play another ball from where the lost ball was struck, but again at the cost of one shot. Rule 10 states that if your ball hits a person (or as they are in Leith, Rattray also adds horses and dogs) you must play the ball where the ball ultimately lies. Rule 11 states that if you are in the process of playing a stroke and for whatever reason stop, this will still be counted as one shot. And Rule 12 states that the player furthest away from the hole should always play first. Furthermore, within the Edinburgh Golfers' Thirteen Rules we see mention of the word 'tee'. Rule 2 states that 'your tee must be on the ground', with your tee then consisting of a small mound of sand. The precise etymology of the word 'tee' is uncertain, but it seems to derive from the Gaelic word *tigh*, meaning 'house', as in the precise area from which you should play your shot and not from the Edinburgh definition of *tea* meaning 'hospitality' as, of course, popularly expressed in the well-known Edinburgh saying 'You'll have had your tea'.

With these Thirteen Rules from the Gentlemen Golfers of Edinburgh the game of golf as an organised sport was truly born. It had taken over 300 years to get to this point, but it was from this first competition in the port of Leith that the development of golf could truly be recorded. In 1768 the Gentleman Golfers built the first clubhouse in the world (long since demolished) and in 1800 changed their name to The Honourable Company of Gentleman Golfers.

By 1831 it was clear that there was no room in Leith for the gentlemen to continue their pursuits and they left the north of Edinburgh to the local population, horses, dogs and 'wattery filth' that, even more than the Church of Scotland, had become the bane of their sporting lives.

The move away from Leith in 1831 now left the way clear for the Society of St Andrews Golfers who had been founded ten years after the Gentlemen Golfers of Edinburgh in 1754. We know that James IV had bought golf clubs in St Andrews in 1506 and that in 1552 a charter allowed, among other things, the local community to play golf – as well as the right to rear rabbits (although presumably not at the same time). Therefore, this means that the Old Course of St Andrews, the most famous golf course in the world, is at least 500 years old and probably considerably older. In 1764 golfers at St Andrews began playing eighteen holes on the Old Course, which is now the standard number of holes in a golf round around the world, although it would not be until 1857 that this was translated into eighteen *separate* holes and the revered golf course that we know today.

After a difficult period at the end of the eighteenth century, when it seemed highly likely that the rabbit farmers, and by definition the rabbits, were on the verge of taking over the entire golf course, the St Andrews Links was sold and The Old Course was saved. And with the Gentlemen Golfers of Edinburgh temporarily out of commission, it was the Society of St Andrews Golfers who gained the patronage of King William IV and became the Royal and Ancient Golf Club of St Andrews, the pre-eminent golf club in Scotland, and by definition, the world.

And what of the good doctor John Rattray, who with his colleagues had drawn up those original Thirteen Rules in April 1744? A silver club was the prize for the winner of that first golf competition in the world and eleven Edinburgh golfers took part, although sadly the most illustrious of their membership, Duncan Forbes of Culloden, who as Lord President of the Court of Session was the most senior law officer in Scotland, was absent. As the best golfer it was not too surprising that Rattray himself won the inaugural silver club and retained the trophy the following year. But in 1746 he was absent from Leith Links, due to the small matter that in the interim he had been persuaded to join the Jacobite cause and become personal physician to no less than the Bonnie Young Pretender. Rattray remained with the rebellion through to the bitter end at Culloden in 1746, ironically the very same Culloden where Duncan Forbes was the laird.

After the defeat and the flight of the Prince, Rattray was captured and imprisoned by the British government forces, but was eventually released and returned to Edinburgh and to Leith Links where he won the silver club once more in 1751. It was said, due to his close association with Charles Edward Stewart, the authorities were set to hang his personal physician on the grounds of treason, and that Rattray was only saved to play his sand wedge once more thanks to the intercession of his old playing partner, Duncan Forbes, who as a lifelong Unionist may have been no supporter of the Jacobite cause, but was never going to abandon his fellow gentleman golfer when conditions got a wee bit tough.

## On a Fairway Near Leven

In the final round of the 1925 Open at Prestwick in Ayrshire, it seemed an inevitability that the great Scottish-American golfer Macdonald Smith, from Carnoustie but long domiciled in the US where he was a regular winner on the US tour, would join his older brothers, Willie and Alex, who had both won The US

Open before the First World War, to become a major champion. He led by five as he teed off and a huge crowd had travelled to the historic golf course to witness the success of the returning Scottish hero. However, with the crowds so great that they enthusiastically spilled out onto the fairways and with minimal stewarding to protect the leading players from well-meaning spectators, Smith found himself jostled and unable to see the greens when playing his shots throughout his round and crashed to a closing 82 and miserable defeat.

For the Prestwick Club and the golfing authorities, the 1925 Open was a terrible embarrassment. Prestwick had hosted The Open twenty-six times, but it was clear that it was no longer big enough or had the requisite facilities to host the huge crowds that attended the greatest golfing tournament in the world. Prestwick was summarily removed as a venue for The Open, replaced by Troon and Turnberry as golfing representatives of Ayrshire and the West of Scotland, and returned to its previous life as a quiet, picturesque, pure dead brilliant seaside town nowhere near Glasgow. However, it was little, forgotten Prestwick Golf Club, and not the royal and ancient St Andrews, that in 1860 saw the birth of the most prestigious and oldest golfing major. And while St Andrews may be honoured as 'the home of golf', it is Prestwick that is 'the birthplace of The Open'.

Golf in the mid-nineteenth century was still the preserve of the middle-class and the well-to-do. Golf clubs and in particular golf balls were expensive to buy, with the 'featherie' golf ball consisting of a stitched leather sphere stuffed with boiled duck or goose feathers. The two dominant golf clubs were at St Andrews in Fife and Musselburgh in East Lothian, the new home of the Gentlemen Golfers of Edinburgh, and in 1843 an epic challenge match was contested over ten days between Allan Robertson of St Andrews and Willie Dunn of Musselburgh, with the St

Andrews man eventually prevailing to be acclaimed as 'champion golfer'.

Allan Robertson is considered to be one of the first professional golfers. He ran a family golf shop in St Andrews that had begun with his grandfather, where they sold golf clubs and golf balls, and played golf matches for money. It is said that Robertson never lost a game without handicaps when there was a financial incentive on offer, and in foursomes he was nigh on invincible as he had as a partner another golfer from St Andrews by the name of Tom Morris, eight years younger than the champion golfer and a man who had worked in the Robertson's shop since the age of fourteen.

The world of golf in the mid-nineteenth century may have continued to slowly evolve as it had for the past two centuries, as a Scottish pastime exclusively played by the leisured classes, if it had not been for the unlikely divine intervention of the Rev. Adam Paterson, also from St Andrews. In 1848 Rev. Paterson invented a brand new golf ball that was made from the liquid rubber of the gutta-percha plant, especially imported from Malaysia. This new ball was called 'the guttie' and would revolutionise the game by making golf balls (and therefore golf) more affordable for the ordinary man and woman.

Allan Robertson was initially resistant to the 'guttie', fearing that it would have a detrimental effect on his business, and when he caught Morris, who was still his employee, playing with the new ball he fired him on the spot. However, within a few years the 'guttie' would replace the 'featherie' as the universal golf ball of choice for the rest of the nineteenth century, and for the thirty-year-old Tom Morris sporting salvation was to come from an unlikely location.

The history of golf up until that point had been personified by the sandy coastal links of the east of Scotland, but in 1851 the Prestwick Golf Club was formed at the Ayrshire seaside resort and appointed Tom Morris as their green-keeper, club professional and with a shop that sold golf clubs and the new 'guttie' balls. But more importantly Morris was tasked with designing a new twelve-hole golf course (the standardisation of eighteen holes was still several decades away) and the golfing professional from St Andrews settled down to a new life on the Ayrshire coast.

Then in 1859 champion golfer Allan Robertson and Tom Morris' former mentor and playing partner suddenly died at the age of forty-six. It was agreed that, rather than a challenge match to decide his successor, a tournament should be held that would be 'open' to all the golfing professionals in Scotland

It was the newcomers Prestwick Golf Club, rather than the established St Andrews or Musselburgh, who took the initiative to host the tournament on the course that Tom Morris had built, and commissioned for the cost of £25 a belt made from red Moroccan leather, embellished with silver clasps that would be awarded to the new 'champion golfer'.

On 17th October 1860, eight professionals assembled in Ayrshire and played three rounds over the twelve-hole course. Tom Morris was the favourite and would play the very first shot – it was his course after all – but he would eventually lose by two strokes to his arch-rival Willie Park from Musselburgh, and it was therefore Park who would gain his place in history as the very first winner of the Open Championship and the very first winner of a golfing 'major'.

Tom Morris and Willie Park were the new dominant golfers in the world of golf. Park won again in 1863, 1866 and 1875 and Tom Morris would win The Open in 1861, 1862, 1864 and 1867 (the oldest man to have done so, even if Tom Watson came heartbreakingly close to passing that particular record down the road at Turnberry in 2009). In 1862 Tom Morris won his second

Open by an extraordinary thirteen strokes, and this in an era where they only played thirty-six holes in total, a record that would last until the year 2000 when a certain Tiger Woods won The US Open by fifteen. There had been no prize money on offer in 1860 – the red Moroccan champion's belt was deemed incentive enough – but in 1864 Prestwick bowed to the inevitable and offered for the first time money to the winner. It was only £6, but £6 went a long way in Ayrshire in 1864, and the history of golf and for that matter professional sport would never be the same again.

## Majors and Minors

Golf in Scotland has long been a family affair, a rare pastime where father and son, brother and brother, but rarely husband and wife, can play year after year, decade after decade, locked in an eternal battle not to look too pleased when your beloved family member once more hits the ball into the water. We already know about the brothers Willie and Alec Ross from Carnoustie who both won The US Open (not forgetting younger Macdonald who had a string of second places), Willie and Laurie Aucherlonie from St Andrews who won The Open and The US Open, respectively, and Fred and Sandy Herd, also from the St Andrews, who repeated this feat in the reverse offer. As impressive was the Park family from Musselburgh, with Willie Senior joined by his brother Mungo, who won The Open in 1874 and his son Willie Junior, champion in 1887 and 1889.

However, it was the father and son dynasty of Tom Morris Senior and his son, Tom Morris Junior, who would be forever immortalised as 'Old Tom' and 'Young Tom', and who would become the most famous family in the history of golf.

*   *   *

Young Tom was born in 1851 in the same year that his father had moved from St Andrews to Prestwick and was already something of a golfing prodigy when he entered The Open of 1868. He was only seventeen years old, but he smashed The Open record by eight strokes, defeating the former champions of Willie Park and his father, who came second by three strokes, and if that was not enough, he had the first recorded tournament hole-in-one in the history of golf.

Young Tom is still the youngest player ever to win a golfing major and reasserted his superiority by retaining the trophy in 1869 and 1870 where, with the somewhat basic golfing equipment of the day, he took only three shots to hole out the mammoth 578 yards first. On completing his hat trick of titles in 1870 it was decided that Young Tom should be awarded the Champion's Belt outright, and a new trophy had to be found.

Prestwick had played host and had organised all the Open Championships from 1860 to 1870, but now agreed to join forces with St Andrews and Musselburgh and jointly commissioned a silver Golf Champions trophy, which would become better known as the most famous trophy in golf, the Claret Jug. Clearly the making of history takes time, as no Open was held in 1871 and the trophy was still not quite ready for the 1872 Championship; with a gold medal (still accorded to the winner today) given as the last-minute substitute.

The 1872 Open was held, as with all previous Opens, at Prestwick. However, for the next twenty years after, The Open would be shared with St Andrews and Musselburgh, before it was opened up (if you pardon the expression) to other golf courses around Britain – although it would never lose the ethos that had been established in 1860 that it was not the British Open or the Scottish Open, but The Open, where professional golfers were welcome to compete no matter where they hailed from.

Young Tom Morris won the 1872 Open, his fourth in

succession and an achievement that has never been matched, and even though he did not receive the Claret Jug in person, he would have the honour of being the first name to be engraved on it. Young Tom failed to add to his Open victories in 1873 and 1874, but was still accepted as the greatest golfer that the world had yet seen, and at such a young age there seemed nothing to stop him achieving victories and fame for decades to come. However, in 1875 the Morris family suffered a triple tragedy when Young Tom's wife and unborn child both died in childbirth, and four months later on Christmas Day Young Tom Morris died suddenly at the age of twenty-four.

By 1875 Old Tom was in his fifties and his best golfing days were behind him. He had returned as the prodigal son to his hometown of St Andrews in 1864 where he remained for the rest of his life as green-keeper. And if his son had been in his short, meteoric career the greatest golfer of the nineteenth century, it was his father who would have the greater influence on the development of the game. Winner of four Open Championships and the player who hit the first shot in Open history, Tom Morris Senior designed the golf courses of Prestwick, and in 1891 the new home of The Honourable Company of Edinburgh Golfers, Muirfield in East Lothian, which has hosted The Open fifteen times.

Perhaps his crowning achievement, however, was his long stewardship of St Andrews itself, where his management of the course and his innovations on the greens and hazards established the science of golf course architecture and made the eighteen holes of the Old Course the standard by which all other golf courses would be compared.

When he died in 1908 he was eighty-seven years old and truly was Old Tom. He had devoted his life to the game that he had loved and had seen golf grow from the first Open in 1860 where only eight Scots participated to a sport that was well on the way to conquering the world. Yet while it should always be remembered that it is thanks to Old Tom Morris that St Andrews became and has remained the spiritual home of golf, it is also thanks to Old Tom Morris that Prestwick and Ayrshire acquired its taste for claret.

## The Iron Man

The question of who is Scotland's greatest-ever golfer is an intriguing and complex one to answer. If we are talking about most successful monetarily then clearly the winner is Glasgow-born Colin Montgomerie with his eight European Orders of Merit and the on- and off-course leader and talisman of numerous Ryder Cup triumphs. Yet 'Monty', like Macdonald Smith seventy years previously, never did win a major tournament and therefore regrettably has to narrowly lose out on the final holes of the final round in the race to the title of Scotland's best. For influence on the history of the game, playing the first-ever shot in The Open and turning St Andrews into the undisputed home of world golf, it is hard to look past Old Tom Morris. But then again, for their brief but extraordinary domination of (respectively) The Open and The US Open before their careers were cut tragically short, one must consider the compelling CVs of both Young Tom Morris and Willie Anderson. However, if one is talking purely on a statistical basis, then although Old Tom Morris, Young Tom Morris, Willie Anderson and for that matter Willie Park Senior all won four major tournaments, there is only one Scottish golfing great who won five.

James Braid was born in the East Neuk of Fife and was no relation to the James Braid from Kinross who is considered 'the father of hypnotherapy', but even though he was born and brought up only ten miles from St Andrews, even hypnosis would not have convinced his disapproving family that golf was an appropriate profession for their son. It was not until he moved to London in 1893 at the age of twenty-three to find work as a club-maker that a sporting career began to become a practical reality. Braid would remain predominantly based in the South of England for the remainder of his golfing life, but his greatest sporting victories were all to take place back in his homeland. A late developer, Braid would not win his first Open title until 1901 at Muirfield, but would go on to lift the Claret Jug four more times at St Andrews in 1905 and 1910, Muirfield again in 1906 and Prestwick in 1908.

James Braid would form a triumvirate of legendary British golfers with Harry Vardon from Jersey and John Henry Taylor from England who won sixteen Opens between them in the years preceding the First World War, with Braid and Taylor winning five and Vardon just one ahead on six.

James Braid might have won even more if he had not retired from competitive golf in 1912, but if anything he would go on to have a greater legacy through his subsequent career as a golf course designer. He was involved in the building, extending and redevelopment of over 200 courses around Britain, including Gleneagles in Perthshire and the improvements to future Open venues Troon in Ayrshire and Carnoustie in Angus. Yet for all the many achievements of James Braid, there is one other Scottish golfer who achieved greatness in both Europe and America who may not quite have won the same number of majors and Opens as Braid or Anderson or Old and Young Tom, but whose career is perhaps the most remarkable of any of the great golfers in the history of the sport.

The years between the two World Wars were difficult ones for Scottish golf. The rest of the world had now embraced the game that had been exclusively nurtured and cherished in Scotland for centuries. Scottish golfers now had to compete with professional golfers from the rest of Britain, the Commonwealth, and in particular the USA, who had more courses, more money and more major tournaments to win with the Masters joining The US Open and the US PGA (that was initially a match-play tournament), leaving Scotland only with the good old Open, and even there the Claret Jug was now regularly competed for across the border in England. Golf had gone international, and while the game honoured its birthplace by following the rules of John Rattray and the template established by Old Tom Morris, they felt no obligation to continue to let Scots win. It was the world's game now.

However, in the interwar years there were still Scottish golfers who were able to hold back the rising American tide to win major tournaments in the US. In 1925 Willie Macfarlane from Aberdeen won The US Open in the most gruelling of circumstances at the Donald Ross-designed Worcester Country Club in Massachusetts. This was the famous tournament where the world's then-greatest golfer, the American Bobby Jones, called himself in the final round, when unbeknownst to everyone but Jones, his ball moved infinitesimally in the rough when his club was addressing the ball. This extra one shot resulted in Jones and Macfarlane being tied after four rounds, and they still could not be separated after an additional eighteen-hole play-off. It would take a second eighteen-hole play-off – 108 holes in total – for the Scot to finally edge one shot ahead and take the title. Macfarlane's eventual victory is generally overshadowed by the credit given to the great sportsmanship of Jones, but while the American became a legend in the game, Macfarlane, the man who defeated him over six rounds of championship golf, is mostly forgotten.

In the 1900s, Jock Hutchison from St Andrews had been part of the exodus of Scottish golfers who had travelled to America to make his name as the game began to take off in the States. Hutchison was a teenager when he first settled in Pittsburgh and it would not be until 1920 that he became the US PGA champion when it was at the time a match-play tournament. Hutchison never won the US Open, although in a long and illustrious career in the States, as well as becoming the long-term honorary starter of the US Masters, he was the inaugural winner of the Seniors PGA in 1937 and demonstrated that old adage that golfers never retire, they just get gradually closer to their score.

The highlight of Jock Hutchison's career, however, would come much closer to home when in 1921 he returned to St Andrews, the town of his birth, to win his one and only Open after a play-off. On the one hand, Hutchison's victory was a favourite son returning home to claim his golfing inheritance and celebrate his victory in the town that he had left nearly twenty years before. But on the other hand, as Hutchison was now a US citizen, when he left 'the home of golf' to return to his new adopted home it was the first time that the Claret Jug had crossed the Atlantic and the clearest indication yet that the New World had superseded the Auld.

There was, though, one final Scot who would find fame, fortune and glory between the Wars. Tommy Armour had been born in Edinburgh and was a keen amateur golfer when he joined the Tank Corps on the Western Front. The First World War was the first time that tanks had been used in conflict, and Armour joined as a young private and survived the carnage long enough to become a Staff Major in 1918. However, also in 1918 his luck finally ran out and he was seriously injured and blinded in both eyes by a mustard gas explosion. After months in hospital, Armour eventually regained his sight in one eye, but not the other, and to help build up his strength he returned to playing the game that he had enjoyed previously as an enthusiastic amateur.

Armour was in his mid-twenties before he began playing golf seriously and immigrated to America in 1920 to further his career. In the US Tommy Armour became famous for his determination, his doggedness and for being the best iron player in the game, an ironic achievement, as it was said that after his injury in the First World War he had required metal plates to be inserted into his shattered right arm. Armour was once quoted as saying that it was not 'good shots that made champions, but making very few bad shots' and he achieved his greatest success when the going was at its toughest. He won the US PGA in 1930 and The US Open at Oakmont, Pennsylvania, in 1927, the last Scot to date ever to do so. And in 1931 he returned home to Scotland and won the first-ever Open to be held at a golf course that has become famous for being arguably the toughest place there is to win a major.

Carnoustie Links in Angus was first laid out by Allan Robertson in 1842, then later extended to eighteen holes by Old Tom Morris and finally modified by James Braid, meaning that three 'champion golfers' had been involved in its design. It was therefore highly appropriate that it was another Scottish great who would be the debut winner there.

Carnoustie has hosted seven Opens to date, and has been the venue for some of the most dramatic moments in Open history, with the great and the good of world golf falling victim to the 'Carnoustie effect', where disaster is but one wayward shot away. This superstition led to Carnoustie being renamed 'Car-nasty' by golfers who had seen a promising round blown off course on the undulating links.

In 1999, The Open had returned to Carnoustie after a twenty-four-year gap amidst much speculation that the course had been tamed of its demons. However, when Frenchman Jean Van de Velde required anything up to a double bogey on the final eighteenth hole to secure his first major title, the course that had been built by Robertson, Morris and Braid showed that it lost none of its devilish tendencies when Van de Velde's ball went into the burn at the final hole, followed by Van de Velde himself, and in tragicomic circumstances the Frenchman ended up taking a triple-bogey, so ensuring the most unlikely play-off in Open history. The unfortunate Van de Velde and the American Justin Leonard would eventually lose the play-off to the previously-unheralded Paul Lawrie from Aberdeen, who had been ten strokes behind at the beginning of the final round and had never been ahead at any point of The Open in regular play. And in the gloomy chill and coastal drizzle of a North East summer's evening, considered ideal golfing conditions in his native Aberdeen, Paul Lawrie became the most recent Scot to win the fabled Claret Jug.

The fortitude and grit shown by Lawrie would have impressed Tommy Armour, who became the first Carnoustie Open winner in 1931, and with the Masters at Augusta not established until 1934, it meant that Armour had won all three major tournaments that were available to him. On the course Armour was often a conservative golfer who concentrated on the elimination of mistakes to keep him in contention, but off the course he was a charismatic, colourful and complex character who was highly popular with the public and was initially nicknamed 'The Black Scot', on account of his trademark dark hair before age inevitably saw him renamed as the no less unmistakable 'Silver Scot'.

Tommy Armour was also a noted raconteur, gambler, drinker and an enterprising businessman who made and lost great fortunes at least once, but such was his gift as a storyteller that nobody was quite sure how much of what he said about his past was true or ever so slightly embellished.

Armour retired from competitive golf in 1935 when his issues with his putter proved insurmountable and it is said that he popularised the term 'yips' for those so afflicted, but he continued to find fame as the world's best-known and most expensive golfing instructor, a noted golf clubs designer and the author of several self-help golfing books that were bestsellers around the world right up to his death in 1968.

Throughout, 'The Black Scot' who became 'The Silver Scot' lived life to the fullest, which was perhaps not so surprising when one considers the adversity that he had overcome to reach the top. This also might explain how, better than anyone, Armour, despite writing a book called *How to Play Your Best Golf at All Times*, was able to make light of the fact that, at the Shawnee Open in 1927, he once took 23 shots on one hole! This remarkable feat still remains the most shots ever to be taken on one hole in the history of US professional golf, as Armour repeatedly hooked his tee shot out of bounds, but if you have just won The US Open only one week before and nine years previously were lying blind and seriously wounded in an army hospital bed, it probably did not seem that big a deal. Even if you do have to have some sympathy for his unfortunate playing partner patiently waiting to take his second shot.

# 3

# *The Footballers*

William McGregor, founder of the Football League

And so we come to football. 'The people's game', 'the beautiful game' and the national game of Scotland, the game of tenements and closes and jumpers for goalposts, and the game of high-definition plasma screens and cyber-space websites that combine the cutting edge of twenty-first-century technology with the views and ideologies of several centuries before. For ever since an enthusiastic group of Victorian Scottish sportsmen adopted a game and set of rules that had originated in the public schools of England, football (or to give it its full, official name, association football) has been – despite the pockets of diehard adherents of rugby, cricket and shinty dotted around the country – the undisputed heartbeat of Scottish team sport for the best part of 140 years, with more players, more clubs, more supporters, more money, and crucially more coverage than all the other team games played in Scotland put together. And once the craze of fitba' had successfully swept the Scottish nation, there was for Scots only one logical next step. And that was, as always, to conquer the world, even if in the early years of association football the world just meant England.

Today the English Premier League is the richest, if not necessarily the greatest, football league in the world, and one of the wealthiest competitions in global sport, with iconic brand names followed by millions of people around the world. And behind all those great global clubs you will invariably find at their birth and underpinning their first flush of success a vanguard of working-class Scots as founders, managers, captains and leading players. For these Scottish football pioneers, as with most Scottish immigrants, the motive was intrinsically economic, drawn south of the border by the greater financial rewards that were on offer on Tyneside, on Merseyside, in the industrial Midlands and mill towns of Lancashire, but so influential would their impact be that without them the world may have never heard of Liverpool FC, Manchester United, Newcastle, Arsenal and Aston Villa, to name but a few.

For the best part of fifty years Scotland was the most important football country in the world, and those pioneering teachers, 'the Scotch Professors' as they were known, spread the gospel of the tenets of the Scottish passing game to whoever would pay. A century later, the teams that they led to greatness in Scotland and England are followed and revered across the globe, even though the names on the backs of the replica shirts are as cosmopolitan as their billionaire owners – multi-national teams for a multi-national age. And though you will struggle to find many Scottish names in the squads of the Champions League usual suspects of the twenty-first century, you do not have to look too far to find a history, a heritage and a manager that was more often than not forged in the cradle of football that was and is the West of Scotland, where in 1872 on a Glasgow cricket pitch international football was born and where over the next 140 years some of the most legendary footballers in the history of the game would first make their name. And then invariably leave as soon as was humanly possible.

## It was Under the Tape!

There have been numerous forms of football around the world for centuries, and kicking a sphere-like object and kicking each other is a pastime and a skill that is not exclusive to any one nation. Rugby union, rugby league, Australian rules and American football are all sports that have the same antecedents and are all first cousins or first cousins once removed of each other. They can all trace their histories back to the nineteenth century and Victorian society's requirement that public enjoyment of physical exertion, as contrasted to private enjoyment of physical exertion (that should of course not be referred to in any circumstances whatsoever), was not acceptable unless accompanied by a strictly adhered to rulebook of laws, regulations and sub-clauses. Therefore, it was in 1863 that the sport of association football was born in London, complete with the requisite Laws of the Game.

There were many football teams playing to varying rules throughout Britain – including Scotland – before 1863, but it was in that year under the leadership of the wonderfully named Ebenezer Morley that eleven clubs came together to form the Football Association and agreed on the fourteen rules of the game (that still included catching and handling the ball by outfield players), that would eventually take over the world (more or less).

The original eleven clubs all came from London and the South of England, and although the association rules began to be used throughout Britain, the strongest clubs were initially from the English public schools who were the original pioneers of the people's game, and we can presume that it was in the south of England that the first Scottish footballers took up the new rules.

In 1870 Charles Alcock, top English footballer and newly-appointed Secretary of the FA, decided to make the fateful decision to organise a challenge match following association football rules between an English eleven and a Scottish eleven. This game was held at The Oval cricket ground in March 1870, with Alcock captaining England and the Scottish team a loose assortment of friends of Alcock's and players with vague Scottish connections living in London or the Home Counties, all of whom had either some understanding of the new game or had been misinformed and turned up with their batting pads.

The first match was an honourable 1–1 draw and four more matches were held at The Oval between 1870 and 1872, with one further draw and three English victories. The games were considered a qualified success, but it was pointed out to Alcock that the Scottish eleven were not actually all that Scottish, with only one member of the original 1870 team, Kenneth Muir Mackenzie from Perthshire, actually born in Scotland. Stung by this criticism, Alcock pointed out these challenge matches had been open to all Scots, and to be fair he had posted adverts in the Scottish newspapers to attract Scottish players, but it had only been the Anglo-Scots who had responded. However, he would now offer a further open invitation that an England eleven would travel to the back of beyond, or even Glasgow, to take on a truly representative Scottish eleven, if there were indeed eleven Scots ready and willing to take up his call.

With the gauntlet thrown down word went out for Scottish

heroes to once more take on the English. National pride was at stake, the cricket season was over and eleven men from the south side of Glasgow stepped forward and changed the history of football forever.

Scotland's oldest association football club, Queen's Park, had been founded in July 1867 and were the top football team in Scotland in 1872, although granted there were probably no more than ten other teams in the whole of Scotland for them to play against and some of them were not very good – a not too dissimilar scenario to Scottish club football today.

In order to get more games against tougher competition, Queen's Park in 1872 had entered a brand new tournament that Alcock had devised, called the FA Cup, and had travelled down to London to play a semi-final against the pride of English football, the Wanderers, who were captained by Alcock and had the best of the public school footballers at their disposal. The game ended in an honourable 1–1 draw, but the London jaunt had exhausted Queen's Park's limited budget and they could not afford the cost of a replay in London and withdrew from the Cup. However, Queen's Park's creditable performance had shown that they could compete with the best of the English, and when Alcock's challenge to play in Scotland was issued, Queen's Park were ready and willing to answer the call.

The game was appropriately arranged for St Andrew's Day, 30th November 1872, and was held at the Hamilton Crescent ground of the West of Scotland Cricket Club in Partick, Glasgow. Robert Gardner, goalkeeper and captain of Queen's Park, took on the task of selecting the Scottish team and unsurprisingly selected the entire Queen's Park first eleven: Gardner, William Ker, Joseph Taylor, James Thomson, James Smith, Robert Smith, Robert Leckie, Alexander Rhind, William MacKinnon, James Weir and David Wotherspoon. Alcock selected a strong English team, but was unable to play himself because of injury, much to the disappointment of the Glaswegian crowd who had been practising several chants in his honour.

The Hamilton Crescent pitch was heavy due to persistent rain in the days leading up to the match and kick-off was delayed by twenty minutes so that the fog could clear. Four thousand curious spectators paid one shilling each to watch this momentous sporting occasion, many watching an association football game for the first time and some no doubt slightly put out about why W.G. Grace wasn't playing.

The Scots played a 2–2–6 formation, which sounds incredibly attack-minded, but it was in fact more defensive than the English 1–2–7 and gave the Scots a strategic advantage. Accounts of the game are not comprehensive and sometimes contradictory, but seem to imply that, while the English team were stronger and specialised in individual dribbling, the lighter Scots coped better with the rain-soaked pitch and as a club team were better at playing together. With both teams cancelling each other out, chances were few and far between, but Robert Leckie almost had the chance to achieve football immortality when his shot headed towards the goal and in these pre-crossbars times hit the tape between the posts. No goal was awarded and the historic first game ended in a 0–0 draw, with many in the crowd commenting that while the match itself had been quite enjoyable to watch, 'wasn't it high time that goal-line video technology was brought in'.

Four months later, on 8th March 1873, Robert Gardner came down the road with his Queen's Park colleagues for a return match against England at The Oval, bolstered by three of the top Anglo-Scots. The second match was somewhat more exciting than the first and 3,000 spectators in London watched the home team defeat the Scots 4–2, with the English having learnt from the previous game and choosing to match the Scottish formation this time around. And five days later, on 13th March 1873 Queen's

Park agreed, with seven other Scottish clubs – including such historic but now mostly forgotten names as Vale of Leven, Third Lanark, Clydesdale, and Kilmarnock – to found the Scottish Football Association to organise the game in Scotland and run the national team.

The events of November 1872 and March 1873 would radically change the history of Scottish, British and international football. The game of association football had its roots in England, but it was in Glasgow that international football was born, with Hamilton Crescent the venue for the world's first official international match. The Partick ground would see two further internationals between Scotland and England in 1874 and 1876, before football internationals left cricket grounds behind and moved to a new Glasgow home at Queen's Park's new ground that went by the name of Hampden Park. Hamilton Crescent returned to its primary and no less exciting existence as the home of West of Scotland Cricket Club, but will always have the honour of not only being the first ground in the world to host a football international, but with Scottish victories in 1874 and 1876 and the draw of 1872, would never witness a Scottish defeat.

The formation of the Scottish Football Association in 1873 also meant that England and the FA were no longer the sole arbiters and guardians of the game and paved the way for other countries to take up the game and form their own associations, making football truly international. Unlike the game of cricket where there were no matches between England and Scotland and it would belatedly take well over a century for the Scots even to consider competing as a separate nation, from 1872–1873 on Scotland was, as far as the world of football was concerned, the international equal of England, a sovereign sporting nation, regardless of and separate to the political and constitutional actuality of the United Kingdom. And thanks to Robert Gardiner, Queen's Park and an Englishman called Alcock, the history of association football (and it could be argued the history of Scotland itself) would never be the same again.

## *Football Heroes and Villains*

By the early 1880s, association football had grown rapidly in England, and by 1881, 128 clubs had joined the FA. The game was flourishing throughout the country and the FA Cup was well established as its premier football tournament.

However, beneath the rosy, optimistic statistics of growth and greater public interest, a dangerous split was beginning to develop in English football. In 1876 a Scottish football international by the name of James Lang was persuaded to join Sheffield Wednesday from his Scottish club of Third Lanark, with the offer of a position in a local Sheffield company to sweeten the move. It soon transpired that Lang had no actual duties as such with the company in question and his real job description was simply to play football for Wednesday, making him possibly the first professional in the history of football.

The problem with this scenario and the reason that we will never know for sure whether Lang was the first professional footballer or not, was that FA rules clearly stated that football was an amateur game, but by the 1880s it was clear that many of the leading clubs in the Midlands and Northern England were either flouting these strictures by finding their star players jobs where they did not have to actually do anything or increasingly paying them under the table for playing. And since most of the best footballers came from north of the border where the game was also technically amateur but more rigidly adhered to, more and more Scots began to appear for the major northern English clubs.

The issue finally came to a head in 1884 when Preston North End, complete with a coterie of Scottish internationals, were expelled from the FA Cup for being a professional team. In retaliation, Preston joined forces with other top teams such as Sunderland and Aston Villa and threatened to leave the FA and form their own professional association. With a North–South divide opening up in English football and realising that it was way too late to halt the scourge of players being paid, the FA were forced to bow to the inevitable. In 1885 English football went professional, much to the annoyance of the Scottish football authorities and Scottish clubs, who did not go professional until 1893 and in the interim saw the stream of Scots heading south turn into a flood.

The club administrator and one of the directors at Aston Villa was a William McGregor from Perthshire, who was a draper by trade and had set up a drapery business in Birmingham. McGregor had joined the administrative side of Aston Villa in 1877, three years after the club had been founded, and formed a formidable Scottish leadership of the club with McGregor in charge off the field and Glaswegian George Ramsay in charge on the pitch as club captain. McGregor was a true football enthusiast, and with the battle for the acceptance of professionalism in England finally won in 1885 he now saw the opportunity to further improve the game.

Other than the FA Cup that was still played on an annual knockout basis, there was no national tournament for ambitious English football clubs to compete for. Friendly matches and local cups were played on an ad-hoc basis, but clubs needed a more regular stream of income and more matches for their supporters to pay to watch, as, after all, all those Scottish footballers still had to be paid for.

On 2nd March 1888, McGregor wrote a letter to Preston, Blackburn Rovers, Bolton Wanderers, Stoke and West Bromwich Albion, proposing the formation of a league of either ten or twelve teams, with home and away fixtures. It soon became clear that the clubs that received the letter were receptive, and at a meeting at Manchester on 17th April the Football League was founded, the first national association football league to be established in the world, with Aston Villa and McGregor's five original correspondents joined by Accrington, Derby County, Everton, Burnley, Wolverhampton Wanderers and Notts County.

All the twelve original clubs came from either the Northwest or the Midlands in order to ease travel costs in their inaugural season, but the name Football League was carefully chosen so as not to exclude the future inclusion of clubs, not just from the east and south of England, but from the rest of Britain as well (including Scotland).

McGregor was elected the first Chairman of the Football League and would later serve as both Football League President and Chairman of the Football Association from 1888 to 1894. He became the leading figure in the organisation and expansion of association football in nineteenth-century football, even if his dream of a united British League, to the great chagrin of both Rangers and Celtic many decades later, would forever be dashed when McGregor's stubbornly independent fellow countrymen formed the Scottish Football League two years later in 1890.

The debut season of the Football League began in September 1888 and was dominated by Preston North End who went through the campaign undefeated, winning eighteen and drawing four. The club would go down in history as 'The Invincibles', with no other club matching this feat until Arsenal in 2003–04.

The Lancashire town of Preston had long had connections with Scotland, a convenient midway point on the journey from

Glasgow to London. Two Scottish armies in 1648 and 1715 had both made injudicious decisions to march into England on behalf of the Stuart cause and both were summarily defeated, although the local populace showed that they were a forgiving lot when they apparently cheered the Jacobite army of 1745 when they marched into the town thirty years later, and no doubt cheered them even more when it became clear that they were not staying.

In 1888–89, six of the unbeaten Preston North End that became the first football champions of England came from north of the border. Jimmy Ross and George Drummond came from Edinburgh, John Gordon from Glasgow, John Graham from Ayr and David Russell and Samuel Thompson from Ayrshire. In fact, the Preston North End of 1888–89 went not one, but two further than the Arsenal team of 2003–04 by defeating Wolves 3–0 in London to win the FA Cup and become the first team to win the League and Cup double, and with Jimmy Ross's older brother, Nick Ross, rejoining the team, would also retain the League in 1889–90.

In England, there was much jealousy and resentment about the domination of Preston and their Scottish professionals, but it became abundantly clear that Preston's blueprint of building a team around the Scottish tradition of teamwork and passing the ball between the players rather than the English tendency to individual play and dribbling was the future, and if Preston filled their team with Scots then their rivals would do so as well. And whatever the concerns about Preston's dominance, William McGregor's notion of a national league had proven to be a success. As quickly as 1892–93 the Football League had grown to two divisions and twenty-eight clubs, and by 1900 it was up to forty. Woolwich Arsenal had become the first London club to join in 1892, but power remained in the north, although the next great champions of England came from the east rather than the west.

\* \* \*

It was a man from Ayr by the name of James Allan who was teaching in Sunderland and decided to found an association football club in the city in October 1879. Allan had just turned twenty-two when Sunderland FC came into being and became the team's centre forward; it was his club, after all.

The club soon became one of the top teams in the north of England, turning professional in 1885, and with their relative geographical proximity were one of the first clubs to recruit players from Scotland. This did not sit easily with James Allan, who saw football in the amateur light of being a recreational pastime, as well as the fact that he was less likely to get a game, and he left the club in 1888.

Their Scottish founder might have left, but the Scottish influence on Sunderland continued to grow, and in the 1890s they became known as 'a team of all the talents', winning the League three times in 1892, 1893 and 1895, with almost all of those talents in question being Scottish. William Gibson, Ned Doig, James Gillespie, John Scott, John Harvey, Hughie Wilson, Donald Gow, Jimmy Millar and Jimmy Hannah played in all three of those Championship wins. John Auld from Ayrshire was their captain and Johnny Campbell from Renton in Dunbartonshire was the top scorer in the League on all three occasions.

In the twentieth century, Sunderland would win a further three League titles, although none since 1936, making them the sixth most successful club in English football history, with crucially two more titles to their name than their arch-rivals Newcastle United, but none of their subsequent teams or any number of lucky black cats can match the achievements of the Scots who played for Sunderland in the 1890s.

The third great team of nineteenth-century English League football was appropriately enough the Aston Villa side of William McGregor, the man who made the League Championship a reality after all. And thanks to McGregor, and in particular his fellow Scot, George Ramsay, Aston Villa became the predominant club in English football as the nineteenth century turned into the twentieth.

Ramsay had first played for Villa in the year that they were formed, 1874, and with the recruitment of another Glaswegian, Archie Hunter, who joined Villa in 1876 and became their star player, they became the first English club to emulate the Scottish passing game. Ramsay retired from playing in 1882, but became secretary of the team in 1884 (the nineteenth-century equivalent of manager) and with Hunter as captain won their first major trophy, the FA Cup, in 1887. Hunter retired in 1890, but under Ramsay's stewardship Aston Villa went on to win five League titles between 1894 and 1900, and in an extraordinary thirty-two-year tenure in charge that would last right through until 1926, Ramsay would win in total six League championships and six FA Cup victories, making Aston Villa the most successful English club of their time.

Unlike Preston North End and Sunderland, the success of Aston Villa was built on English rather than Scottish players, with the notable exception of James Cowan from Dunbartonshire, who played in all of their first five League titles, but even today the Scottish legacy on Villa's golden age is still commemorated by the Scottish lion rampant that, thanks to William McGregor, first appeared on their shirts in 1879 and is now incorporated on their club crest.

The era of supremacy of English football by Scottish professionals at the close of the nineteenth century was coming to an end. They had been known as the 'Scotch Professors' in recognition of the intelligence of their play and their tactical acumen, had revolutionised association football in England through professionalism and were at the forefront of turning football from an elitist amateur game of the south of England to a game that was dominated by the urban and industrial towns and cities of the North and Midlands. Inevitably, English footballers would eventually become the equals of their Scottish teachers, and with the professionalism of the Scottish game it was to prove more difficult to recruit wholesale teams of Scots and generate instant success.

However, throughout the twentieth century, Scottish footballers would continue to follow the pioneering 'Scotch Professors' south and achieve fame and fortune in the higher echelons of English football, even if by the twenty-first century this tended to be more the second tier of the Championship rather than the actual Premier League.

And arguably even more influential were the Scots who followed the lead of George Ramsay from Glasgow, the first of the tradition of the great Scottish managers in England that at the beginning of the 2011–12 season saw seven men from the West of Scotland managing Premier League clubs. But above all, it was thanks to a Scot from Perthshire that the oldest and at present the richest football league in the world was founded in 1888 and why still being able to watch *Match of the Day* will remain a key issue in any negotiations concerning an independent Scotland.

## Our Cup Final Overfloweth

Robert McAlpine from Lanarkshire, the original Bob the Builder, has many claims to fame. A pioneer in concrete, the company that he founded in 1869 and takes his name is one of Britain's leading construction firms, with recent developments including the building of the Emirates Stadium in 2006 and the London Olympic Stadium in 2012. In Scotland, McAlpine is perhaps best known for the magnificent Glenfinnan Viaduct on the West Highland Line that was completed in 1901, and thanks to a certain young wizard is now appreciated by millions of 'muggles', not all of whom are necessarily aficionados of Victorian railway engineering. And in England, McAlpine was the builder of another iconic construction that captured the imagination far beyond the not-so-deathly hallows of its turf.

The original Wembley Stadium was built in only 300 days in 1922–23 and for seventy-seven years was both the home of English football and one of the most famous, if not *the* most famous, sports stadium in the world. It hosted England internationals, the rugby league Challenge Cup Final from 1929, five European Cup Finals, the European Championship Final of 1996 and apparently sometime in the 1960s, some match between England and Germany. For Scots, Wembley was a biennial pilgrimage to gatecrash and occasionally ransack the citadel of English football pre-eminence and show that the heritage of the game was as much ours as theirs. Yet for everyone else, Wembley became synonymous with the hosting of the FA Cup Final, the highlight of the English football calendar.

In the twenty-first century, the FA Cup Final has lost some of its lustre, what with the closure of the original Wembley in 2000 and the omnipresent influence of the twin economic towers of the Premier and Champions League, but until relatively recently the thirty-nine steps it used to take to lift the FA Cup at the original Wembley had a romantic resonance that far outreached what was, in truth, a secondary domestic trophy. And it was the very first match to be played at Wembley in 1923 that more than any other was responsible for creating the myth and legend of what became one of the greatest sporting events in the world.

When Wembley played host to the FA Cup Final between Bolton Wanderers and West Ham United on 28th April 1923, the oldest football tournament in the world had already been in existence for over fifty years. As mentioned earlier, the FA Cup had begun in 1872, two years ahead of the Scottish Cup in 1874, but in those early innocent amateur days there was no prohibition on Scottish clubs entering their English equivalent. Queen's Park, the pioneers of Scottish association football, who had organised and provided the entire team in Scotland's first international, were the undisputed kings of Scotland. They did not lose a single game from their foundation in 1868 until 1876 and won the Scottish Cup eight times between 1874 and 1886, in the years before the formation of the Scottish League in 1890, and it was therefore understandable that they were keen to take up the offer to compete in the FA Cup.

Sadly, however, Queen's Park as a strictly amateur club found it difficult to afford the cost of regular travel and loss of earnings to play in England. Thus, their initial southern excursions were haphazard and irregular, if not without some level of success. And in both 1884 and 1885 the pride of Scotland managed to stay in the tournament long enough to reach the FA Cup Final itself at the Kennington Oval in London, but on both occasions they were defeated by Blackburn Rovers, and sadly Queen's Park would never add the English FA Cup to their list of extraordinary achievements as the greatest football club in the world at the time. For in 1887 the Scottish FA decreed, in another early demonstration of sporting Scotland's determination to go it alone, that Queen's Park and all other Scottish clubs would be from that point on prohibited from playing in England's Premier Cup tournament, a decision that no amount of campaigns for any notional 'British Cup' over the next 125 years has ever been even close to reversing.

Blackburn Rovers were one of the new elite of English football clubs. Based in the north of England rather than the south, one of the instigators of the English game turning professional and a founding member of the Football League in 1888, Blackburn dominated the FA Cup in the 1880s. After their two victories against Queen's Park in 1884 and 1885, they completed the hat trick in 1886 (the last club ever to achieve this) and won again in 1890 and 1891. And the manager of Blackburn Rovers was a Thomas Mitchell from Dumfries. Mitchell would eventually leave Blackburn in 1896 and become in 1897 the short-lived first professional manager of an up-and-coming London club by the name of Woolwich Arsenal, but it was his five FA Cup victories and his role in the professionalism of English football that would be his legacy.

Only one manager has ever won more than Mitchell's FA Cups, and it is not, at the time of writing, Alex Ferguson, who won his first FA Cup in 1990 but has been stuck on five since 2005. The record instead lies with the Glaswegian George Ramsay, who in a career as manager of Aston Villa that, as far as longevity is concerned, even Sir Alex will struggle to emulate, won his first FA Cup in 1887 and his sixth and final thirty-three years later in 1920 – not that anyone would dare rule out Sir Alex still being in charge at Old Trafford in 2023.

Wherever you look in the early years of the FA Cup, Scots are prominent. In 1894 James Logan from Troon in Ayr became only the second of three players to date ever to score a hat trick in an FA Cup Final, when he starred in Notts County's 4–1 victory over Bolton. This was the only major honour that Notts County, the oldest surviving professional football in England, have ever won, but although it was a surprise it was nothing compared to the winners of the 1901 FA Cup – perhaps the biggest shock in the history of a tournament where until relatively recently great sporting upsets were almost a matter of course.

In 1898 John Cameron from Ayr probably thought his career was in decline. He was an alumnus of Queen's Park and had made his name with Everton and Scotland, but had now signed for a club outside the Football League – Tottenham Hotspur. The following year Cameron was appointed player-manager and in the 1901 FA Cup led the non-League Spurs on a remarkable run through to the final, where Tottenham drew 2–2 with Sheffield United. One week later at a replay in Bolton, Tottenham found themselves 1–0 down at half-time before Cameron popped up to equalise, and with only three minutes remaining another son of Ayrshire, striker Sandy Brown, scored the decisive goal that would seal Tottenham a 3–1 victory. Brown had also scored both Tottenham goals in the first final and is one of only a select number of players to have scored in every round of the FA Cup, while Cameron became the first of an even more select group of two men (along with Kenny Dalglish for Liverpool in 1986) to win the Cup as a player-manager, and in a record that is highly unlikely ever to be repeated, the only manager to lead a non-League club to win the FA Cup.

Tottenham's FA Cup victory in 1901 was the first occasion that a major trophy had been won by a club from London and at the 1901 FA Cup Final a new world record crowd of 110,000 had crammed into the Crystal Palace to watch the game. London and the South were finally emerging as a force in English football that could compete with the North and the Midlands and the construction of Wembley was the next stage in the development of football in the capital. The new stadium would have a capacity of 125,000 – 2,000 less than the 127,000 that had attended the Scotland vs England international at Hampden Park in 1912, but still considerably greater than any previous football match in England.

The organisation of the 1923 FA Cup Final and the opening of the stadium were all rather rushed. Incredibly when one considers what would happen to the much-delayed second Wembley, the original stadium built by McAlpine had been completed almost one year ahead of schedule, and it was a last-minute decision by the FA to hold the Cup Final there. As nobody expected there to be 125,000 Bolton and West Ham fans wanting to attend, the fateful decision was made to make the final a non-ticket affair. An hour before kick-off there was already a huge crowd inside the stadium, and it was clear that Wembley had reached full capacity and that the organisers had underestimated the appeal of the first match ever to be played at the new national home. It was decided to close the gates, but with tens of thousands still outside it was impossible to keep them out. Nobody knows for certain how many people attended the 1923 FA Cup Final. The official attendance was the capacity of 126,000 who actually paid, but estimates have ranged from a cautious 180,000 (probably the police figure) to as many as 250,000 – the highest attendance ever to watch a football match anywhere in the world.

The crowd was so vast that they were forced to go onto the pitch to avoid being crushed, and amidst the chaos there seemed to be little hope of a game of football actually taking place. Somehow the crowd was pushed back just far enough that the pitch was visible, but with spectators crowded along the very edge of the pitch and behind and almost in the goals; however, against all expectations and amidst all the chaos, the game kicked off only forty-five minutes late. After two minutes Bolton took an early lead, but only a few minutes later the crowd had surged back on the pitch and play was suspended.

Abandonment seemed inevitable, but once more the crowd were persuaded back and the game continued, although there were several instances of full-backs and wingers finding themselves entangled in the crowd, and not unexpectedly, much of the game was played in the centre of midfield.

The key moment of the game took place in the fifty-third minute. The teams had no choice but to stay on the pitch at half time, and in the second half against the run of play Bolton made a break down the wing. It seems likely that the ball was actually going out of play and was kept in by a supporter, but the referee waved play on and the ball was crossed into the middle where it came to Bolton forward Jack Smith.

Smith hailed from Glasgow and was, unusually for the time, the only Scot on either side. His shot went past the West Ham players towards the goal and immediately rebounded back. As far as West Ham were concerned, Smith's shot had hit the post, but in the referee's view the ball had crossed the line and had come back into play after hitting the crowd that was pressed against the net. A goal was awarded to give Bolton a decisive 2–0 lead.

The remainder of the game was played out with the clear and present danger of further crowd invasions, and it was probably a relief for all concerned, including West Ham, when the final whistle was blown.

King George V, who like most of the crowd had not paid for his ticket, presented the FA Cup to the victorious Bolton team, and incredibly considering all that had taken place in the previous few hours, the massive throng dispersed without one serious injury. Against the odds and despite the complete shambles that had taken place, the inaugural FA Cup Final at Wembley had made sporting history and a new glorious chapter of the FA Cup had begun.

Learning the lessons, all future matches at Wembley would be all-ticket with a maximum capacity of 100,000, and it was therefore once more Hampden Park that would reclaim the title of the largest football stadium in both Britain and the world until 1950 and the opening of the 200,000 capacity stadium Maracanã in Rio de Janeiro.

As for the FA Cup, there would be numerous other Scottish entries to the legend of the oldest football tournament in the world from managers to players to the communal hymn 'Abide With Me' that was written by theologian Henry Francis Lyte from the Scottish Borders and has been sung at every Final since 1927. But no matter what the future holds for the tournament, it is difficult to imagine that there will be many who will be able to emulate the managerial success of Thomas Mitchell and George Ramsay, the achievement of John Cameron of leading the only non-League side ever to lift the trophy and the strange footnote in sporting history of Jack Smith from Glasgow, who scored a goal in front of the largest crowd ever to watch a game of football, and did so with only one person out of a crowd of 250,000 spectators of the opinion that the ball had actually crossed the line.

## Scots Never Walk Alone

Aston Villa and Sunderland had been the leading clubs in 1890s English football, but as a new century dawned with a new king and a new era, a new force would rise to the top of the Edwardian decade, and as had been the case with Sunderland, 'the team of all the talents', their rivals from the North East, Newcastle United, would base much of their success on recruiting players from Scotland.

Newcastle United had been founded in 1892 and in 1895 they recruited Frank Watt from Edinburgh as their club secretary and *de facto* unofficial manager. Watt would remain in that position for over three decades through what would be the most glorious chapter in the history of the club. One of Watt's first and most crucial decisions was the signing of the Ayrshire-born defender Andy Aitken who became club captain when they were promoted to the First Division in 1898, and in 1905 led the Geordies to their first League Championship. Aitken left the club at the end of the following season, but this did not stop further honours being brought to Tyneside – much to the chagrin of their Wearside neighbours, especially when in 1904 Newcastle signed their Scottish international defender, Inverness-born Andy McCombie, for a then-colossal world record transfer fee of £700 and so intensifying the Tyne–Wear football rivalry that remains to this day.

Newcastle United, renowned for their attacking and entertaining play, would win three League titles in 1905, 1907 and 1908, as well as finally lift the FA Cup in 1910 after a run of four final defeats. There were six Scots in the team that won the FA Cup in 1910 and three of them had also played in all of their successful League campaigns: goalkeeper Jimmy Lawrence from Glasgow, who was at the club for eighteen years and still holds the record for most appearances; midfielder Jimmy Howie from Ayrshire and Peter McWilliam, from Inverness and nicknamed 'Peter the Great', who would later be the manager of Tottenham when they won the FA Cup in 1921. However, of all the significant Scots who have featured in Newcastle United's golden age, the 'greatest' would be the Airdrie forward and Bellshill-born Hughie Gallacher.

Gallacher had made his Scotland debut in 1924 in an international career that would see him star as one of the 'Wembley Wizards' who defeated England 5–1 in 1928, and he would score an extraordinary twenty-three goals in only twenty matches, making him still to this day the third-highest goal scorer in Scotland's history, after fellow greats Denis Law and Kenny Dalglish, both of whom played in far more games than Gallacher ever did. He was the most wanted player in Scotland and had inspired Airdrie to their only major honour, the Scottish Cup in 1924, but it was Frank Watt and Newcastle who finally signed him in December 1925.

Gallacher was a revelation in English football, his skill and strength belying his five-foot-five-inch frame, and despite the regular brutal treatment meted out to him by defenders, he became a folk hero in the North East, scoring 133 goals in only 160 appearances between 1925 and 1930.

He was only twenty-three years old when he was appointed club captain at the start of the 1926–27 season and led Newcastle to their first League title since 1909, scoring a club record thirty-six goals in the season. For all his incredible record at Newcastle and the success he brought to the club, Gallacher was often a combustible and controversial personality, and in 1930 he was transferred. He continued to score goals in the First Division until 1936 and appeared for Scotland until 1935, but the 1930s were less kind to Gallacher compared to his glory days at St James' Park, and retirement from football saw him beset by financial and personal problems that were exacerbated by alcohol.

Hughie Gallacher committed suicide in his adopted home of Tyneside in 1957 at the age of fifty-four but remains to this day one of Scotland's greatest-ever footballers, and remains over eighty years later and despite all the many famous players who have subsequently played for them, the hundreds of millions of pounds of investment and the fanatical and loyal support of a club that is one of the giants of the game, the last man to lead Newcastle United to a League Championship title.

The club that Hughie Gallacher was transferred to in 1930 and where he was reunited with fellow 'Wembley Wizard' Alex Jackson was Chelsea. And even back then they were considered amongst the *nouveau riche* of English football.

Chelsea Football Club had been founded in West London in 1905 and elected to the Football League the same year. They hired Glasgow architect Archibald Leitch to design their Stamford Bridge Stadium and recruited Dumbarton-born defender John

Robertson, who had won three League titles for Rangers, as the club's first player-manager.

It would be Robertson who would score Chelsea's first-ever competitive goal, but he would surprisingly resign after only one season, and in 1907 Chelsea appointed another Scot, David Calderhead from Hurlford in Ayrshire, as manager. He remained in charge until 1933, where, despite regular sojourns in the Second Division, Chelsea became one of the best-supported and wealthiest clubs in England and gained a reputation under Calderhead for entertaining, attacking football. Calderhead was not shy in taking fellow Scots to the Bridge, but despite the recruitment of Hughie Gallacher and regularly leading the First Division goal-scoring charts, Chelsea were unable to turn this into elusive silverware. Calderhead left in 1933 without any major honours, but remains with a tenure of twenty-six years, by some way the club's longest-serving manager, a record that, considering the average tenure of Chelsea managers today, seems highly unlikely ever to be beaten.

If Newcastle is one English city that Scotland has always said to have a natural affinity for, then it is Liverpool, who is the other. Both are northern ports that have grown, prospered and declined through trade, industry and shipping and have become celebrated and often caricatured for their pride in their city, pride in their culture and pride in their working-class heritage. They may come from three distinct geographical regions and have three distinct histories, but Geordies, Scousers and Jocks have far more in common than distinctive accents and for centuries Scots have been making their home on either side of the north of England.

In the nineteenth century, the Scottish brothers David and Charles McIver established themselves in Liverpool as ship owners and would go on to run the Cunard Line services from

Liverpool to New York and Canada, and at the end of the same century Scottish footballers would also begin to find themselves leading football clubs on Merseyside.

Everton were the first team to emerge from the city of Liverpool. Formed in 1878 they were one of the founding members of the Football League in 1888, and in 1891 they became the second club to win the League Championship. As with 'The Invincibles' of Preston North End, the first club to attain this title, the Everton side of 1891 was dominated by Scots, with no fewer than six in the title-winning team. Their formidable defence, moreover, was led by captain Andrew Hannah from Renton in Dunbartonshire and one Dan Doyle from Paisley, a brilliant but tempestuous defender who was as controversial as he was successful.

After winning the English League title with Everton, Doyle returned to Scotland to join Celtic as arguably the most important signing in their history, even though the club were nominally still 'amateur'. With Doyle leading their defence, Celtic would become one of the dominant clubs in Scottish football, winning their first four League Championships between 1893 and 1898, with Doyle himself becoming a legendary figure for Celtic supporters and a captain of Scotland, while still somehow managing to leave a trail of chaos in his flamboyant wake.

Even with the exit of Doyle, everything seemed set for a period of Evertonian dominance south of the border, but only one year later in 1892 a bitter internal dispute within the club resulted in the formation of a rival team in the city, Liverpool FC. As part of the final agreement about how the club should be divided the new club (Liverpool) would inherit Everton's former home of Anfield, with Everton moving to a new ground at Goodison Park, but Everton would retain the playing squad and their position in the League.

Unsurprisingly, Liverpool's directors followed the tried and trusted route for English football clubs looking for instant success and recruited an entire squad of Scots to play for them, including as captain Andrew Hannah, the same Andrew Hannah who had captained Everton to their League title the year before. The original Liverpool side would become known as 'the team of the Macs' on account of so many of their players' surnames beginning with that prefix, making them the first, but certainly not the last, English team to actually have no English players. Liverpool were elected to the Football League Second Division in 1893 and on 2nd September of that year Malcolm MacVean from the Vale of Leven scored the club's first-ever League goal. The Scottish influence continued throughout the decade as Liverpool were promoted to the First Division and culminated in the team of 1900–01 that included five Scots, becoming the first champions of the new century and earning the first League title for a club that had not been in existence ten years before, with poor old Everton back in seventh place.

The captain of the first Liverpool title-winning side was a twenty-two-year-old centre-half from Polmont. Alex Raisbeck had already played for both Hibernian and Stoke City before he joined Liverpool in 1898, and he immediately became established in the first team as an athletic and commanding defender who showed leadership qualities beyond his years. He was first appointed captain of Scotland in 1900 when only twenty-one. Raisbeck was the golden boy of both Liverpool and Scotland in the 1900s, as admired for his fair-haired good looks and his endless determination as much as for his defensive skills.

Raisbeck was Liverpool's best player of the 1901 team, and when the club was surprisingly relegated in 1904 Raisbeck only enhanced his popularity at Anfield by staying with the club and leading them to immediate promotion, and in 1905–06 their second League Championship title.

Raisbeck last played for Scotland in 1907 and left Liverpool in 1909, but his legacy of having helped Liverpool FC establish themselves as one of the strongest clubs in the nation lived on.

Following Raisbeck, Scots would play an integral role in almost all of Liverpool's subsequent successes domestically and internationally, as is of course only appropriate for the team that was originally christened 'the team of the Macs'. But the honour of being Liverpool's first superstar player and the first man to captain a Liverpool title-winning side will always remain with Alex Raisbeck from Polmont, for as another illustrious Liverpool centre-half might have said, 'You win nothing without Scots.'

## The Wizard of North London

In the moments before the announcement of the hosts of the 2018 and 2022 FIFA World Cup in 2011, that wily old fox Sepp Blatter increased the tension by prefacing the opening of the envelopes that contained the winner with a short oration on the history of football, and in particular the intrinsic part Britain had played as the birthplace of the beautiful game. For those listening to his warm and generous words, it was apparent that by so explicitly highlighting this heritage the FIFA President was signposting the impending humiliation that was about to hit the bid by England to host the 2018 Finals, where they ignominiously came fourth out of four in the voting.

However, what was also interesting about his remarks was that Blatter specifically mentioned both England and Scotland as the pioneers of football, which might have been an additional dig at the unsuspecting and guileless English, who somehow had convinced themselves they still had the chance of winning, but was also a diplomatic and historically accurate summary of the early years of association football.

We have already seen the influence of the many 'Scotch Professors' in the development and growth of football in the nineteenth century, but Scotland's domination of the Victorian era was even more marked when it came to the international game. The first official international had been played between Scotland and England in Glasgow in 1872, with Wales and Ireland joining in 1876 and 1882, respectively. In Scotland's first forty-three full internationals between 1872 and 1891 they only lost three times and, even more remarkably, only lost once between 1874 and 1887.

The superiority of the Scots was more clearly demonstrated in three extraordinary internationals against England between 1878 and 1882, when Scotland won 7–2 in Glasgow in 1872, 5–1 in Glasgow in 1882 and most convincingly on 12th March 1881 when Scotland crushed England 6–1 at The Oval in London, a result that still remains England's heaviest defeat at home. Playing in all three of those mighty Scottish victories was captain and defender Charlie Campbell from Coupar Angus, who was also a long-standing stalwart for Queen's Park, winning eight Scottish Cups in his career, and only appearing on the losing side once in thirteen years of representing his country.

Whether it was complacency brought on by their position of being the top football nation in the world (even if the world then consisted of only four countries) or due to the growing reluctance of the SFA even to select players for the national team who played for English clubs, by the early twentieth century when football began to develop and grow throughout continental Europe and South America, Scotland remained firmly cocooned in their own insular world of domestic leagues and cups and the British Home Championship. And while the also innately isolationist England first ventured into playing internationals in Europe in 1908, Scotland criminally did not follow suit until 1929 – a deplorable fifty-seven years after their first international – and found to their cost that the world had moved on and overtaken them.

There was, though, to be one final hurrah for the legend of Scotland as international world-beaters, although granted it would once more take place down the road in London on 31st March 1928 at Wembley.

In 1928 the Scottish national team were going through a lacklustre period and for the match at Wembley it was England with home advantage and a strong team who were considered the favourites, and even more so when the Scottish team was announced. Not one of the Scottish forward line was over five foot seven inches – surely no match for the powerful English defence. However, what the Scots lacked in height, they more than made up for in skill and trickery and were almost without question the greatest quintet of forwards in Scottish football history.

On the wings was Alex Jackson from Renton, the tallest of the five, and a League Champion winner with Huddersfield Town, and Alan Morton from Glasgow, the legendary 'Wee Blue Devil' who, with nine Scottish League titles with Rangers, is one of their greatest players. At inside right was Jimmy Dunn, also from Glasgow, who would become a League Champion and FA Cup Winner with Everton in the 1930s and completing the five, two boyhood friends from Bellshill in Lanarkshire by the names of Hughie Gallacher and inside left Alex James who in 1928 plied his trade with Preston North End.

Eighty thousand fans – a large contingent from north of the border – watched, amazed, as the diminutive Scots tore England apart with their control, speed, vision and cunning. Morton crossed three times for Jackson to score and Gallacher and James combined twice for the Preston man to score. Scotland were

5–0 up before England scored a consolation in the last minute, but nothing could take away from the team who would be given the name of 'the Wembley Wizards', the worst defeat England have ever suffered at the national stadium, even if, as was typical of the vagaries of the Scottish selection policy of the time, the eleven men who represented Scotland that day would never play together for their country again.

However, for Alex James, the creator and pass master of the side, 1928 was the beginning of a remarkable period of success and glory, where he would supersede Gallacher as the leading figure in English football and would be instrumental in the rise of one of the world's great football clubs.

Woolwich Arsenal had been the first club from London to join the Football League in 1893, with Thomas Mitchell from Dumfries appointed as their first manager in 1897. Mitchell had already achieved great success at Blackburn Rovers; however, he only lasted one season at Woolwich Arsenal, where success was to prove elusive for the next two decades. It was only in 1913, with the move to a brand new stadium in Highbury, North London, as designed by famous Glaswegian football architect Archibald Leitch and a subsequent name change from Woolwich Arsenal to simply Arsenal, that the club became established as a mid-table First Division club after the First World War. And in 1929, legendary Arsenal manager Herbert Chapman signed Alex James from Preston to become the playmaker of the new side that he was building.

In 1930 Alex James scored Arsenal's first goal in a 2–0 victory over a Huddersfield team that included fellow 'Wembley Wizard' Alex Jackson to win the FA Cup – the first major trophy in the club's history. From there, Arsenal went on to dominate the decade, lifting the League title in 1931 and three years in succession from 1933 to 1935, culminating in another FA Cup Final victory in

1936, with Alex James given the honour of captaining the side to lift the trophy.

The Arsenal side that was assembled by Chapman was full of talent. At one stage seven of the England side played at Highbury, but it was Alex James who pulled the strings, an archetypal modern playmaker long before the concept of a creative fulcrum for a team's attacking play came into vogue.

Arsenal's success on and off the pitch made them the first club from the capital to break the hegemony of the north and show that the southern softies could truly mix it with the best of them. The fact that they were then also the best-funded club in England was a not insignificant factor and saw them christened 'the Bank of England club' – a highly appropriate moniker when one considers that it was Scotsman William Paterson who founded the Bank of England in 1694.

Arsenal were also pioneers in organising summer tours abroad, and Alex James, with his trademark extra-baggy shorts to cover up the long johns he wore for his rheumatism, was the main attraction and was known as 'Le Miracle'. Not because it was miraculous that someone could play football so well when wearing shorts so big, but at the remarkable way that one man in one position could unerringly dictate the flow and direction of an entire game. In 1930s English football, Alex James was the most influential player of the decade and someone who could have had his pick of clubs to play for, but chose to remain dedicated to the rise and rise of the new and, as it would turn out, enduring force in world football. Lucky, lucky Arsenal.

In 1971 after a period of relative mediocrity that had seen North London not win the League since 1953, Arsenal became the fourth club to win the League and FA Cup double, and as with all their predecessors (Preston North End in 1888, Aston Villa in 1897 and Tottenham Hotspur in 1961), Scots would play a prominent role. Defender Frank McLintock from Glasgow was their captain and is, along with Alan Hansen in 1986 with Liverpool, one of two Scottish captains to have won the English double. And playing alongside McLintock in the 1971 Arsenal double side was George Graham from Bargeddie in Lanarkshire, an elegant striker-turned-midfielder who was christened 'Stroller' for his ability to create without ever seeming to break stride. George Graham left Arsenal for Manchester United in 1972 in the days when such a move was not unthinkable and few at Highbury would imagine that fourteen years later this laidback entertainer would be returning to the club as their new disciplinarian manager.

Under George Graham Arsenal won their first League title since 1971, when in the legendary match of May 1989 where Arsenal required an unlikely 2–0 away win in the final game of the season in, of all places, Anfield to snatch the title from League leaders and defending champions, Kenny Dalglish's Liverpool, and in one of the most astonishing denouements in football history, did so in the very last minute of the game.

Arsenal won the League again in 1991 and for all George Graham's playing reputation as the creative 'Stroller', he established a new Arsenal reputation that was at its core centred on a formidable work ethic and a long-standing defensive discipline (now somewhat forgotten) that turned the playing of the offside line into an almost telepathic art form.

Graham remained at Highbury until 1995 and in the process returned the club that had been built sixty years before around the bandy-legged figure of Alex James back to the summit of the English game. 'One–nil to the Arsenal' was the triumphant cry that rang out around Highbury, and if you didn't like it, well, as they say in as Lanarkshire, 'Stroll on' – or words to that effect.

# 4
## *The Racers*

Chris Hoy

Scots like to travel. From Auckland to the Algarve and Melbourne to Málaga, the history of Scotland is one long journey of a restless nation who are either imbued with an insatiable desire to experience and explore new lands and cultures so as to further advance their knowledge and understanding of the world that we universally share, or alternatively are just wanting to get away from Scotland as quickly and as economically as possible.

Scotland is, of course, not unique in being a country that is predisposed to foreign excursions, but what perhaps sets the Scots apart is their determination to make the logistics of travel as efficient and precipitous as possible. In the nineteenth century, the major maritime routes of the world that criss-crossed the Atlantic, Pacific and Indian Oceans were invariably run and managed by Scottish owners in ships that were more often than not designed and constructed by Scottish shipbuilders on the yards of the Clyde. On dry land, Glasgow was also one of the world's largest manufacturers of locomotives, built in Springburn and exported overseas, where Scottish railway engineers opened up the continents of the world as they built a global train network. And in the air, Glaswegian Arthur Whitten Brown was one of the two men who, in 1919, became the first to cross the Atlantic Ocean, a remarkable feat of aviation when you consider that the world's first flight had only taken place sixteen years before.

And with all this longstanding Scottish predilection for speed, endurance and technical ingenuity, it is therefore not so surprising that, when it came to sports where such qualities were a prerequisite to success, Scots have from the beginning excelled on the international stage. Whether it be on two legs, four legs, two wheels or four wheels the legend of 'The Flying Scot' dates back the best part of four centuries. From a time when Scottish royalty laid the foundations for one of the world's most enduring and lucrative sports, then on to the nineteenth century when Scottish inventors inspired a global sporting movement, and finally on to the twentieth century when Scots were regularly and dazzlingly the fastest and most talented sportsmen on the planet. For as the auld song goes, you can take the high road, and you can take the low road, but odds-on the Scots will be at the finish afore ye.

## All Bicycles Great and Small

Even 450 years after the end of the historic 'Auld Alliance' between France and Scotland there is not much, in truth, that divides the two nations. Scotland still enjoys and admires the best of French culture – the wine, the cuisine, the perfume, the fashion, the art, the Stella Artois, the weekends in Paris and their antipathy to the *rosbifs* – while the French reciprocate by drinking whisky and defeating us at rugby every year. Yet if there is one thing that disrupts this *entente ginger cordial* it is the vexed question of who invented the bicycle.

As far as the French (and most of the rest of the world) were concerned, the pedal-driven bicycle was invented in France around 1865 by either Ernest Michaux or Pierre Lallement, who were the first to have pedals attached to the front wheel, the first to begin producing these *vélocipèdes à pédale* commercially and the first to patent their innovation. *Et voilà* – the bicycle was born, and it was indisputably French.

'But, wait a minute!' said the Scots. Hold your hobby-horses. Had not Gavin Dalzell from Lesmahagow built a two-wheeled vehicle that was driven from the rear wheel by pedals hanging from the front around 1846 – twenty years earlier than Michaux and Lallement? And then, in the 1890s the mystery deepened when a descendant of Kirkpatrick Macmillan, a blacksmith from the village of Keir Mill, near Thornhill in Dumfries and Galloway, stated that the Dalzell bicycle of 1846 was but a copy of a bicycle that Macmillan had built in 1839! *Zut alors!*

Unfortunately for the claims of both Macmillan and Dalzell, neither of these two men ever patented or left any written or photographic records of their contraptions, and any replicas of their original inventions, such as the bicycle attributed to Dalzell that resides in the Glasgow Transport Museum, were built after the first French *vélocipèdes* of the 1860s. So we will never know for certain when or, for that matter, *what* exactly Macmillan and Dalzell built in their Scottish workshops – even if it is now generally accepted (except in France) that, as stated on the little plaque that can be found on the place where Kirkpatrick Macmillan's smithy in the village of Keir Mill used to be, 'He builded better than he knew'. Which at least gives us the room for a linguistic and semantic compromise between the rival countries, as in if we accept that it was the French who 'built' the first bicycle, then the French can in turn accept that it was the Scots who were the first to 'builded' one.

Therefore, when it came to the invention that would revolutionise the history of the bicycle and turn the bike into a worldwide phenomenon, we will find that to avoid any future controversy there was not one, but two, Scottish inventors who would take credit for the pneumatic tyre, and crucially both of them had legitimate patents.

By 1887 the bicycle had become established throughout Europe and America as a new method of travel. However, there was one major problem. For all the developments in the construction of the bicycle that were making it lighter, faster and above all safer, there was still the issue of the wheels to be considered. To this point wheels were wooden with iron rims, or possibly made from solid rubber, but whatever the material, they could not prevent the cyclist from feeling the full impact of the surface they were riding on, leading to the early bicycles gaining their alternative name of 'boneshakers'.

John Boyd Dunlop came from the village of Dreghorn, near Irvine in Ayrshire, but lived in Belfast, where he worked as a vet. Dunlop was a practical man, and when he saw the difficulties his young son was encountering on the cobbled streets of Belfast while riding his new tricycle fitted with solid rubber tyres, he decided to do something about it.

Dunlop took thin strips of rubber that he wrapped around the tyres and then inflated them, so providing a cushion of air. The results were impressive. Dunlop patented his pneumatic tyre in 1888 and his poor son was made to ride the streets of Belfast in his new-improved tricycle for far longer than was strictly necessary.

There had been organised cycle races from almost the first time that bicycles had been commercially produced in France in the mid 1860s, and Dunlop was now determined to see his invention tested out in competition. In 1889 he persuaded local Belfast cyclist Willie Hume to purchase a bicycle fitted with pneumatic tyres, and on 18 May 1889 at the Queen's College Sports in Belfast, Hume competed in and won all four races he entered at the Queen's College playing fields. Hume may have won all the races anyway, but it was clear that the new tyres gave him a clear advantage and astonished all those spectators who had initially laughed at Dunlop's 'sausage wheels'.

When Hume repeated his Belfast success in races in Liverpool, Dunlop realised that the idea that had come to him so that he could help his children had a much wider commercial appeal. In 1889, with the support of investors, he co-founded the Dunlop Pneumatic Tyre Company, and within two years was producing tyres in both Dublin and Birmingham. Everything seemed set for global domination, but Dunlop suffered a sudden puncture to his plans when it transpired that, unbeknownst to him, fellow Scot and serial inventor Robert William Thomson from Stonehaven had, back in 1846, already developed and patented the use of pneumatic tyres. Furthermore, Thomson had successfully demonstrated said tyres on a horse and carriage in London, with the tyres thankfully on the carriage rather than the horse.

Nobody had any idea what to do with Thomson's invention back in 1846 and it had long been forgotten by 1887, with Thomson himself having died in 1873, but his patent still stood and undermined Dunlop's claim of exclusivity to pneumatic tyres.

Dunlop sold out the shares of his own company in 1896, but by the end of the 1890s the demand for pneumatic tyres and bicycles had become so great that Dunlop's loss of exclusivity could not prevent Dunlop the company from becoming both one of the most famous manufacturers of tyres and one of the most famous producers of sporting equipment in the world.

In motor sport, Dunlop have been producing tyres for over a century and in their heyday were the undisputed premier tyre manufacturer, winning twenty-three Le Mans, eight Formula 1 World Championships between 1958 and 1969 and twelve 500cc World Motorcycle Championships between 1949 and 1975. Away from tyres, Dunlop began producing golf balls in 1910, tennis racquets in 1917 and became a market leader in sporting equipment for squash and badminton. Legendary tennis champions Lew Hoad, Rod Laver, John McEnroe and Steffi Graf all used Dunlop tennis racquets to win their Grand Slam championships, and in the case of McEnroe, no doubt broke more than a few along the way.

As for John Boyd Dunlop, the Scottish vet who became the second inventor of pneumatic tyres and founder of arguably the most famous sporting equipment company in the world, he settled in Dublin where he lived to his death in 1921. The money from his shares meant that he had a comfortable retirement and never had to bother expectant cows again, but he missed out on the untold riches that would have come his way if he had remained in his own company, or if he had indeed been the one and only inventor of pneumatic tyres, but as our cycling friends from France would philosophically say – *c'est la vie!*

## Indiana Wants Me

It was a Scottish architect from Midlothian, Alexander Ralston, who in 1821 was tasked with the responsibility of laying out the city of the new capital of the state of Indiana, Indianapolis. The much-admired city centre that Ralston designed has remained, in essence, untouched to this day, however Ralston cannot take credit for the sporting event that one most associates with Indiana's state capital – America's most famous and historic motor race, the Indianapolis 500. First run in 1911 and currently drawing a crowd of 400,000 spectators a year, the race has attracted many famous drivers from around the world, and amongst their number you will find more than one Scot who has felt as much at home in Indianapolis as the Scottish architect who built the city.

Dario Franchitti from Bathgate moved to the USA in 1997 and has become one of America's most successful figures in motor sport (and arguably the best-known Scottish sportsman in North America today). To date, Franchitti has won the IndyCar Championship (the premier motor racing series in North America) four times in 2007, 2009, 2010 and 2011 and has won the Indianapolis 500, the unquestioned showcase of the IndyCar season, on two occasions in 2007 and 2010. Yet for all Franchitti's success in the most iconic event in US motor racing, even he would have to allow another Scot who was also a champion at Indianapolis to overtake him in the pantheon of legendary racing drivers.

There have been five drivers so far who in their career have won the Indianapolis 500, the pinnacle of motor racing in America, and the Formula 1 World Championship, the pinnacle of motor racing in the rest of the world. Graham Hill, Mario Andretti, Emerson Fittipaldi and Jacques Villeneuve were four of them, but only one man has managed the extraordinary feat of winning both the Indianapolis 500 and the Formula 1 Championship in the same year. And the driver in question was a farmer from the Scottish Borders by the name of Jim Clark.

When the question of who was the greatest of all the legendary drivers to have raced in Formula 1 since the first World

Championship in 1950 is raised, four names in particular tend to generate most heated debate. Statistically, Juan Manuel Fangio and Michael Schumacher are the two who have won the most World Championship titles, but for those who know their Grand Prix history even the remarkable achievements of Fangio and Schumacher cannot match the claims of the Brazilian Ayrton Senna and the Scotsman Jim Clark, who were both recognised as the greatest drivers of their generation, were both multiple World Champions and both tragically died young at the peak of their careers.

Jim Clark was born in Kilmany in farming country in Fife, but moved with his family at an early age to a farm in Chirnside, near Duns, close to the English border. He began racing as a teenager, and in 1960 made his Formula 1 debut at the age of twenty-four for Colin Chapman's Lotus team, a relationship based on mutual friendship and loyalty that would endure throughout Clark's career – even during the seasons where, although Clark was clearly the fastest driver in Formula 1, Lotus was clearly not the fastest car.

Clark's breakthrough year came in 1962 when he won the Grand Prix in Belgium, Britain and the US and went into the final race of the season at South Africa knowing that victory would gain him his first World Championship. Clark had qualified on pole position and from first place on the grid he led for more than half the race before engine trouble forced him to retire – and a first Scottish World title would have to wait.

There were no such setbacks in 1963 when Clark was in dominant form, winning seven Grand Prix out of ten to become at the age of twenty-seven the then-youngest driver ever to become World Champion.

The year 1964 saw three further Grand Prix wins, but once more Clark would lose out on the World title through an oil leak on the last lap of the final Grand Prix at Mexico, with victory in sight. However, it was 1965 that was to prove Clark's greatest year, when he won six Grand Prix to comfortably earn his second World title and then flew to America to win the Indianapolis 500 in one of the most impressive performances ever seen in Indiana, with Clark leading for 190 of the race's 200 laps.

The 1966 and 1967 seasons were more problematic for Clark, as no matter how brilliant his driving, the Lotus struggled for reliability, but when Clark won the first Grand Prix of the 1968 season at South Africa, it seemed that a third World title beckoned.

On 7th April 1968 at a Formula 2 race at Hockenheim, Germany, in an era when the world's top drivers also regularly drove in non-Formula 1 races, Jim Clark's Lotus went off the track and crashed into the surrounding trees. Sadly, he would die from his injuries before he reached hospital. He was only thirty-two.

There had been no shortage of horrific accidents and tragic fatalities in Formula 1 during the 1960s, but Clark's death sent the world of motor sport and sport in general into shock and mourning. Clark's driving had been so consummate that, unlike many of his fellow drivers, he had suffered remarkably few accidents in his career, which made his death even more difficult to comprehend. An inquiry would later show that it was a deflating rear tyre that had caused his car to go off the road.

For seven years Clark had been at the very pinnacle of his sport. Out of the seventy-two Grand Prix he had started, he had been on pole position thirty-three times and won twenty-seven, both records at the time. He won five British Grand Prix (still the equal most victories), won four Belgium Grand Prix in succession, and as well as his victory in the Indianapolis 500 in 1965, he came second in the same event in 1963 and 1966.

Jim Clark was so versatile that he could turn a wheel in touring cars, sports cars, stock cars and rally cars and raced and won all over the world. But for all the glamour and fame that came his way, Jim Clark remained at heart the shy, unassuming but completely professional son of a Borders farmer that he had always been.

At his funeral at his family home, the greatest names in motor sport all congregated in the little church at Chirnside. They all came to honour their friend and rival, the most naturally gifted, the most talented and the most successful of his generation, and despite all the other legendary drivers who have graced Formula 1 in the past sixty years, just possibly the greatest driver the world has ever seen.

## Paisley's Miles Better

There have been many prominent visitors to the historic Holyrood Park at the foot of the even more historic Royal Mile in Edinburgh, which amongst its more curious characteristics is that, to the bemusement of almost all visitors and despite being Scotland's most famous street, it is not at any point actually called 'The Royal Mile'. Furthermore, The Royal Mile is not, in fact, one mile long, but is actually 1.1 miles long, as it was based on the measurement of the old Scots mile that was used in Scotland until the Act of Union in 1707 when it was replaced by its English imperial equivalent that is roughly 0.1 miles shorter. However, this anomaly is not often reported as when it comes to The Royal Mile there is perhaps only so much bemusement that visitors can take.

Holyrood Park would also make sporting history in March 2008 when it would be the venue for the World Cross Country Championship and would witness the sixth World Cross Country title for arguably the greatest middle-distance runner of all time – the Ethiopian Kenenisa Bekele.

Holyrood Park and 2008 was the second time that the World Cross Country Championships had been held in Scotland, thirty years after the 1978 Championships were held in Bellahouston Park in Glasgow. And even the peerless Bekele may have balked at the adverse weather conditions that the world's elite runners faced in Glasgow in November 1978, but for true aficionados of the sport, what would cross-country be without biting winds, torrential rain, a smattering of sleet and a course where there is more water than grass?

It could even be said that there must be something deep in the Scottish psyche that is somehow strangely attracted to cross country and the concept of running through mud and snow in the middle of winter, wearing only a vest and unfeasibly short shorts.

Holyrood Park hosts the annual Great Edinburgh International Cross Country Race that remains one of the most prestigious competitions on the middle-distance calendar, despite the fact that it takes place in Scotland in, of all months, January. And while the World Cross Country Championships only began in 1973, the first International Cross Country Championship ever to be held dates back to 1903 and was held at the Hamilton Park Racecourse, one of Scotland's historic horse racing venues, in conditions so difficult that even the watching horses could be seen shaking their heads.

However, in Scotland as in the rest of the world, it is on the track and on the road, rather than the grass and the mud, that true recognition of middle- and long-distance running is won and lost, with Olympic and World medals and championships to compete for, and by breaking a world record the ultimate achievement of becoming the fastest the world has ever seen.

Scotland's greatest distance runner was never actually a world record holder, but for guts and bravery and sheer determination, and for being the only person on *A Question of Sport* ever to use the word 'United' in reference to the team from Dundee rather than Manchester, there was nobody to beat her. Liz Lynch (better known as Liz McColgan) from Dundee was twice Commonwealth Champion, twice winner of the London Marathon and in 1988 won Olympic silver at the 10,000 metres in Seoul. Her achievements in Korea had already made McColgan Scotland's most successful long-distance runner, but three years later she returned to Asia for what was at the time described by no less than Brendan Foster as 'the greatest performance by any distance British athlete, male or female'.

McColgan was a front-runner and not noted for her sprint finish. She had to burn off her competitors to negate their greater acceleration on the last lap. In Seoul in 1988, all but one had succumbed to the pace set by the Dundee runner, but when it came to the even more hot and humid Tokyo of August 1991 and the final of the 10,000 metres World Championship, McColgan attacked from the very first lap and never let up. Conditions were as far removed from Broughty Ferry as one could imagine, but 'Super Liz' destroyed the best runners in the world to come home twenty-one seconds in front and become Scotland's first and so far only athletics World Champion. If that was not enough, only a couple of months later McColgan ran her first-ever marathon and duly won in New York. Liz McColgan was an inspiration for thousands of women and men who have taken up running and found the pleasure and pain curiously addictive, even if they could really do without the obligatory charity raising. Thanks to athletes such as Liz McColgan, long-distance running has rarely been so popular as a participatory pastime; however, when it comes to the athletic events with the greatest prestige and the most illustrious sporting history even the marathon and the 10,000 metres cannot compete with the one mile.

It was in the one mile in 1954, in perhaps the most momentous

240 seconds in athletics history, that an Englishman by the name of Roger Bannister ran 3:59.4 and became the first man to break the four-minute barrier. And thirty years later, in the early 1980s, the world watched, spellbound, as the two great English rivals, Steve Ovett and Sebastian Coe, raced around Europe, but not against each other, taking turns at breaking the world mile record on an almost weekly basis.

However, if Roger Bannister gained sporting immortality in 1954 for becoming the first man to break the four-minute barrier, what about the Scottish runner who held the world mile record for five years and in doing so would break a record that had stood for sixteen years and many thought unbreakable?

People had always raced each other for either fun or money, but in the nineteenth century, interest in contests between the top runners of the day would attract large crowds and even larger wagers. By the mid-nineteenth century, the first specifically-built running tracks were being put down, athletics clubs were being founded and accurate times rather than guesswork were being recorded to show who was the fastest man on earth – even if at that point in athletics history, as with many other sports, the earth appeared to consist solely of the British Empire. So popular did top races become and so much money was generated in betting on their outcome that the best runners in the country could afford to go professional, which was what an eighteen-year-old from Paisley, William J. Cummings, decided to do in 1876.

Cummings raced over various distances competitively and became the Champion Miler of England in 1878. Over the next five years, Cummings was the undisputed top middle-distance runner in Britain, and on 14th May 1881 at his home track in Preston, Lancashire, he broke the world mile record that had stood since 1865. He ran 4:16.2 to prove that a man could indeed run a sub-4:17 mile after all.

This achievement brought Cummings considerable acclaim and financial reward, and it would not be until 1885 that his supremacy would be challenged by Englishman Walter George. George was the leading amateur runner of his time, but had turned professional so that he could take on Cummings. They agreed to race a series of three distances of one mile, four miles and ten miles in London and Edinburgh. Huge crowds saw Cummings win the two longer races, but it would be George who won the one mile race in London, although Cummings' world record of 4:16.2 remained intact.

With honours more or less even between the two great and well-matched runners, there was huge demand for a re-match and in August 1886, Cummings and George met again in southwest London, where 25,000 people saw them run what would be called the 'Mile of the Century'. The two ran lap for lap and stride for stride, keeping well within world record schedule. Then, with one lap to go, Cummings took the lead, seeming to have finally broken his great rival, but in the last seventy yards George fought back and hit the front. For Cummings, the unexpected comeback of George was too much and he collapsed through exhaustion; however George, unaware of this, continued to sprint for the line. The London crowd had been loudly cheering and roaring the two men on, but now the applause would turn to pandemonium when it was announced that not only had George broken the world mile record, but that his time of 4:12.8 was an extraordinary improvement of three seconds better than the previous best by Cummings.

William Cummings and Walter George would compete against and defeat each other several times and at varying distances after 1886, but it would be the 'Mile of the Century' race for which they would be remembered, and George's winning time would remain the world record for an incredible thirty years until it was finally bettered in 1916.

Although Walter George and especially William Cummings are names that have become footnotes in the history of athletics, in the era before the revival of the modern Olympics and the re-ascendancy of amateurism, at the time they were two of the most famous men in sport and their rivalry was akin to that of Coe and Ovett nearly one hundred years later. And perhaps given Cummings' repeated dominance over George in the longer distances where they raced against each other, it could be argued that if the 'Mile of the Century' had been over the Scots mile distance of 1.1 miles rather than the English one mile, it might well have been Cummings who would have proven ultimately victorious. However, if George would prove the Victorian archetype of Sebastian Coe and William Cummings his Steve Ovett contemporary, it does beg the question – who was Steve Cram?

## My Sporting Kingdom for a Horse

For a monarch who played such a pivotal role in the history of Britain and the English-speaking world, James VI of Scotland, who would become James I of England in 1603, is often portrayed as a surprisingly marginal historical figure sandwiched halfway between the tumultuous Tudors and the catastrophic Civil Wars, with a reputation as confused as his two names. However, it cannot be denied that James was the monarch who united the two crowns of England and Scotland, a Union that, over 400 years later, even the staunchest of Scottish Nationalists shows no inclination to tear asunder. He was also the monarch who promoted the mass immigration of English and Scottish Protestants to Northern Ireland; the king who established the first permanent English settlement in North America (Jamestown in Virginia); and also gave his name to both the Jacobean golden age of English letters that included the greatest works of William Shakespeare and Francis Bacon, and the King James Bible, one of the most important, influential and best-selling books of the last five hundred years – although James did not actually write a word of it. But even less known than all of the above is the integral part he played in the history of international sport, even if it was almost entirely accidental.

James may have been the son of the pioneering golfer Mary, Queen of Scots, but there is little in the way of evidence to show that he inherited his mother's golfing genes. True, it was when James made his royal progress to London that the English got their first glimpse of a curious pastime involving sticks and a small spherical object played in the countryside for hours on end, but although golf was reputedly played in Blackheath in London from 1608 on, it was other members of the Scottish royal court, rather than the king, who caused panic amongst the English populace with their wayward drives.

James's sporting interests tended more towards hawking and hunting, and it was thanks to these passions that we find the king in Suffolk in February 1605. Apparently some inclement weather forced the monarch to abandon his day of hunting and repair for the evening to an inn called The Griffin in a nearby village. When James awoke, having no doubt been fortified by the establishment's fine array of wines and spirits, the weather had cleared and he was rewarded with his first vision of Newmarket Heath. James was clearly taken by this vista, and from 1606 onwards, he made regular returns to Newmarket with his entourage. Soon he also began purchasing property and land in the village and saw the construction of Newmarket Palace, perhaps not the grandest of all his royal residences, but increasingly the one in which James felt most at home. And for those who thought it curious that James would prefer to spend so much time in an obscure East Anglia village, when you consider that he had just survived the Gunpowder

Plot of 5<sup>th</sup> November 1605, it is perhaps not that surprising that he was keen to get out of London as much as possible.

James may have been more of a huntsman, but it was clear that Newmarket Heath and the surrounding countryside were ideal for horse riding. The first recorded horse race was held in Newmarket in 1622 and the first Cup race was held at Newmarket in 1634, during the reign of James's son and successor, the Dunfermline-born Charles I. As king, Charles continued the family tradition of Newmarket as a royal residence and furthermore oversaw the construction of the first grandstand on the heath.

Charles was himself a keen and fearless rider and an enthusiastic competitor in the early races at Newmarket, which we can only surmise presumably would have followed many of the Scottish horse racing traditions of the time. And it would be fair to say that while he may have had to defer to his father when it came to political competency, military strategy and keeping one's crown and one's head, he would have been a comfortable winner over a one mile gallop.

Newmarket Palace did not survive the Civil Wars brought about by Charles' inability to form any sort of working relationship with the English Parliament and his ultimate and terminal defeat to the Parliamentary forces in 1649, despite the initial odds being 9/4 in his favour.

However, with the Restoration of Charles II in 1660, Newmarket once more became a popular royal residence, and horse racing continued to flourish there. In 1750, the Jockey Club was established at Newmarket to organise and control British horse racing. And today Newmarket and its environs are home to more than 2,500 thoroughbred horses, the two British Classics of the 1,000 and 2,000 Guineas and is accepted not only as a global centre of international horse racing, but the birthplace of horse racing as an organised sport.

\*    \*    \*

As for the man who started it all, it was in the city of Stirling that James VI spent most of his childhood and early life, and it was in Stirling nearly 400 years later that Scotland's most successful and greatest jockey was born. It is probably lost somewhere in the mists of Suffolk whether the term *jockey* for the rider of a racehorse was coined in recognition of the Scottish influence on the beginnings of the sport. Or probably more likely, the word jockey derives from the Northern English *jock* meaning 'lad', rather than the Scottish *jock* meaning 'John', as a 'lad' or 'young man' were invariably lighter than older men and therefore ideal for riding in horse races. But although we will probably never know for certain what the true etymology of *jockey* is, perhaps no one epitomises both of the possible alternatives more aptly than Willie Carson, who was Scottish and only five feet in height.

Carson was born in 1942, in the same year as another not particularly tall giant of sport named Billy Bremner was also born in Stirling. Like Bremner, Carson left Stirling as a teenager to begin his career in England and rode his first winner in 1962. In his early racing years, Carson struggled to make an impact and his breakthrough year would not take place until 1972 when he became Champion Jockey for the first time and won his first British Classic, the 2,000 Guineas, appropriately enough at Newmarket.

Over the next two decades Carson remained at the very top of flat racing. He surpassed one hundred winners in a season on twenty-three occasions and was Champion Jockey again in 1973, 1978, 1980 and 1983. Despite these accomplishments, his most successful year was in 1990 at the age of forty-eight when he rode 187 winners, including an extraordinary six in one day at Newcastle, but still came second overall in the race to be Champion Jockey for that year. Between 1974 and 1996 Carson won ten Irish Classics at The Curragh, including the Irish Derby twice in 1979 and 1990, as well as the Prix du Jockey Club at

Longchamps in 1980. However, it was the British Classics and in particular, the most famous of them all, the Epsom Derby, for which Carson is best remembered.

Carson would win seventeen British Classics in total between 1972 and 1994 that included a clean sweep of all five historic races – the 1,000 Guineas, the 2,000 Guineas, The Oaks, The St Leger and the Derby. Carson's four Derby wins were on Troy in 1979, Henbit the following year in 1980, Erhaab in 1994 and possibly the best of them all, Nashwan in 1989, who had also, with Carson on board, already won the 2,000 Guineas that year – the first horse since 1970 to achieve that double.

When Wille Carson finally retired in 1997 at the age of fifty-four, he had overcome numerous falls and injuries (at least one life-threatening). He may never have been the most talented jockey of his generation, but nobody could question that he could not be beaten on determination and competitive spirit. It was this irrepressible spirit that saw him achieve a career record of 3,828 winners, the fourth highest in history, behind only Gordon Richards, Lester Piggott and Pat Eddery, and made him not only a wealthy man, but also brought more wealth to those knowledgeable punters who consistently backed him more than any other figure in the history of Scottish sport. No wonder he was always so popular.

Even more successful in terms of Classic wins than Carson was a man who was born in Aberdeen but moved to England as a child. Henry Cecil gained his trainer's licence in 1969 in, of course, Newmarket, and began one of the most extraordinary careers that flat racing has ever seen. He first became Champion Trainer in 1976 and would win the accolade a further nine times between then and 1993. For the best part of two decades Henry Cecil was nigh on unbeatable, training 200 top horses at his stable's peak and forming legendary partnerships with jockeys Steve

Cauthen, Lester Piggott and Pat Eddery – although surprisingly not his fellow Scottish-born Willie Carson – to go with his ten Champion Trainer titles.

In the mid-1990s, Cecil's career went into what seemed like terminal decline as the titles, Classics and horses dried up, but a decade later Cecil defied the odds to return to the winning enclosure, and in 2011 he produced a new champion wonder horse in the form of Frankel, the most exciting colt of his generation. To date, Henry Cecil has won twenty-five British Classics, including four Derbys, and has achieved more victories at Royal Ascot than any other trainer in history. He remains 'the Master Trainer' and perennial friend of the punter (royal, commoner and Aberdonian alike), and if you can persuade a citizen of the Granite City to open his wallet then that is high praise indeed.

As a final royal postscript to Scotland's involvement in the history of horse racing, in 1977, the year of Queen Elizabeth's Silver Jubilee, the monarch who had long been a passionate follower of the turf and all things equine was also the owner of the horse that won both The Oaks and The St Leger that year. The horse in question was called Dunfermline, as in the same Dunfermline that was the birthplace of Charles I, and the winning jockey was, of course, Willie Carson from Stirling, who was born in the same city where James VI learned to ride, but on balance was far less likely to lose his way.

## King of the Hills

Back in 1839 and the early 1840s when Kirkpatrick Macmillan rode whatever it was that he rode, he could be said to be the fastest cyclist in the world as he was the only person in the world to actually have a bicycle. Not that anyone in France will ever agree. However, even Macmillan's staunchest admirers would have to admit that being the fastest of the reputed one billion and rising cyclists there are thought to be in the world today, rather than the fastest of just one, is quite an impressive achievement. Why, even the French had to grudgingly accept that, for once, the Scots might actually have *la crème de la crème* of track cycling, as Chris Hoy from Edinburgh kept defeating both the best French sprinters and the best sprinters from the rest of the world year after year after year.

Hoy won his first gold medals at the World Cycling Championships in 2002, with victories at the 1km time trial and the team sprint (as part of a three-man team that also included Craig MacLean from Grantown-on-Spey). So began a period of domination that has seen him win further World Championship gold medals in the 1km time trial in 2004, 2006 and 2007, in the team sprint in 2005, the individual sprint in 2008 and the keirin in 2007, 2008 and 2010.

In the Olympics, Hoy won a silver in the team sprint (with MacLean) in Sydney in 2000, before winning his first gold at Athens in 2004 in the 1km time trial and then surpassing even that achievement in Beijing in 2008 by winning three gold medals in the individual sprint, the keirin and the team sprint. This meant that for the 2008 Olympics medal table Hoy was on equal terms with the entire teams of Canada, Poland and Brazil and had also equalled the greatest number of gold medals won by any male cyclist in the history of the Olympics. The only title to elude him so far in his career, however, is the 1km world record, where Hoy's attempt in 2007 saw him fail by only 0.005 seconds, just to show that he was human after all.

Hoy's remarkable achievements have sparked a renaissance of interest in the sport of cycling. Today thousands of Scottish adults are returning to cycling as both a pastime and as a favoured mode of transport, and thousands of Scottish children have been inspired to take up cycling and become budding Chris Hoys in the making, only for thousands of Scottish parents to then inform them that, 'No, you can't go on the road!' And interest in cycling is not solely reserved for track cycling, in which Hoy excels, but has seen increased coverage and appreciation for the ultimate road cycling events of strength, skill and endurance, and the greatest and most historic cycling event of them all, the Tour de France.

There are three Grand Tours that dominate the cycling calendar, but with all due respect to the Giro d'Italia and the Vuelta a España, the Papa of world cycling is Le Tour de France, arguably the greatest sporting event in Europe. Since its inception in 1903 the race has given the world such legends as Anquetil, Merckx, Hinault, Indurain and Armstrong, and even inspired Kraftwerk to write one of their most iconic tunes.

Within the Tour, there is the title itself and the race to wear the yellow jersey, the individual stages, and the Tours within the Tour, with possibly the toughest and most gruelling of them all, the battle to be crowned the King of the Mountains.

To become the King of the Mountains one has to be the fastest rider in all the stages that are classified as 'mountain' stages and feature considerable levels of climbing – or in other words one has to conquer the Pyrenees and climb and climb and climb some more to the point of exhaustion and beyond. And in 1984, it would be an unheralded Scot from Glasgow who would shock the cycling *cognoscenti* and upset the European *cart de pomme* by winning this prestigious title.

In his heyday during the 1980s Robert Millar would gain overall podium finishes of second place in the Vuelta a España in 1986 and second again at the Giro d'Italia in 1987, but his greatest moments came in the mountains of France, and especially in the town of Pau, which was incidentally the same Pau where in 1856 Scottish ex-pats built the first golf course in continental Europe. Between 1983 in his first tour and 1989 Millar was to win three Mountain stages in total, but it was in 1984 that he had his greatest tour. Millar won the Mountain stage between Pau and Guzet-Neige, was crowned King of the Mountains and in the overall Tour came fourth, with the only people ahead of him being Laurent Fignon, Bernard Hinault and Greg Lemond – multiple Tour winners all.

Before Millar, no rider from outside continental Europe had ever won the Tour, and Millar was first in the peloton of a new wave of cyclists from around the world to take on and compete against the top riders from continental Europe and make the Tour a truly world event. Millar's fourth place overall in the Tour of 1984 was the greatest ever finish by a British rider, until it was equalled by Bradley Wiggins in 2010. But Millar still remains the only cyclist from an English-speaking country (Lance Armstrong included) to ever become King of the Mountains.

As King of the Mountains, Robert Millar received the prestigious white with red polka dots jersey that is awarded to the winner (well, it is France after all), and with apologies to Kirkpatrick Macmillan, it is fair to say that it is Robert Millar who is unquestionably Scotland's greatest and most successful road cyclist to date. And to be honest, from the little that we know of the life of Kirkpatrick Macmillan in 1839, you can't really see him wearing white with red polka dots as he cycles to Dumfries.

## *Making Sense Never Stops*

In 2011, Paul Di Resta from Bathgate and cousin of two-times Indy 500 Champion Dario Franchitti made his Formula

1 debut with Force India. At age twenty-four, Di Resta made an immediate impact on the Formula 1 grid with a string of accomplished performances and consistent point scoring with what was, after all, a middle-ranking car. Already expectations are high for the man from West Lothian as he follows in a long line of 'Flying Scots' in Formula 1, with his immediate predecessor the perennially-overlooked David Coulthard from Dumfries.

It is often forgotten that in his fifteen-year Formula 1 career David Coulthard was in the final three of the Driver Championship standing on five occasions and won a highly impressive thirteen Grand Prix that included two victories at Monaco (a feat that even the great Jim Clark never achieved). Sadly, Coulthard never had the good fortune, the consistency of results or the advantages of being the clearly designated main driver of one of the title-chasing constructors to win the ultimate prize, and even when he did become the number one driver in 2005 for a brand new team to Formula 1, it was typical of Coulthard's luck that Red Bull only began their rise to the front of the grid in 2009, a year after he retired. However, what cannot be taken away from David Coulthard is a longevity at the very top of Formula 1 that twenty or thirty years previously would have been considered unthinkable.

It had been as a consequence of Ayrton Senna's tragic death at Imola in 1994 that Coulthard had made his Formula 1 debut, but what had made Senna's death so shocking was not just because he was seen as the greatest driver since Jim Clark, but because safety on the track had improved greatly and fatalities had mercifully become very rare and a far cry from the carnage of the 60s and early 70s when it was statistically more probable that drivers racing for five seasons or more would lose their lives in racing accidents. And at the forefront of these changes would be Scotland's second legendary Formula 1 Champion.

\* \* \*

In the 1950s and early 1960s the blue metallic cars of Ecurie Ecosse were a familiar feature at the great racetracks of the world. Founded in 1952 by Edinburgh businessman and racing driver David Murray, Ecurie Ecosse (French for 'Team Scotland') were based in Merchiston, Edinburgh, from where they competed with the great marques of motor sport. In Formula 1 Ecurie Ecosse only made a handful of undistinguished appearances, but they would make their greatest impact at the 24 Hours of Le Mans, the world's greatest and oldest endurance motor race.

In 1956 Ron Flockhart from Edinburgh and Ninian Sanderson from Glasgow were the co-drivers who won Ecurie Ecosse's first Le Mans against the best of Ferrari and Jaguar, and to show that this was no fluke, Flockhart and Ecurie Ecosse repeated this feat the following year. Ecurie Ecosse were to withdraw from competitive motor sport in the mid-60s, but their legacy continued in the experience that they gave to a generation of young Scottish drivers who may otherwise never have had the opportunity. Two of those Scots were Jimmy Stewart from Milton near Dumbarton and his younger brother Jackie.

Jackie Stewart would progress from his early outings with Ecurie Ecosse to make his Formula 1 debut in 1965 at the age of twenty-six, winning the Italian Grand Prix in his first season. In 1968 he won three Grand Prix and came second in the World Championship, but the following season in 1969 he would not be denied, winning six Grand Prix and his first World Championship, becoming, after the late Jim Clark, Scotland's second Formula 1 World Champion.

Stewart and Clark had been close friends and Clark's death in 1968 affected Stewart greatly, but he continued with his racing career and between 1969 and 1973 dominated the Formula 1 grid, winning two more World Championships in 1971 and 1973, both by a significant distance. In his time in Formula 1, Stewart won at Monaco three times, three times in France and Germany, and twice at the British and Italian and ended his career with twenty-seven Grand Prix victories, two more than Clark and at the time the most Grand Prix victories in Formula 1 history.

Back in 1966, mechanical failure whilst leading with only eight laps to go had prevented Stewart from winning the Indianapolis 500 at his first attempt, but otherwise he had achieved everything in motor sport and had decided in advance to retire at the end of the 1973 season, irrespective of the six Grand Prix victories he won that year.

1966 had also been the year that a younger Jackie Stewart had survived a near fatal accident at Spa and he had lived through the deaths of so many friends and colleagues when racing – including of course Jim Clark. After Spa, Stewart had become a consistent and dogged advocate for improved safety and medical facilities in Formula 1, and this stance would see Stewart at odds with the racing authorities and even many of the Formula 1 teams who associated the dangers involved with even greater box-office numbers. Progress was painfully slow, but through time and Stewart's continued calls for action, safety barriers, crash helmets that protected the whole head and significantly improved medical and fire services were all eventually introduced.

In his heyday, Jackie Stewart was one of the most famous figures in the world of sport, a three-times World Champion and one of the greatest motor racing drivers ever, but perhaps his greatest legacy was to make Formula 1 an international multi-billion-pounds soap opera of glamour, politics and high-octane chicanery off and on the track, avidly followed by over 500 million people around the globe – petrol-heads and non petrol-heads alike – safe in the knowledge that statistically there will be less death and destruction on view than the Sunday *Eastenders* omnibus that immediately precedes it.

*   *   *

Between the years 1962 and 1973 Jim Clark and Jackie Stewart won five Formula 1 World Championships and established a reputation for 'Flying Scots' in motor sport that through David Coulthard, Dario Franchitti and now Paul Di Resta, has continued to this day. It is a remarkable heritage and one that is made even more extraordinary by the fact that Scotland has never hosted a Grand Prix and has not had a Scottish-based team in Formula 1 for more than fifty years.

Thanks to Jim Clark and Jackie Stewart, Scotland's place in the pantheon of the great Formula 1 nations is more than secure. However, when one looks to the future there is of course one intriguing hypothesis: If Red Bull can become the leading constructor in Formula 1, then what about another soft drinks company slightly closer to home? Now that would truly be phenomenal.

## Bordering the Unbeatable

When the Fife-born, Borders-raised Jim Clark tragically died at the age of thirty-two in Germany in 1968 there was little dispute that he was the greatest motor racing driver of his generation. Even further, many experts were of the opinion (and remain so to this day) that Clark was also the greatest motor racing driver of any generation, so talented and natural was his ability with a car. Yet Jim Clark was not the first Scot to have become a legend in motor sport, and in the year that Clark was born, 1936, another Borderer whose career would have distinct parallels was also being crowned the greatest of his time.

When it comes to media coverage of sport in the twenty-first century, a clear hierarchy can be identified. At the top of their increasingly debt-laden tree we have football, as it has been for decades, masters of all they survey and seemingly impervious to economic recession, institutional corruption and the need for goal-line technology. A long way behind, but still maintaining a high profile in days of the week that don't have a 'y' in them we have, in no particular order, golf, rugby union, Formula 1, horse racing, cricket (in England), Wimbledon and down on points and holding on for dear life in the final round, boxing. And finally we have a whole series of worthy and distinguished sports that we all get incredibly excited about every four years, and then immediately ignore again as soon as the Olympics is over.

However, there is one sport that has for decades attracted a loyal, devoted and substantial fan base that have disregarded and if anything thrived on the minimal media exposure that has come their way. And if you want a demonstration of how massive this unrecognised sport truly is, then witness the 140,000 fans who attend the British Moto GP weekend at Silverstone every year.

The World Motorcycling Championships officially began in 1949, as any biker obsessive will happily tell you, one year before the birth of Formula 1. But just like motor racing, motorcycling had been staging Grand Prix competitions that attracted huge crowds throughout Europe well before the outbreak of the Second World War. And of all the major motorcycle races that were competed for, the greatest of them was the Isle of Man TT.

If one was stretching a point then one could claim the Isle of Man TT as another great Scottish sporting invention on the basis that the Isle of Man had once belonged to the Scottish crown. However, said Scottish sovereignty had come to an end in the fourteenth century, long before 'the Manx Missile' Mark Cavendish first turned on his after-burners, when there was no internal combustion engines, and for that matter, no bicycles, and for the next 500 years the Isle of Man was more or less left to its own idiosyncratic, three-legged devices.

Neither part of England, Scotland, Ireland, nor for that matter Wales, the Isle of Man's unusual constitutional position of being a United Kingdom crown dependency, but not answerable to their laws, was the principal factor in their unlikely place in sporting history. The Isle of Man had no UK speed limit for road vehicles (it still doesn't) and in 1907 the first race on the island was held for the growing number of motorcycle riders who wanted to go faster than a horse. The winner would receive the Tourist Trophy, better known as the TT. From such humble beginnings the most famous motorbike race in the world was born, and when the World Motorcycling Championship began in 1949 the Isle of Man would naturally become the venue for the British Grand Prix that it would stage until 1976 when growing safety concerns and a series of high profile fatalities saw the Grand Prix finally leave the island and move to the British mainland.

In its post-war heyday, however, the Isle of Man TT had witnessed multiple successes by such motorcycling greats as Giacomo Agostini, Mike Hailwood and John Surtees, not forgetting Glasgow-born rider Bob McIntyre who won the double of the Senior TT (500cc) and Junior TT (350cc) in 1957. But for many, the classic era of the TT had been in the 1930s when motorcycling came of age and found a mass audience fascinated by the bravery and incredible riding skill of the men who rode their bikes at unimaginable speeds, with disaster only one tiny slip away. And at the pinnacle of 1930 motorcycling was Jimmie Guthrie from just outside Hawick.

Guthrie only came to biking by accident. He was eighteen when he joined up for the First World War and was shortly afterwards wounded at Gallipoli in 1916. It was only once he had recovered from his injuries that he was given a job as a motorcycle despatch rider. He remained in the Middle East and on the Western Front until the end of the War, but had caught the biking bug, and in the 1920s was an enthusiastic amateur racing along the country roads of the Borders, honing his skills by avoiding any unsuspecting stray sheep. In 1930 he had his first major success when he won the Lightweight 125cc TT on the Isle of Man and the German 350cc Grand Prix. And in 1931 he joined the British Norton team, for whom he would have his greatest success.

Between 1930 and 1937 Guthrie would win nineteen Grand Prix, thirteen at 500cc and six at 350cc, including multiple victories at both Germany and Spain, and six TTs that included the Senior and Junior TT double of 1934. At the Grand Prix of Europe that would crown the European Champion, and by definition the best in the world, Guthrie was imperious and won the 500cc title three years in a row between 1935 and 1937, also adding the 350cc title in the last year for good measure. If this was not enough, in 1935 Guthrie travelled to Montlhéry in France where he set a series of time and distance world motorcycling records and smashed the one-hour record at an unbelievably rapid average time of 114 mph.

Throughout, Jimmie Guthrie remained an extremely consistent and tactically astute rider, with a whole string of second places to complement his victories. And despite all the inherent dangers of racing at such high speeds he suffered surprisingly few injuries, with all the years of avoiding farm animals and absent-minded tractor drivers in the Borders standing him, or technically sitting him, in good stead for whatever came his way on the racetracks of Europe and the roads of the Isle of Man. And for all his formidable determination when racing, off the track Guthrie was an unassuming man who was hugely popular everywhere he rode.

Nowhere was Guthrie more highly thought of as in Germany, a Germany that by the mid-1930s was firmly under the grip of the Third Reich, but where nevertheless even that unlikely motorbike fan Adolf Hitler was an admirer. On 8th August 1937 over 200,000 spectators crowded into the Sachsenring circuit in Saxony to see the best German and European riders take on the great Guthrie for the 500cc German Grand Prix. Guthrie was forty years old, one of the oldest men on the circuit, and he had privately intimated that this would be his final year in competitive motorcycling. He was unquestionably still at the peak of the powers, having retained his European Championship title earlier that year, and at Sachsenring he was going for a hat trick of successive victories in Germany. As the race developed, Guthrie gained a substantial lead, and with only one lap to go, he had a two-minute advantage and was in complete control.

The German crowd were hoping for a home victory, though were still ready to rise to acclaim the admirable Scot who was unquestionably the greatest rider in the world. But Guthrie never appeared. As the seconds went past, it soon became clear that something serious had occurred and when a German rider was first to cross the finish line, word began to spread that Guthrie had suffered an accident on the final lap.

In a scenario that would be tragically similar to the fate of Jim Clark in 1968, Jimmy Guthrie was found off the road in a ditch next to some trees. It was clear that he was in a serious condition, but because of the immense crowds around the circuit it would take two hours for an ambulance to reach Guthrie and transfer him to hospital. He died of his injuries the same day.

Nobody knows for certain what happened on that final lap. The general consensus was that Guthrie's bike suffered serious mechanical failure, but other hypotheses suggested that a rival rider might have accidentally, or more sinisterly, deliberately driven Guthrie off the road. Tellingly, there was never any speculation that Guthrie himself might have been responsible for any driving accident, for Jimmie Guthrie did not make those sort of mistakes, and especially not on the final lap of a Grand Prix where he was comfortably in the lead.

The world of motor sport mourned the loss of their most

popular and successful rider, and his Borders hometown of Hawick would come to a standstill to honour his funeral, just as in 1968 the Borders village of Chirnside would for another Scottish racing legend.

In Germany, the Guthrie Stone that was erected at Sachsenring following his death remains to this day a commemoration of the respect and affection accorded to him in the country where he lost his life.

In the seventy-plus years since the accident in Germany, Scotland has been blessed with many great names in motor sport, and Jim Clark, in whose career one can see so many parallels, and Jackie Stewart, were two of the greatest of all time. But it was Jimmie Guthrie from Hawick, the Borderer who survived the First World War and became the fastest and best in the world, who was first.

# 5
## *The Team Players*

Mike Denness

One of the many contradictions of Scotland since the Act of Union with England in 1707 has been that, while the Scots have appeared to be either relatively content with, or perhaps indifferent to, the major political and economic decisions being made for them, they have at the same time single-mindedly and ruthlessly sought positions of power and influence throughout the rest of the world.

Four Prime Ministers of New Zealand, two Prime Ministers of Australia and two Prime Ministers of Canada have, to date, been born in Scotland, just a small fraction of the countless Scottish politicians, trade unionists, military leaders and industrialists who have made their mark around the world. And in London at the mother of parliaments there have been, to date, seven Scots who have sufficiently succeeded in climbing the greasy pole of UK politics to gain the ultimate prize of the keys to Number 10.

So when it comes to the great global team sports of the current era – and yes there is more than one great global team sport, even if in Scotland you would hardly think it – Scots have played their part in making these sports truly international. In North America, Bobby Thomson, Charlie Gardiner and Lawrence Tynes became iconic legends of baseball, ice hockey and American football, respectively, and in cricket, rugby union and rugby league there have been historic Scottish sporting figures that have become international captains, World Cup winners, teenage prodigies and cornerstones of some of the greatest sporting team sides of all time.

For when all is said and done (and regardless of their individual sport's lowly profile in the Scottish psyche where football is king and everything else is only played by incomers and public schoolboys and girls), if anywhere in the world you put together a group of eleven, thirteen or fifteen people and one of them happens to be a Scot, then the likelihood of said Scot taking over remains disproportionately high. Except, of course, in Scotland itself, where the tendency still remains to do what they are told.

## Disdain Stops Play

There is undoubtedly not a sport that divides Scots as much as cricket. 'Too English', 'too upper-class', 'too effeminate', 'too boring (five bloody days and still nobody wins!)', are but some of the typical and more polite descriptions expressing the antipathy and at times vitriol that many in Scotland feel towards the world of *Test Match Special*, tea and cakes and silly mid- on.

Cricket has an innate ability to get under Scotland's skin like no other sport. And yet, and yet, there are tens of thousands of the silent minority who play cricket in Scotland and far more again who follow the game. And although cricket is indeed a game that was introduced to Scotland by England, then the same can be said for both football and rugby, and compared to those two sports, cricket in Scotland has a far older history.

The first recorded cricket match in Scotland goes all the way back to 1785 in, of all places, Alloa. The oldest existing cricket club in Scotland was founded in Kelso in 1821, and by the middle of the nineteenth century cricket clubs and cricket pitches were springing up all over Scotland. When the first-ever football international match was played between Scotland and England in 1872, it was at the Glasgow cricket ground of the West of Scotland Cricket Club. And ten years later, in July 1882 at the Grange in Edinburgh, Scotland defeated an Australian team that one month later would irrevocably change the history of cricket by winning a Test match in England for the very first time.

As part of the Australian tour of Britain in 1882, the Australian tourists had agreed to travel north to play a combined Scottish team in a non-Test match three-day game. Unsurprisingly, considering the relative playing strengths of the two sides involved, the Australians comfortably won the match by an innings within two days, with a day to spare, and it was agreed that so as not to disappoint the Scottish public, a one-off one-day game would be played on the third day.

It would be fair to say that perhaps the Australians did not take this additional game as seriously as other matches on their itinerary. Their legendary fast bowler, Frederick 'The Demon' Spofforth, was rested, many of the remainder of their side were recovering from the boisterous celebrations in Edinburgh the night before, and to show what they thought of the abilities of their opposition, the Australians decided to bat in reverse order with their best batsman bringing up the rear. However, for the thousands of Scottish cricketing aficionados crowded into a packed Stockbridge to witness a legendary home victory, a win is still a win, and 130 years later this still remains the only time that Scotland has defeated a major cricket nation.

Yet for all the enthusiasm in Scotland for cricket as their summer sport of choice, Scotland never established a culture or crucially a team that could compete with the English. Unlike football and rugby where Scotland vs England internationals were introduced in 1871 and 1872, there was never any impetus for cricket to follow suit, or even for Scotland to join the English County Championship, and so Scotland remained an isolated northern outpost where rain invariably stopped play. Perhaps more than any other reason it is this inability to be competitive, to have no team to follow, and to be reminded of this fact for day after day, week after week, month after month of an English cricket summer series that most rankles with your typical cricket-phobe. For, as every Sporting Scot knows, what is the point if ye cannae win?

However, even in cricket you will still find Scots who would make their mark. Alec Kennedy from Edinburgh was a medium-slow bowler who played five Tests for England in the 1920s, but is better known for his lengthy career at Hampshire for whom he played for the best part of thirty years, from 1907 to 1936, and his career total of 2,874 first-class wickets remains the seventh highest of all time. Yet even more remarkable, and ultimately tragic, is the career of Archie Jackson from Rutherglen.

Archie Jackson came from a sporting background. His uncle, Jimmy Jackson, was captain of Woolwich Arsenal in the 1900s, but young Archie immigrated to Sydney as a child and settled with his family in the historic suburb of Balmain, which incidentally had been named after William Balmain from Perthshire, a surgeon in the First Fleet who sailed and settled in New South Wales in 1788. Jackson was a cricketing teenage prodigy and first played Sydney grade cricket at the age of fifteen, for New South Wales at the age of seventeen and on 1ᵗ February 1929 at the age of nineteen was selected to play for Australia at Adelaide in the Fourth Test of the 1928–29 Ashes series.

England had unexpectedly proven dominant in the series and would win the first four Tests, but on his debut at Adelaide Jackson demonstrated a precocious brilliance far beyond his teenage years. He scored 164 in his very first Test innings, and was at the time the youngest player ever to score a Test century. (And to this day he still remains the youngest batsman ever to score a Test century in an Ashes series.) Truly, this was the first sighting of a new cricketing superstar.

However, Archie Jackson was not the only young, up-and-coming Australian batsman to make his debut in the 1928–29 Ashes series. A certain Donald George Bradman, one year older than Jackson, who had been Jackson's batting colleague and some-time rival in the New South Wales batting line-up, scored his maiden Test century in the Fifth Test of the series; however by the time of the 1930 Ashes tour of England, with both Bradman and Jackson selected, it was still Jackson who was perceived as the greater talent.

The Australians would win the 1930 Ashes series 2–1. But while Bradman scored over 900 runs to announce himself as the greatest run-scorer Test cricket had ever seen, Jackson, out of form and suffering from poor health, was only chosen for two Tests; although in the decisive Fifth Test at The Oval Jackson scored 73 in a 243 run partnership with Bradman that would ultimately take the game away from England – much to the chagrin of Aberdeen-born English bowler Ian Peebles – in the only occasion to date when Scots have played Test cricket on opposing sides.

Despite his setbacks in England Archie Jackson was still only twenty years old and a glittering career lay ahead of him, but in 1931 after only eight Tests he collapsed after coughing up blood. He had been suffering for years from persistent health problems and was eventually diagnosed as having tuberculosis. As a result, he was ordered to have total rest and give up cricket until he was fully recovered. Archie Jackson would miss the next Ashes series versus England, the infamous 'Bodyline' series of 1932–33, but against his doctor's wishes he could not resist playing the occasional game of club cricket.

In February 1933, Archie Jackson collapsed after playing cricket in Brisbane and suffered a brain haemorrhage. At the same time as Jackson was fighting for his life in hospital, the decisive Fourth Test of the Ashes was also being played at Brisbane. And on the last day of the Test, with England controversially regaining the Ashes at Brisbane, Archie Jackson died. He was only twenty-three.

Unlike those other Sporting Scots who died tragically young, golfer Willie Anderson and ice hockey player Charlie Gardiner, Archie Jackson did not live long enough to reach his peak sporting years. However, at his funeral back in Sydney thousands came to honour the young Scots-born cricketer who had already demonstrated in his short career that he was one of the most elegant and stylish batsmen that Australia had ever seen. Sadly, we will never know if Archie Jackson would have fulfilled the promise of his teenage years to become one of the legends of the game, and while it is probably unlikely that he or anyone could have matched the phenomenal heights of the run machine that was his contemporary, Donald Bradman, it is fair to say that the stylish Archie Jackson from Rutherglen would have been a lot more fun to watch. Why, even the cricket-averse Scottish sporting public might have been mildly impressed – but then again, probably not.

## Try, Try and Try Again

The twenty-first century has so far been almost universally kind to the leading nations of international rugby union. In Europe, England, France, Ireland and Wales have all savoured successful winning campaigns in the Six Nations Championship. In the southern hemisphere, New Zealand and South Africa have won the World Cup, while Australia have lifted the Tri-Nations and defeated the British & Irish Lions. And with both Argentina and Italy also making great strides to join the international elite, sold-out stadiums, increased sponsorship and media coverage, ever more lucrative contracts and rewards for players and with the World Cup itself attracting a global television audience of over four billion people, it could be said that the sport has never been in greater shape. That is, with the one notable exception of the country where international rugby union actually began.

It has to be said that Scotland has a curious relationship with its oldest international team sport. It is, with football, the only team game where Scotland has consistently competed at the highest world level, and have done so for the best part of 140 years. As recently as the 1990s Scotland were World Cup semi-finalists in 1991 and European champions in 1999. And even the past decade of the twenty-first century has witnessed the occasional fleeting moments of backs-to-the-wall Scottish rugby glory.

However, for Scottish rugby, the general backdrop of the twentieth century has so far been one of disappointment, financial crises and diminishing returns as dark and gloomy as the Edinburgh sky on an autumnal and spring evening, after yet another Test match at Murrayfield where Scotland have somehow managed to fail to score a try.

And when you combine a predilection towards pessimistic despondency with a deep-seated stereotyping by many in Scotland that rugby is merely a posh boys' affectation of a sport, played solely by the privileged few of Edinburgh and some farmers in the Borders with too much time and not enough sheep, and is no more than an inconsequential and irrelevant minor denomination when compared to the people's religion that is fitba', you might very well think that the future of Scottish rugby is as doomed as the prospects of a Scottish winger scoring a hat trick. But yet, the Scottish rugby team in their long and (very occasionally) illustrious history have weathered many similar periods in the past where the only question before an international was how many points Scotland would lose by, and still the public have always come back for more.

For, despite all the defeats, the perception of privilege and the complete absence of attacking back-play, there still remains a considerable groundswell of support and affection for Scotland's other national team that reaches far beyond the number of Scots who have actually played the game. And given a half-decent side, and a complimentary ticket or two, you will still see Murrayfield Stadium in Edinburgh once more in its rightful place as one of the greatest international rugby sporting venues in the world, for it was in Edinburgh in 1871 that international sport truly began.

Rugby football, as compared to any sort of football, began in Rugby School, Warwickshire, with its first set of rules published in 1845 by three Rugby pupils. Incidentally the headmaster of Rugby in 1845 was one Archibald Campbell Tait from Edinburgh. However, Tait was more interested in the spiritual rather than the sporting well-being of his students and would leave Rugby for a greater calling in the Church of England, culminating in his being ordained as Archbishop of Canterbury from 1868 to 1882, where any inclination to play rugby would have been seriously restricted by the dangers of his mitre falling off.

The game of football that loosely followed the Rugby rules arrived in Scotland when it was exported from the fee-paying schools of England and was taken up in the 1850s by the fee-paying schools of Edinburgh. With the oldest record of a game following 'rugby' rules in Scotland taking place at Edinburgh Academy in 1854 and the Academy's former pupils founding the Edinburgh Academical Football Club on 26th December 1857, and as the rules for association football would not be written until 1863, this would make Edinburgh Academicals not only Scotland's oldest continuous rugby club but Scotland's oldest continuous football club as well.

In 1858, Edinburgh Academy began to play another Edinburgh school, Merchiston Castle School. Merchiston Castle School had been founded in the former home of noted mathematician and inventor of logarithms, John Napier, and the Academy vs Merchiston fixture remains the oldest continuous fixture in world rugby, with the teams having played against each other for over 150 years and counting.

As the game of 'football' grew in popularity, more schools throughout Scotland began to play the game, but the lack of an agreed set of rules would often lead to disputes and sporting conundrums about who had exactly won that even Napier himself would have struggled to solve. In England this vexed question of what should and what should not be allowed would lead to the 1863 attempt to codify 'football' with one set of rules that everyone could adhere to. However, it soon became clear that there was a clear unbridgeable divide between those who saw 'football' as primarily a handling game and those who saw 'football' as primarily a kicking game.

When the meetings that led to the founding of the Association Football and the publication of the Laws of the Game had taken place in London in 1863, there had been a concerted attempt to find a compromise and it was initially accepted that handling and running with the ball would be allowed. However, consensus would break down on the question of legitimate and illegitimate tackling with the leading representative of the 'rugby rules', Blackheath from London, refusing to concede that 'hacking' and 'tripping' would not be permitted. And from that moment on the divide between association and rugby football irrevocably came to be.

Association football now had their own set of rules and with attempts at unifying the various codes now at an end, the Football Association swiftly prohibited the handling and running with the ball for all bar the goalkeeper. For the remaining 'football' clubs who had not agreed to follow the FA rules it would not be until 1871 and the formation of the Rugby Football Union in London that a new and improved, codified set of rugby rules (which incidentally outlawed both hacking and tripping – the very sticking points from eight years earlier) was agreed.

The impetus for this long overdue unification of what we now know as rugby had been a letter to *The Times* on 4th December 1870 that called for 'a code of practice' to prevent differences between clubs. It was co-written by Benjamin Burns, the Secretary of England's leading 'rugby' club, Blackheath, who although he worked and played rugby in London, was a Scot by birth and a former pupil of Edinburgh Academy. Burns had written his letter in the hope that he would gain a positive reaction to his plans for unifying and codifying the game, but he would not have been expecting the response that appeared from the land of his birth a mere four days later.

The circumstances behind the conception of international rugby would prove to be uncannily similar to the birth of international football eighteen months later. In football, it had been the publication in the press of a letter by the secretary of the FA, Francis Alcock, issuing a challenge to the association football players of Scotland that had led to the first match. And in rugby, it was Burns' letter to *The Times* that would lead to a reply on 8th December 1870, from the captains of Edinburgh Academicals, Merchistonians, Glasgow Academicals, West of Scotland and St Andrews stating that a representative Scottish team would be more than happy to take on a representative English team in a twenty-a-side game (in the days before fifteen became the accepted norm), playing rugby rules in either Edinburgh or Glasgow, where the Scottish captains promised their visitors 'a hearty welcome and first-rate match'.

For Burns and Blackheath this was too good an opportunity to miss, and despite being engrossed in the negotiations that would lead to the establishment of the RFU in January 1871, Burns also accepted this unexpected gauntlet of an international match and began to organise an English team. A date was set for 27th March 1871, with the location being Raeburn Place, in the leafy district of Stockbridge, Edinburgh – an appropriate choice, as it was the home ground of Edinburgh Academicals and the birthplace of Scottish rugby. Even though the RFU had been founded two months earlier none of the Scottish rugby clubs had been involved in its formation and with a new set of rules not published by the RFU until June 1871, a specially-agreed set of rules had to be decided on for the first Scotland v England challenge match.

It was agreed that the match would be played over two halves of fifty minutes each. The English would play in all white with a red rose emblem; the Scots would wear white flannels with brown shirts and a thistle emblem. Leading the Scottish team would be the Edinburgh Academicals captain and co-author of the public challenge, Francis Moncreiff, and crucially the umpire would be

Glasgow-born Dr Hely Hutchinson Almond, the headmaster of Loretto School in Musselburgh and the man who had done more than anyone to promote rugby in Scotland, having been an enthusiastic supporter of its virtues since the 1850s.

The match between England and Scotland captured the sporting imagination. There had been three challenge matches played in London between England and a Scottish eleven at association football prior to March 1871, but none of these had been widely covered and were not seen as being representative as there were hardly any Scots actually in the Scottish team and the first official association football international was still another twenty months away. Furthermore, association football was still nothing more than a fledgling sport in Scotland, with Queen's Park becoming in 1868 the first of only a handful of clubs actually playing the new code, and even if rugby may have been back then primarily a pastime for the privileged, then association football was not exactly a game of the people either in 1871.

Four thousand spectators congregated in Stockbridge to watch the world's first rugby international and the world's first football international of any kind. There was no agreed points system to decide the winner and no penalty kicks on offer, as obviously gentlemen did not cheat. Even scoring a 'try' was not sufficient, as a 'try' only entitled you to have a 'try for a goal', what we now know as a conversion, and only counted as a score when said conversion was successful – so constituting 'a goal'.

The first half of the first-ever international match saw much committed play between the two well-matched teams, but no tries or goals, and the decisive moment would come in the second half when the Scottish team were awarded a scrum near the English line. As was the Scottish rather than the English tradition, the Scottish forwards kept the ball in the scrum and drove the scrum over the line, claiming the try with Angus Buchanan from Inveraray and the Royal High School in Edinburgh being given the credit. Contemporary reports of the time are unclear about how controversial the scoring of the Buchanan try was, how much the English team queried the score and whether the England team were actually aware of or had agreed to the Scots attempting a pushover from a scrum. Any disputes by the England team, however, were given short shrift by the good Dr Almond, who said the try was legitimate, and with William Cross of Glasgow Academicals successfully kicking what we now call a 'conversion', it was Scotland who had scored the first 'goal' in international rugby.

In the remainder of the game, both sides managed to achieve one further 'try' each, but as neither 'try' was converted they did not count. And when Almond brought the game to an end, it was Scotland who had proved victorious by one goal to nil. For the English, defeat had both been unexpected and humbling, as they had not appreciated that Scottish rugby was of such a quality that they could compete with them at what was their own game after all. And if there was any grumbling about the result and the Scottish officiating, it was relatively restrained in keeping with what would be expected from English sporting gentlemen. Although, even this stiff upper lip might have quivered somewhat if they had known that umpire Almond, as he would later admit, had absolutely no idea if Buchanan had actually scored or not, but had awarded this momentous and historic try on the grounds that 'when an umpire is in doubt, he is justified in deciding against the side which makes the most noise, as they are probably in the wrong.'

The English would gain their revenge the following year with victory at The Oval in London in 1872, but what Scotland had shown with their victory at Raeburn Place was that they could play England on equal terms, and the Scotland vs England fixture became established as an annual contest and the oldest fixture in international rugby.

After the initial March 1871 match, Edinburgh Academicals and four other Scottish clubs joined the RFU, but following a goal-less third match draw at Hamilton Crescent in Glasgow, on the evening of 3rd March 1873, all of the Scottish clubs left the RFU and founded the Scottish Football Union, so officially confirming the advent of rugby as an international sport with national teams and now national administrations for more than just the one country.

Intriguingly, the Scottish Football Union did not include the word 'rugby' in their original title, and this remained the case all the way through to 1924 when they were renamed the Scottish Rugby Union. And even more symbolically, the Scottish Football Union would be founded in Glasgow ten days before the Scottish Football Association, on 13th March 1873, therefore meaning that, for all the years of association football, rather than rugby, being considered the national team game of Scotland, it is rugby club Edinburgh Academicals who are Scotland's oldest football club; it is rugby ground Raeburn Place in Edinburgh that hosted the world's first football international; and it is the Scottish Rugby Union rather than the Scottish Football Association that can call themselves Scotland's oldest national football body. But as with most things in Scottish history, the truth usually comes a distant second when compared to mythology, and in sport second is nowhere.

Angus Buchanan never played rugby for Scotland again after 1871, and although he did go on to represent Scotland at cricket, he will always be remembered as the man who scored the first try in international rugby. Granted it was a debatable score, with Buchanan merely falling on the ball over the line after some sustained pressure by the forwards rather than the conclusion of some mazy, jinking attacking play by the backs, but then long-suffering Scottish rugby fans watching the Scotland of today would have expected nothing less, other than mild surprise that Buchanan did not knock on as he fell over the line.

As for Benjamin Burns, the Scot who had played such a prominent role in the history of rugby through his role in the formation of the Rugby Football Union and the organisation of the first international, he had one other unique claim to fame.

When the English team arrived in Edinburgh in March 1871, they were missing one player who had not turned up. With no substitutes or replacements in their party (and at twenty-a-side there was already quite a lot of them as it was) it was Burns who stepped into the breach, making him the first rugby international to play for a country not of his birth, and so beginning a tradition that has continued to this day and one that all the leading nations could not do without.

As far as we know Burns showed no shortage of commitment for his adopted country on the ground that he had played on when at school at Edinburgh Academy, but for the unfortunate England team, it was yet another portent that they were never meant to win the first rugby international in the world. It was bad enough that the Scots had 4,000 spectators and the umpire on their side, but having one of them on your own side as well was just taking things too far. The only consolation for the English as they nursed their carafes of claret in the watering holes of Stockbridge afterwards was at least they did not have to play in brown.

## In a League of Someone Else's

The 26th of October 1991 was the closest Scotland has ever come to winning the Rugby Union World Cup. A year before Scotland had clinched their third Grand Slam victory in their history, after 1925 and 1984, with that famous 13–7 victory over England at Murrayfield when the Scottish team slowly marched onto the pitch, when even the well-to-do denizens of Edinburgh West briefly considered not paying the Poll Tax and when, for better or probably worse, 'Flower of Scotland' became an anthem for a nation.

The Scots went into the 1991 Rugby World Cup with a distinctly un-Scottish mood of optimism. True, they were not one of the favourites for the tournament, but immediately after their Grand Slam in 1990, Scotland had travelled to New Zealand and had come within a dubious decision or two from becoming the first Scottish team in history to win a Test against the mighty All Blacks. And with a favourable draw and home advantage Scotland cruised through the Group stages and Quarter-Final to reach the Semi-Final where they would once more meet the team they had sent homewards the year before. On paper and on the pitch the English were favourites, but they had their Murrayfield ghosts to exorcise, and although the larger English forwards dominated possession they somehow could not find a way to convert this into a lead. Incredibly, the score remained tied at 6–6 deep into the second half, when against the run of play Scotland were awarded a penalty in front of the English posts to possibly, or considering how few chances there had been, probably, win the game. And then Scotland's best player, Grand Slam hero and leading points-scorer Gavin Hastings stepped up and inexplicably put his kick wide! With that, Scotland's best and only chance had gone and England dropped a late drop goal to win 9–6, and then almost as inexplicably lost the Final at home to Australia by changing the habits of a lifetime by actually trying to play attacking rugby.

For the Scots, defeat, no matter by such an agonisingly close margin, was still a defeat and almost immediately national amnesia set in as Murrayfield 1991, as has been the case with so many Scottish defeats in the past, was put to one side in favour of honouring the memory of Murrayfield 1990. It is the Scottish way and proves that it is not always the victors who get to rewrite history.

The Scottish team of the early 1990s is arguably the greatest rugby team that Scotland has ever produced: World Cup semi-finalists, champions of the northern hemisphere, and key players Finlay Calder and Gavin Hastings would both become captain of the British & Irish Lions. Yet possibly the greatest Scottish rugby player of that era was not even in the squad.

Alan Tait from Kelso had made his debut for Scotland as a centre in the inaugural Rugby Union World Cup of 1987. In less than a year he had become established as one of Scotland's most important players and a rare talent, but after the Five Nations Championships of 1988 he shocked the conservative world of Scottish rugby by turning professional and changing codes to join top English rugby league team Widnes.

The great schism in rugby had taken place in 1895 and was all to do with money. By 1895, rugby football in England had followed the same pattern as association football. The top teams in England were in the north and the top players in the north wanted to be paid. In football, the establishment had been forced to back down and in 1885 grudgingly accepted the concept of professionalism, but in rugby the empire struck back and refused to abandon amateurism. The northern clubs had no choice but to go it alone and in 1895 professional rugby league was formed. Over time, the two games of rugby union and rugby league diversified with rugby union featuring fifteen players and rugby league thirteen, and as the decades went by the two codes would develop their own respective traditions, tournaments and heartlands and never the twain should meet.

In its early years, rugby league was called the Northern Union, a working-class game with its roots and adherents in the north of England, but in Scotland where up north was actually down south, rugby league made minimal impact. Amateur rugby union remained predominantly the game of choice for the fee-paying schools of Edinburgh and Glasgow and the farming communities of the Borders, and the vast majority of leading Scottish rugby players neither had the inclination nor the financial necessity of actually playing rugger for a living. And despite what one would think would have been the natural affinity the game of the industrial north might have had with the industrial Central Belt of Scotland, as far as most Scots were concerned, they were so used to disregarding one rugby code that it was not too much of a stretch to disregard another.

Alex Laidlaw of Hawick was the first prominent Scot to take the northern shilling when he joined Bradford in 1897, but over the next century the number of his fellow countrymen who followed Laidlaw to play at the highest level of rugby league would only just about make up a Caledonian XIII, and when Alan Tait joined Widnes in 1988 he was the first Scottish rugby international to switch codes for over thirty years.

Tait would make an immediate impact in his first season in rugby league, playing as full-back in a star-studded Widnes side that also included two other famous converts from union – Martin Offiah and Jonathan Davies. And in the 1988–89 season Widnes would win the Championship, the Premiership and to complete the set, defeated Canberra Raiders from Australia to be crowned World Club Champions.

Alan Tait would go on to have a hugely successful career in rugby league, playing for Widnes and then Leeds, and winning fourteen caps and scoring six tries for Great Britain. However, when rugby union finally went professional in 1996 (101 years late and predictably against the better judgement of the SRU),

Alan Tait was one of the first to return to the game where he had first made his name. He was thirty-one and his league career was entering its twilight years, but it did not take him long to show what union had been missing over the previous eight years. He became an integral member of the British & Irish Lions that, against all the odds, defeated the world champions South Africa in 1997, with Tait scoring a try in the First Test, and resumed his career for Scotland that would have an unexpected renaissance in 1999 with Scotland's victory in the 1999 Five Nations Championship.

Tait finally retired from international rugby after the 1999 Rugby Union World Cup, twelve years after his first, and he is the only Scot to become a union international, then a league international, then a union international again and to have played for Great Britain in both codes. And while we will never know what would have happened if Tait had been playing in that 1991 Murrayfield Semi-Final against England (Tait was not a goal-kicker after all), unlike all the other greats of 1990s Scottish rugby he did actually play in a World Cup Final when he came within inches of scoring the winning try in Great Britain's epic 10–6 defeat against Australia at Wembley in the Rugby League World Cup Final of 1992.

However, Tait was not the first Scot, nor the first Scottish full-back, to taste narrow defeat in the premier tournament of international rugby league. George Fairbairn played international rugby from 1975 to 1982, winning seventeen caps for Great Britain and kicking three penalties in Britain's last-minute 13–12 loss to Australia in the 1977 World Cup Final held in Sydney. He was first-choice kicker throughout most of his career, and in an era when there were separate English and Welsh teams as well as the combined Great British Lions, Fairbairn also found himself making sixteen appearances for England. He scored 118 points in his sixteen matches for England, which curiously means that a man from Peebles still holds to this day the all-time English international scoring record.

If both George Fairbairn and Alan Tait were to suffer ultimate heartbreak in attempting to win the World Cup, then two Scots were to prove more fortunate. As with so many other innovations in rugby, from professionalism to sin bins and from video referees to championship play-offs, rugby league was once more well ahead of their union first cousins (once removed) when it came to holding a Rugby World Cup. Thirty-three years before the first Union tournament, the inaugural Rugby League World Cup was held in 1954. Four teams took part: Australia, Great Britain, New Zealand and the hosts France, who were at the time a major force in rugby league. The staging of the first World Cup was a step into the unknown for rugby league and there were no clear-cut favourites, with all four competing nations capable of defeating each other. Great Britain had defeated the Australians at home in 1952, but had lost the rugby league Ashes in Australia in 1954 and the British team that travelled to France in 1954 had been handicapped by a series of injuries and withdrawals, so expectations were not high.

Surprisingly considering how few Scots had ever played in rugby league, there was two of their number in the Great Britain team of 1954. David Rose from Jedburgh had won seven caps for Scotland on the wing between 1951 and 1953 before joining Huddersfield, where he teamed up with the more experienced Dave Valentine from Hawick, who had won two caps in the Scottish pack in 1947 before heading down north in 1948.

Playing in the Huddersfield pack, Valentine played a key role in winning the 1948–49 Championship and became established as a Great Britain international, making fifteen appearances between 1948 and 1954, and with other leading players unavailable, was named captain of a very inexperienced side for the World Cup in France.

The World Cup was played on a league basis, with each side playing each other once and the top two teams then meeting in the Final. To the surprise of many, it was Great Britain and France who went through the group undefeated (with the group game between the two of them resulting in a 13–13 draw in Toulouse) and they would meet again on 13<sup>th</sup> November 1954 at the final in Parc des Princes in Paris.

So far, the first World Cup had been an unquestionable success with exciting games, a high standard of rugby and the largest crowds watching rugby league ever seen in France. The Final did not disappoint. The French team playing in front of a passionate home crowd played with considerable attacking flair, but they could not break the strength of the British pack that were anchored at loose forward by captain Valentine.

On the wing David Rose once more crossed the try line to complete a remarkable scoring record of having scored a try in every one of Britain's four World Cup games, and in the second half Great Britain began to take control to complete a narrow but ultimately decisive victory of 16–12.

Since 1954, the captains of winning World Cup teams have included such rugby league legends as Clive Sullivan, Graeme Langlands, Wally Lewis, Mal Meninga and Brad Fittler, but it was Dave Valentine from Hawick who was the very first man to lift the trophy. And although his incredible achievement is often overlooked it is Dave Valentine from Hawick and David Rose from Jedburgh who remain the only Scottish rugby players to be able to call themselves World Champions.

The successes of Valentine and Rose, as with the subsequent glittering careers of George Fairbairn and Alan Tait, may have been disregarded in their native country where despite its geographical proximity rugby league remained a foreign game in a foreign land, but as another famous son of Hawick, Bill McLaren, might have said, in November 1954 as two Scots lifted rugby's first World Cup, 'They will be dancing in the streets of Huddersfield tonight.'

## The Original Lion King

Things were going well in the world of rugby in 1884. The game had become established as fifteen-a-side rather than the original twenty-a-side (not that this initially seemed to make much of a difference to the rate of scoring, where 0–0 draws were still a common theme). The issue of professionalism that would result in the union–league split of 1895 was still over a decade away, and with the spread of the game to Ireland and Wales in 1882–83 rugby saw the introduction of the first International Championship, the forerunner of today's Six Nations, once more ahead of association football, who followed suit the following year.

England and Scotland remained the strongest of the four nations and were undefeated as they headed for the decisive encounter at Blackheath in London on 1st March 1884. For the Scots, wins in London were as rare back in the 1880s as they are today, and when coupled with the fact that the previous international in 1883 had seen England win in part thanks to a disputed score, one can but imagine the excitement and tension when Scotland went one try up, within touching distance of a victory on English soil and becoming, for the first time, Triple Crown champions. With England pressing, there was a lineout near the Scottish line and the ball was knocked backwards from a Scottish hand. The English grabbed possession and crossed over for a try that was converted to give them the lead, and then it really kicked off.

Back in the first rugby international of 1871 it had been Scotland who had benefited from a referee's interpretation of the rules and had awarded Angus Buchanan's decisive try, reluctantly but grudgingly accepted by the sporting English visitors, but in 1884, for anywhere between ten and thirty minutes (accounts vary), the match was halted as the Scots protested about the validity of the try, for in their Scottish interpretation of the rules if the ball had been deflected from the lineout then the game should be stopped and therefore the try was null and void. As far as the English were concerned, by their rules nothing untoward had happened at all , but still the Scots kept on complaining and the game was only continued when the referee agreed that the whole matter of the legality of the 'try' should be decided at a later date. The match then continued amidst much ill feeling and confusion, but no further scoring. However, when the dust had settled and the decision was eventually reviewed, the English Rugby Football Union, who as also the sole arbiters of the laws of the game, unsurprisingly decided to reject the Scottish interpretation of what had happened and upheld the decision of the referee to confirm both the English try and the English victory.

The game of rugby had been born out of amateurism and sportsmanship, but the dispute of 1884 showed how competitive international rugby had become, and that the concept of different countries following their own slightly different rules and one country having the final say was unsustainable.

The Scottish Union, as thrawn as any Scottish sporting organisations over the years, refused to let the matter lie and not only refused to play England in 1885 as a mark of protest, but set in motion discussions with Ireland and Wales that would result in the formation in Dublin in 1886 of the International Rugby Football Board (who, as the International Rugby Board, would become the guardians and legislators of the world game) as a rival to the pre-eminence of the English and a neutral organisation to make judgements on the laws of the game.

Predictably, the English refused to have anything to do with this upstart organisation. It was their game, their rules and their oval ball, after all, but when the three founding members of the IRB refused to let them participate in the Championships of 1888 and 1889, and with nobody left to play against the English, Rugby Football Union were finally forced to accept the new realities of federalism (which is something that the English have never found particularly easy). In 1890 they finally agreed to join the IRB, and rejoined the International Championship the same year. Not that England ever elicited much appreciation from their Celtic rivals for their return to the fold, as was demonstrated every time they visited Edinburgh, Dublin and Cardiff for the next 120 years.

The captain of the Scottish team, and presumably one of the principal protestors in that historic match in London in 1884, was Bill Maclagan from Edinburgh. Maclagan had begun his rugby career at the birthplace of Scottish rugby, Edinburgh Academicals, and made his debut for Scotland in 1878. He moved to London in 1880 where he worked as a stockbroker, but continued a remarkable rugby career that saw him continue to play for Scotland until 1890, captaining his country on eight occasions and, with twenty-six caps, become the then-most capped Scottish international.

By 1891 Maclagan had finally retired from representing Scotland and was winding down his club career with London Scottish. Then unexpectedly he was given the opportunity for one final international campaign.

Three years earlier, in 1888, an unofficial and motley assortment of British rugby players had undertaken a tour of Australia and New Zealand that lasted five months and did much to enhance the profile of the game in the southern hemisphere. The 1888 tour had not been sanctioned by any of the national unions, no

Test matches were played and economically it was not a success, but the concept of a team representing the British Isles overseas as international rugby missionaries was one deemed worth persevering with.

The South Africa Rugby Board had been formed in 1889 and decided to invite a British team to tour and would underwrite the costs. In 1890, the English Rugby Football Union, who after their years of exile were in a mood of winning friends wherever they might be, agreed to sanction the tour for the following year. A touring party of twenty-one was chosen, predominantly made up of English players, and was often described at the time as an English team, but crucially selected four Scots (including future Scottish captain Robert MacMillan) and one Irishman, and appointed the venerable Bill Maclagan as their captain.

The tour began in Cape Town in June and would last for three months. While the British team included players from England, Scotland and Ireland, the South African team also saw a union between the British colonies of the Cape and Natal and the independent Boer republics of Transvaal and the Orange Free State, who would combine to form a South African team that, you will not be surprised to hear, did not include any players not of European origin.

This South African team would play three Tests against the tourists, but the more experienced British Isles would prove too strong, winning all three matches as well as all their remaining seventeen games against regional teams to go through the entire tour undefeated. Bill Maclagan captained the tourists throughout the tour and therefore became, on 30th July 1891 at Port Elizabeth, the first man ever to lead a British Isles rugby team in a Test match. His long and illustrious international career would finally come to an end in the Third Test with a victory at Cape Town that was rounded off with the captain scoring a try. However, Maclagan had one final contribution to make to rugby history.

The British Isles touring party of 1891 had sailed to South Africa on the Castle Shipping Line that was owned by Greenock-born Donald Currie. Currie had made his name and reputation by sailing the route from London to Cape Town and was a prominent figure in South African affairs. He was also a keen patron of sport and in 1889 had provided a Currie Cup trophy for the best cricket team in South Africa that would continue as the main first-class domestic cricket tournament for over a century until 1990.

In 1891, Currie accompanied the British team on the journey to the Cape and brought with him a gold trophy that he gave to Maclagan, with instructions that this should be presented to the local team that gave the tourists the hardest game. Griqualand West from Kimberley were the lucky recipients of the trophy, and the following year they donated the trophy to the South African Rugby Board to be competed for on an annual basis and to this day the Currie Cup remains the premier rugby tournament in South Africa.

As for Maclagan and his players of 1891, there was no trophy to commemorate their achievements, but the success of the tour would prove a defining moment in the global history of rugby. In South Africa, the tour of 1891 and the introduction of the Currie Cup would provide a springboard in their rise to become, with New Zealand, one of the two most powerful rugby nations of the following century. While back in Britain, the 1891 tour was deemed so successful that officially sanctioned trips to the southern hemisphere became regular highlights of the international rugby calendar, and for English, Scottish, Welsh and Irish rugby union players still remains, despite the advent of professionalism and the Rugby World Cup, the ultimate tour to be selected for.

\* \* \*

Today, the British Isles rugby union team is better known as the British & Irish Lions, and even here there is a decided Scottish connection. The Lions name, rather than that of the British Isles, only came into prominence for the 1950 tour of New Zealand and Australia; however, from 1910 to 1938, the British Isles team had worn a jersey that was the dark blue of Scotland and until 1930 a Scottish lion rampant badge had complemented this dark blue Scottish shirt. Six years earlier in South Africa in 1924, there had been no lion rampant on the dark blue jersey, but the players all wore the lion rampant emblem on their official ties, and it was from that point on that the 'Lions' nickname was first coined. Ironically, it was the same 1950 tour when the term 'The Lions' was first used on an official basis that the British Isles replaced the dark blue jerseys from which the whole 'Lion' connotation had first been originated with the now famous red Lions jersey that we know today. But then again if you can accept the notion of a team representing Britain and Ireland wearing as an emblem that well-known native British and Irish animal, the lion, in, of all countries in the world, South Africa, then it is clear that irony is not really a major consideration.

## Of Mighty Mouse and Men

On 1st March 1975 the Scottish rugby team played the Welsh rugby team in Edinburgh. This was the era of the great Wales side of the 1970s, with legendary figures such as JPR Williams, Gerald Davies, Mervyn Davies and the greatest of them all, Gareth Edwards. The Scottish team, to be fair, was also not too shabby, including amongst their number such famous players as Sandy Carmichael, Gordon 'Broon from Troon' Brown, Jim Renwick and Andy Irvine – and while the Welsh were the pre-match favourites, with home advantage the Scots were expected to make the contest highly competitive.

As expected, the match remained close throughout, but with the home pack gaining the narrowest of advantages it was Scotland who ended up victorious by 12–10. However, what made the Scotland–Wales match of 1975 truly historic was that, while the Murrayfield capacity at that time was officially 80,000 spectators, there were in fact 104,000 Scottish and Welsh fans crowded into Murrayfield that day, including more than a fair percentage of Welsh supporters who had still not made it home from the previous game two years before.

The 104,000 attendance of 1975, while dangerously overcrowded, was the first time that a rugby game of either code had topped the 100,000 mark in the history of the sport and would remain the world record until 1999 and the opening of Stadium Australia in Sydney. Realising how close they had been to a health and safety disaster, the Scottish Rugby Union would in the future ensure that all internationals would become the increasingly exorbitant all-ticket affairs that we know and love today; however, what could not be denied was that the events of 1975 had been yet another milestone for a stadium that had been opened fifty years earlier in another game that would take on legendary status.

In 1897 the Scottish Football Union, as they were still called before their name change to the Scottish Rugby Union in 1924, purchased the land for their first national ground, Inverleith Park in Stockbridge, Edinburgh, but with the growing popularity of rugby in the twentieth century, the re-branded SRU as they had become decided that a larger purpose-built stadium was required. An appropriate site was located in Murrayfield, in the West of Edinburgh, and construction of the new stadium would be completed for the climax of the 1925 Five Nations

Championship, with France having joined the party in 1910.

The Scots began the 1925 Five Nations in impressive style, with a comfortable home victory over France at the old ground of Inverleith, followed by away wins in Wales and Ireland, but they still had in front of them the small matter of a final encounter against the then-leading side in European rugby, England, who had won back-to-back Grand Slams in 1923 and 1924 and were led by their greatest-ever player, Wavell Wakefield. Attendances at Inverleith for internationals had reached a perfectly respectable 25,000, but nearly 70,000 Scottish supporters would make the short journey to Murrayfield on 21st March 1925 to witness the first-ever game at the largest rugby stadium ever to be built in the northern hemisphere, which by lucky circumstance would also prove to be the decisive fixture in the destiny of the 1925 Five Nations Championship.

The Scottish team of 1925 was built on a typical doughty and hard-working pack, but what set them apart was an electric three-quarter line of Aitken, Macpherson, Smith and Wallace, all of whom had played their rugby for Oxford University, and in an early sign of Scotland's liberal interpretation of nationality, only one of them was actually Scottish. Aitken was a New Zealander, and the flying wings, Ian Smith and Johnny Wallace, were Australians, leaving centre and captain George MacPherson from Newtonmore in the Highlands as the only bona fide Scottish representative.

The match fluctuated from the first whistle with both sides taking the lead and then proceeding to lose it again. With five minutes to go, the English were ahead, but then fly-half Herbert Waddell from Glasgow popped up to score the crucial drop goal that put Scotland 14–11 ahead, and roared on by the 70,000 home crowd, Scotland somehow managed to hang on to the end of the game and complete their first-ever Grand Slam.

No one could have imagined a more dramatic or glorious first game for the new national stadium, and as the exultant crowd began the deceptively longer-than-you-think journey back to the city centre of Edinburgh, there truly was dancing in the streets of Murrayfield that day, and considering the cosmopolitan make-up of their team, a fair amount of dancing in Oxford, Melbourne, Sydney and Wellington as well.

Fifty years later, in 1975, it was the Ayrshire-born prop forward Ian McLauchlan who was captain of the Scottish side that defeated Wales in front of the Murrayfield world record crowd. McLauchlan had been a late entrant to the world of international rugby, being nearly twenty-seven when he made his debut in 1969, but for the next decade he was the unmovable cornerstone of the Scottish pack. He came into a Scottish side where the magical dawn of Murrayfield in 1925 had long since clouded over. Scotland may well have a world-class stadium, but on the pitch, no matter how many ringers they recruited from overseas they had not won the Championship since the Triple Crown season of 1938, that with France temporarily out of the tournament was almost (although not quite) as good as a Grand Slam. Yet for Ian McLauchlan, playing well for Scotland, despite the perennial lack of success in the Five Nations, did offer the opportunity of selection to an even more august body – the British Lions touring side of the best players from England, Ireland, Scotland and Wales that had first been captained by fellow Scot Bill Mclagan in 1891.

Ever since the great pre-war Scottish captain Mark Coxon Morrison, who had led Scotland to two Triple Crowns in 1901 and 1903, but had in 1903 become the first captain of a British Isles side to lose a test series in South Africa, the balance of rugby power had decisively shifted from north to south of the equator. And for the remainder of the twentieth century no side from the

British Isles had ever won a Test series in either South Africa or New Zealand.

In 1971 the British Lions were set to tour New Zealand, and while many thought that this was one of the more talented groups of players to be selected from Britain and Ireland, it still seemed unthinkable that the All Blacks' undefeated record against the Lions could be in any way threatened. However, just to be on the safe side, the visitors would be subjected to a prolonged amount of provocation in the provincial games that preceded the four-match Test series, and would culminate in a brutal encounter against Canterbury in Christchurch, when both of the Lions' first choice props were invalided out of the tour.

One of those props was Sandy Carmichael from Glasgow, a player noted as much for his fair play as for undoubted talent. He suffered a fractured cheekbone from a particularly vicious assault, and it was only with his departure from the tour that Ian MacLauchlan, Carmichael's partner in Scotland's front row throughout his career, found himself the only Scot selected for the crucial First Test on 26th June.

The Carisbrook ground in Dunedin on the South Island of New Zealand was the venue for the First Test and would became known as 'the House of Pain' for its reputation as a ground where visiting sides would come to grief. But Dunedin was also that most Scottish of cities, founded in 1848 by the Scots William Cargill from Edinburgh, and the Rev. Thomas Burns from Mauchline in Ayrshire, who was also the nephew of the slightly more secular national bard Robert Burns. Dunedin was established as a Scottish Presbyterian settlement, with the name Dunedin itself deriving from the Gaelic form of Edinburgh, *Dun Eideann*, and with this background it is perhaps not too surprising that it was here that McLauchlan would play the most important game of his life.

The Lions of 1971 included some of the greatest players ever to come from the British Isles – Gareth Edwards, Barry John, JPR Williams and Gerald and Mervyn Davies from Wales, Willie John McBride and Mike Gibson from Ireland – but against a second-choice Lions front row the mighty All Blacks, captained by their greatest-ever player, Colin Meads, was expected to prove too strong, especially in the forward battle.

Particular scepticism was expressed about the selection of McLauchlan who, at only five foot eight inches, was seen as the weak link in the Lions pack. But as Dunedin's founder Rev. Thomas Burns' more famous uncle might have said, 'Now's the day and now's the hour.' For much of the game the Lions were, as expected, under repeated pressure, but their defence remained firm and the scrum stayed solid, and it was the Lions who ran out narrow 9–3 victors, with the most unlikely figure of the prop Ian McLauchlan charging down an All Blacks kick and crossing the line to score the only try of the game. Scots wha' hae indeed.

The All Blacks, stung by defeat in their most impregnable fortress, fought back in the Second Test at Christchurch with a convincing 22–12 victory to square the series. For the Third Test at Wellington, McLauchlan was joined in the Lions side by lock forward and fellow Scot Gordon Brown, an irrepressible figure on and off the pitch who would star on three consecutive Lions tours and was universally known as 'Broon from Troon'. At Wellington, the Lions would be inspired by a virtuoso performance from fly-half Barry John, who scored all of his side's points in a 13–3 victory that would see the visitors take a 2–1 lead to go into the final test at Eden park in Auckland.

With national honour and their undefeated record at stake, the All Blacks threw everything at the visitors, but the Lions held on – just – to a 14–14 draw and a 2–1 series victory, with 'Broon from Troon' requiring twenty stitches for the punishment inflicted upon him as the Lions pack held firm. And for the first time in the twentieth century, British and Irish rugby had overcome all that Middle Earth had thrown at them to record their greatest-ever triumph. However, there was still another equally formidable rugby empire that had to be overcome, and in 1974 the Lions went to South Africa.

Both cricket and the Olympics had by this stage refused to compete against a country that was openly and constitutionally racist and selected its athletes and players on the basis of colour rather than talent, a sporting boycott of an apartheid-run South Africa that would culminate in the Gleneagles Agreement of 1977, signed by the Commonwealth leaders in the famous Perthshire hotel, with the bar staff under strict instructions to hide all the Stellenbosch merlot. However, in 1974 the sport of rugby union saw no problem in the Lions touring South Africa, and the majority of the best players from Britain and Ireland were all present and correct on the white-only *veldt*, determined to repeat their success in New Zealand of three years previously.

Ian McLauchlan and Gordon Brown featured in all four Tests for the Lions, along with Yorkshire-born centre and future coach Ian McGeechan. Billy Steele from Langholm in the Borders played on the wing in the first two tests, and Scotland's most promising new talent, future captain and three-times Lions tourist, Andy Irvine from Edinburgh, replaced Steele for the final two of the series.

The South Africans of 1974, like the New Zealanders of 1971, attempted to weaken the threat posed by the Lions and their formidable pack by inflicting as much violence on them as possible, but learning from what had happened to Sandy Carmichael against Canterbury the Lions had decided to get their retaliation in first with the infamous '99' call, that meant that if any Lion was under attack anywhere on the pitch, then '99' would be shouted and every member of the Lions team would take out whatever Springbok was nearest to them, innocent bystanders included – not that many of the 1974 South Africans could be described as innocent.

The Lions would go through the entire South Africa tour undefeated, repelling everything the Springboks threw at them. They were convincing winners of the first three Tests and were only denied a clean sweep by some contentious refereeing in the Fourth Test that resulted in a 14–14 draw. There were many legendary performances from the Lions of 1974, but none would surpass 'Broon from Troon', who scored an unheard-of (for a lock forward) eight tries on tour, including a try in the Second Test at Pretoria and the crucial opening try at Port Elizabeth in the Third Test that confirmed a Lions series victory.

The Lions that toured New Zealand and South Africa in 1971 and 1974 were the greatest and most successful group of British and Irish rugby union players ever to be assembled in the history of the game. Over the two victorious tours five players would play in every Test in both of those tours – the legendary Irishman Willie John McBride, who was captain of the unbeaten 1974 team; three of the greatest Welshmen ever to play the game in Gareth Edwards, Mervyn Davies and JPR Williams; and at the coalface of the scrum, the immovable prop who played his rugby at Jordanhill in Glasgow, Ian McLauchlan. After the 1971 tour of New Zealand, McLauchlan had been nicknamed 'Mighty Mouse' on account of his diminutive stature and his formidable capacity for getting the better of bigger and heavier opponents, and while success proved elusive in his ten-year career for Scotland, when it came to the Lions he was the mouse that roared.

As one final postscript to the 1974 Lions tour, it was in South

Africa that Billy Steele, the winger from Langholm, decided that it would be a good idea for the Lions to have a team song to sing. He chose a not especially well-known Scottish folk song that had only been written nine years previously, but with the support of fellow Scot Gordon Brown, the song was adopted by the entire touring party and was sung with gusto before and after matches and on the team bus. The Scots were the small minority in the Lions tour of 1974, compared to the English, Welsh and Irish, but this did not stop the players from the other countries enthusiastically joining in, and the song in question has subsequently become a familiar sporting national anthem. And once again we can but wonder at the often-overlooked tolerance and good nature of the English, and in particular, the English players in the 1974 Lions tour as they belted out the words of 'Flower of Scotland' over and over again.

## Climb Every Eildon Hill

The advent of the World Cup in 1987 as the new pinnacle of the game of rugby union where all the leading nations of both the southern and northern hemisphere would compete every four years to decide who was the best in the world was seen by many as ringing the inevitable death knell for the ethos of the British & Irish Lions. After the glory years of 1971 and 1974, the Lions had lost their roar and had returned to their traditional position of being outfought and outplayed, with the number of defeats only being matched by the number of wounded Lions being forced home through injury. And by the 1980s, with England, Scotland, Wales and Ireland all sending their own representative teams on tours to the southern hemisphere most summers, there was a lot riding on the British and Irish tourists, who after a six-year gap went to Australia in 1989 with the very future of the Lions possibly depending on the result.

Finlay Calder from Haddington was the captain of the 1989 Lions and the Test series could not have had a more disastrous start, as Australia won the opening Test in Sydney by a crushing margin of 30–12. Humiliation and a series defeat was looming when the Lions played the Second Test at Brisbane, but with a try five minutes from time from Scottish full-back Gavin Hastings, the tourists fought back to square the series with a 19–12 win. The deciding Third Test was once more played at Sydney Football Stadium, and thanks to five penalties from Hastings and a catastrophic but highly enjoyable mistake from Australian great David Campese that gifted the visitors a crucial try, it was the Lions who edged a 19–18 victory to clinch the series and show that there was still considerable pride in the concept of the Lions.

Finlay Calder had become the first Scot since Bill Maclagan in 1891 to win a Test series as the captain of the British Isles, a feat even more remarkable when you consider that he had not even been captain of Scotland eight months earlier. Four years later in 1993, it was Gavin Hastings who continued the Scottish leadership of the Lions by leading them to New Zealand in what would be the last tour of the amateur era. Despite a comprehensive victory at the Second Test in Wellington, the Lions would lose the series 2–1, and with the advent of professionalism in 1995 there was renewed speculation that the Lions' tour of South Africa in 1997 might well be the last.

Ian McGeechan, the Yorkshire-born Scottish centre and coach, had been in charge of the Lions in 1989 and 1993 and would be undertaking his third tour as Lions coach in 1997. There would be no Scottish captain this time around, and in the shape of things to come, only five Scottish players had made the original thirty-five-man touring party. As well as being the first

Lions tour of the professional age, this was also the first Lions tour to take place in a post-apartheid South Africa that now had Nelson Mandela as their democratically-elected President, when in 1974 he had been a prisoner on Robben Island, and the South Africans had a rugby team who were reigning World Champions and overwhelming favourites against an inexperienced group of players who had been written off before they even left home. However, what the Lions did have amongst their number was an assistant coach from Melrose who had been defying the rugby odds for over thirty years.

When in 2007 the SRU decided that for economic reasons it was preferable to have two under-performing and uncompetitive professional franchises rather than three, it was Edinburgh and Glasgow rather than the unfortunate Border Reivers who were saved to fly the Scottish flag and be knocked out at the Group stages of the Heineken Cup. The decision did not mean the end of rugby in the region, as the amateur Borders clubs would continue to compete as they had done for the previous 130 years, but the concentration of elite rugby in the two centres of Edinburgh and Glasgow saw Scottish rugby turn full circle, back to the beginnings of the sport when the game was exclusively played in the fee-paying schools of those two cities.

Yet for over a century it had been the Borders that had been the true heartland of Scottish rugby, in a region where there is no football club in the Scottish league but the most famous clubs in Scottish rugby. The Borders League established by Gala, Hawick, Jed-Forest, Melrose and Langholm in 1901 remains the oldest rugby union league anywhere in the world and Borderers have provided some of the greatest players, captains and coaches in Scottish rugby history.

The most famous of the historic Borders towns is arguably Melrose, with their medieval ruined Abbey that is the final resting place of the heart of no less a figure than King Robert the Bruce. And as rugby became established in the Borders in the late nineteenth century, Melrose Rugby Club was founded in 1875 and one of their notable early players was a certain Ned Haig.

Ned Haig was actually born in Jedburgh, but had moved to neighbouring Melrose where he found work as a butcher. In 1883, the fledgling Melrose Rugby Club were looking to find ways to improve their somewhat impoverished finances and Haig came up with the idea of a rugby tournament between the local Borders teams. But in order to make this a viable proposition he came up with the idea of making the games only fifteen minutes long and reduced the number of players in each team from fifteen to seven, although crucially the game would still be played on a full-sized pitch, therefore making sevens more high-scoring and exciting for the spectators and considerably more knackering for the poor unfortunate players.

On 28th April 1883 eight Borders teams played in the inaugural Melrose Sevens, the first rugby sevens tournament in the world, with the home side featuring Haig defeating Gala in the final and receiving the Ladies' Cup, the trophy that had been donated by the good ladies of Melrose, who no doubt expected a more than adequate supply of sausages from Ned Haig's butchers in return.

The inaugural Melrose Sevens was judged a great success, and the abbreviated game became a popular event throughout the Borders but struggled to gain a foothold elsewhere until 1976. In that year, Hong Kong, the most Scottish of British colonies, where the Scottish merchants William Jardine and James Matheson and their descendants had established the island as a major international commercial centre from the 1840s onwards, decided to host the first Hong Kong Sevens and invited teams throughout Asia and the southern hemisphere to participate. Since 1976, the Hong Kong Sevens has become one of the major rugby tournaments in the international calendar and the world's premier rugby sevens trophy. Moreover, sevens has also become a global sport, with the speed and skill of the players only matched by the ferocity of the tackles, some of which were occasionally even against an opponent who had the ball. Before long, as has happened throughout Scottish sporting history, the game that had been invented in Scotland had been taken over by New Zealand and Fiji and the rest of the world, but Ned Haig's legacy was not forgotten, as in 1993 the first Rugby Sevens World Cup was held at Murrayfield, with the winners lifting the specially commissioned Melrose Cup in honour of the game's historic birthplace, even if the Bruce's brave heart may have had palpitations that the first holders of the Melrose Cup ended up being, of all teams, England.

Throughout the twentieth century the Borders and Borders clubs provided generation after generation of Scottish internationals as well as a select few such as Great Britain captain Dave Valentine from Hawick, who made a career out of rugby by switching codes and playing thirteen-man rugby league. But of all the Borders rugby greats few would have the enduring influence of player, captain and coach, Jim Telfer, who although born in Midlothian made Melrose his rugby home.

Jim Telfer played twenty-five times for Scotland and eight Tests for the British Lions between 1964 and 1970, in a career that was brought to a premature end through injury, with the highlight being his captaining and scoring the winning try in an improbable 6–3 victory over France in Paris in 1969. In 1980 Telfer was appointed national coach and over the next four years Scotland responded with a series of memorable performances after decades of underachievement. In 1982 Scotland won in Wales for the first time in twenty years and won a Test match in Australia – still to this day the only Scottish victory in the southern hemisphere against any of the big three of Australia, New Zealand or South Africa – and in 1983 Scotland defeated the English at Twickenham (for only the second time since 1938). However, despite these successes Scotland were not one of the favourites going into the 1984 Five Nations, but with victories away in Cardiff and Dublin and at home against England they completed their first Triple Crown since 1938. However, for Telfer and the Scots there was still the small matter of a Grand Slam decider against the also undefeated French side of Jean-Pierre Rives, Serge Blanco et al.

Ten of the Scottish fifteen (captain Aitkin, Deans, Tomes, Leslie, Paxton, Laidlaw, Rutherford, Baird, Robertson and Dods) that started the game at Murrayfield on 17th March 1984 played for either Hawick, Gala, Melrose, Jed-Forest, Selkirk or Kelso in what was a golden era for Borders rugby. Roy Laidlaw from Jedburgh formed with stand-off John Rutherford from Selkirk Scotland's greatest-ever half-back pairing, and in the front row hooker and future captain Colin Deans from Hawick was joined by prop Jim Aitkin from Penicuik who played for Gala.

France were the pre-match favourites, but with a passionate home support, five penalties from Galashiels-born full-back Peter Dods and a late try from flanker Jim Calder from Haddington (who with his twin brother Finlay were mainstays in the Scottish back-row for a decade, but remarkably never at the same time), Scotland won 21–12 to complete only their second Grand Slam in their history and their first for fifty-nine years. Jim Aitkin joined George MacPherson in the select list of Scottish Grand Slam-winning captains, and unlike in 1925, this Scottish team had done so without any southern hemisphere playing assistance.

Thirteen years later, Jim Telfer, the architect of the 1984 Grand Slam and driving force behind Scottish rugby for two decades, was appointed assistant coach to Ian McGeechan for the mission impossible that was the 1997 Lions tour to reigning world champions South Africa.

It was not the first time that the McGeechan–Telfer combination had worked together. Telfer had been assistant coach in the slow march of Scotland's third Grand Slam of 1990. Furthermore, for Telfer the Lions tour of 1997 meant unfinished business, as his previous tours with the Lions as a player in 1966 and 1968 and as coach in 1983 had resulted not only in three series defeats, but in each case the Lions had failed to win a single Test.

In 1997 Telfer was given the responsibility for the Lions forwards and turn them into world-beaters in a space of a few weeks against bigger and more experienced opponents who were playing on their home turf – and few gave him any chance. However, throughout his coaching career Jim Telfer had specialised in making the most unheralded group of players into highly competitive and disciplined units that could, with the hard, athletic driving forward play that was his speciality, take on and defeat the best in the world.

For the First Test at Newlands in Cape Town, the Lions deliberately picked a lighter and more mobile pack that out-manoeuvred and disrupted the supposed superiority of the Springboks pack and against all expectations ran out 25–16 winners to take a 1–0 lead in the series.

For the Second Test at Durban on 28th June, the shocked and wounded Springboks were in no mood to allow a repeat performance. The element of surprise that had caused their downfall in Cape Town was no longer a factor and from kick-off South Africa dominated both possession and territory. The Springboks had learned all the lessons from the previous defeat – except for one: they had not selected a proven goal-kicker. And although they outscored the Lions by three tries to zero they missed all their numerous penalty opportunities. The Lions, despite being comprehensively outplayed, clawed themselves back in the game by scoring all their penalties, and against all the odds, took the lead with a late drop-goal to win 18–15 and take an unassailable 2–0 lead in the three-Test series. It was only the second time in a century that the Lions had won a series in South Africa, and much of the credit was given to the hard, abrasive assistant coach from the Borders who, irrespective of the egos and feelings of the individuals concerned, had moulded the Lions pack into history makers. In a famous speech before the First Test, Jim Telfer had told his players that this would be their Everest, but so fearsome was his reputation that if he had said that this would be their Lammermuirs it would have probably had the same effect.

In 1998 Jim Telfer had one more crack as Scottish national coach. Expectations for the Scots before the 1999 season was as usual no more than modest, and with away fixtures at Twickenham and the Parc des Princes, mid-table respectability was as much as could be reasonably expected, but Telfer had overcome the seemingly impossible throughout his career, and for all the dilution of the Borders influence that had been the backbone of the legendary team of 1984, the team that he had put together in 1999 still contained at its heart a trio of Borderers as illustrious as any of the Borders greats of the previous 120 years. Centre Alan Tait, who had returned to union after a glittering career in rugby league, and the mercurial stand-off from Galashiels, Gregor Townsend, had both played integral roles in the 1997 Lions victory and were joined by scrum-half, captain and survivor of the 1990 Grand Slam team, Gary Armstrong, who although born in Edinburgh had, like his Number 9 Scotland predecessor Roy Laidlaw, made his name and reputation at Jedburgh.

Even though Scotland would narrowly lose, as like so many Scottish teams had done over the decades, in London, comprehensive home victories over Wales and Ireland saw them go into their final game against France on 10<sup>th</sup> April with an outside chance of winning the championship for the first time since 1990.

It was in the springtime in Paris, on 10<sup>th</sup> April 1999, that saw the culmination of all the decades of Jim Telfer's hard work and a vindication of his philosophy that Scotland should be a modern, attacking rugby nation with forwards and backs working in cohesive unity. Alan Tait scored two tries and Gregor Townsend one as Scotland confounded everybody to score five tries in a scintillating first half and eventually ran out 36–22 winners. And with England losing the following day to Wales, it was Scotland who would lift the 1999 Championship and end the century as they had begun, as the champions of the northern hemisphere.

Although nobody knew it at the time, it was the end of an era. Jim Telfer, Gary Armstrong and Alan Tait would soon all retire from international rugby. And in 2002, the revered commentator and son of his beloved Hawick, 'the Voice of Rugby' Bill McLaren, who had witnessed all the highs and many lows of Scottish rugby for over fifty years, also retired.

The twenty-first century has so far proven a trying time for Scottish rugby, as Scotland has found itself more often at the bottom than the top of the international standings. There have been, of course, similar long periods of disappointment in the past, and Scottish rugby has always come back, so for the half-glass-full optimists there is always the hope that Scotland will rise once more like the lone piper above the Murrayfield gloom. Yet if history tells us anything about rugby in Scotland, it is that without a renewed flourishing of its one true heartland that has over the past 130 years given the world Ned Haig, rugby sevens, Jim Telfer, Bill McLaren and some of the greatest players and teams Scotland has ever produced, the journey back to the summit of international rugby will be Bordering on the impossible.

## *I'm a Jock, Not a Pom*

As we have seen, the first rugby union international in the world was held in Edinburgh in 1871 and the Scottish Football Union (that would become the Scottish Rugby Union) was formed in 1873. The first association football international in the world was held in 1872 and the Scottish Football Association was formed one year later. However cricket, the game that in Scotland had preceded both of those upstarts and in the 1870s was far more popular than both of them combined, did not form a national Scottish Cricket Union until 1879 and then swiftly abandoned said Scottish Cricket Union four years later. It was not until 1908 that a longer-lasting Scottish Cricket Union was established, by which time Test cricket had been up and running for thirty years; however, even then there was no attempt for Scottish cricket to follow their rugby and football counterparts and compete at an international level.

Over the next eighty-six years the West Indies, New Zealand, India, Pakistan, Sri Lanka and even Zimbabwe would see the list of Test-playing nations rise from three to nine, but in Scotland, where cricket had been played for 200 years, there was no such initiative. It was not until 1994 that Scotland finally joined the International Cricket Council as an Associate Member, the level below playing Tests, which even by cricket standards was exceptionally slow.

Therefore up and until 1994, Scotland found itself and furthermore chose to remain in cricketing purgatory. They had a cricket union but did not play international cricket, other than the occasional and haphazard friendly against touring teams with time on their hands and relatives to visit. They accepted England as their cricketing overlord, but never appeared to have the inclination or desire, as Glamorgan of Wales did in 1921, to join either the English County Championship or the Minor County Championship (for all the remaining lesser-known counties ending in –shire). This curious and unsatisfactory state of affairs, that inexplicably was allowed to remain in place for over a century, meant that unless you were someone like Archie Jackson who had immigrated at a young age to Australia and learned the game in his adopted country, any young Scottish cricketers with a modicum of talent had no other choice but to move to England if he wanted the opportunity to play first-class and Test cricket.

Before the Second World War, Alec Kennedy from Edinburgh, who played for Hampshire, and Ian Peebles from Aberdeen, who played for Middlesex, played five and thirteen Tests, respectively, for England. In the decisive fifth and final Test of the 1930 Ashes, with the series tied at 1–1, Peebles produced his best Test performance by taking six wickets in the first Australian inning at The Oval. Unfortunately, his six wickets came at a cost of 204 runs, as Bradman scored a double hundred and Jackson a delightful 73, sending England crashing to an innings defeat and a series loss. After Peebles played his last Test in 1931 and Jackson tragically died in 1933, it would be another thirty years before the next Scots played Test cricket in the shape of Middlesex opening batsman Eric Russell from Dumbarton and Northamptonshire fast bowler David Larter from Inverness.

Russell and Larter both made their Test debuts between 1961 and 1962, and both played ten Tests for England, but they never appeared on the same Test team at the same time. Of the two, it was Larter who, at six foot seven, was an exceedingly tall and at times unplayable fast bowler, who made the greatest impact. But his career was bedevilled and eventually curtailed by injuries. His highly impressive 5 for 68 against South Africa at Trent Bridge in Nottingham in 1965 marked not only the confirmation of a world-class fast bowler, but also Larter's final Test. If the Test career of David Larter was over before it had really begun, then the next Scottish bowler to make his name in international cricket was a prime example of persistence and hard work.

Peter Such from Helensburgh was, at twenty-nine, a well established if unspectacular off-spinner on the County Championship circuit when he made his Test debut in 1993 against Australia. Such would play eleven Tests in total between 1993 and 1999, but it would be for his debut in the First Test of The Ashes at Old Trafford in Manchester that he is best remembered, with an astonishing 6 for 68 in the Australian's first innings. Or he would have been best remembered, if it had not been for the fact that in the English reply a certain young leg-spinner by the name of Shane Warne bowled Mike Gatting with his very first delivery in what would become known as 'the Ball of the Century' and inspire a famous Aussie victory. Or as they say in Helensburgh – 'Such is life.'

Defeat to the Australians, and often crushingly so, has been an occupational hazard not just for Scots playing for England, but for all English cricketers for over a century. Having your noses rubbed in it by colonials with ideas above their station is bad enough at home, but there are few lonelier places in international sport than that of a losing English cricket captain in Australia. Battered, bruised and mercilessly sledged both at the wicket and in the stands by up to 100,000 baying Aussies with their taste for English blood only surpassed by the necessity for more amber nectar to be cracked open, with even the most restrained show of disappointment only exacerbating the cries of 'whingeing Poms'. And of all the English captains who suffered this Antipodean torment, few suffered more than the only Scot to have been a Test cricket captain.

*　　*　　*

The town of Bellshill has a remarkable sporting heritage. Hughie Gallacher, Matt Busby, Billy McNeill and Ally McCoist are amongst the many great players and managers to hail from this North Lanarkshire football nursery, but perhaps unexpectedly Bellshill was also the hometown of Mike Denness, Scotland's best-known cricketer. Denness began his first-class career with Kent in 1962, and in 1972 became county captain. He had become a respected and successful middle-order batsman in county cricket, scoring over 25,000 runs in his career, but it was still somewhat of a shock when he was appointed English captain for the 1974 tour of West Indies.

Denness had made his Test debut in 1969, but had only played nine Tests in the next five years, had never scored a Test century and had not been in the English team for over a year. Furthermore, he found himself in charge of an experienced and established side that included such proven world-class players as Knott, Underwood, Tony Greig and a certain Geoffrey Boycott, all of whom had been passed over in favour of the unproven Scot.

There were few tougher places to tour in 1974 than the Caribbean, and Denness and England made an inauspicious start with a crushing seven-wicket defeat in the First Test in Trinidad. England remained on the back foot for the next three Tests and only narrowly managed to escape without further defeat, but at the series finale, once more at Trinidad, fought back in a low-scoring match to sneak a thrilling victory by only twenty-six runs and against all expectations square the series 1–1 – a perfectly acceptable result in the circumstances and the last time for thirty years that any English team would return from the Caribbean undefeated.

As a batsman Denness had struggled in the West Indies with a top score of 67, but as a captain he was given credit for the English fight back and continued in charge through the following summer, where England remained undefeated in home series against both India and Pakistan and finally demonstrated that he was worth his place in the side as a batsman, rather than just as a captain, by scoring his first two centuries in Test cricket.

The year 1974 was a busy year for English cricket, and after having already played eleven Tests and remained undefeated, there was still the small matter of a tour that winter and the ultimate challenge for all English cricket teams, playing Australia in Australia for The Ashes. England had held the urn since 1971 but were an ageing team, while the Aussies under the abrasive and astute captaincy of Ian Chappell were on the rise. England's chances were further handicapped by the withdrawal of their leading batsman, Geoffrey Boycott, who had never been reconciled to Denness being appointed captain, while Australia were about to unleash, for the first time, one of the most lethal fast bowling attacks in cricket history with Dennis Lillee joined by the even more explosive Jeff Thomson.

It was carnage from the very beginning, and after three Tests, a battered and bruised England were 2–0 down, and to the delight of the home crowd were facing humiliation in chants of, 'Ashes to ashes, dust to dust. If Lillee doesn't get you, then Thomson must.' Desperate measures were called for, but no one expected what would happen next.

England went into the Fourth Test at Sydney knowing that they had to avoid defeat to have any hope of retaining the Ashes, and for Mike Denness, who had only scored 65 runs in six innings so far, there was only one thing to do. He made the unprecedented sacrifice of dropping himself from his own team. It was an honourable decision from an honourable man for the benefit of the greater good of his side, but while some hailed Denness as being brave and courageous, many were of the opinion that a captain should never abandon his ship, and especially so when said ship was listing badly and in imminent danger of capsizing. Sadly, the gamble by the captain failed and Denness remained a helpless bystander as Australia secured a comfortable victory at Sydney, earning a 3–0 lead with two to play to regain the Ashes. And with so many English batsmen injured from having to face the onslaught of Lillee and Thomson, Denness had no option but to return to captain the side for the remaining two Tests.

At the final Test at Melbourne, with Australia 4–0 up and Lillee and Thomson both injured, Mike Denness finally gained some small satisfaction from the tour from hell when he led his team to an innings victory, with the highlight being a brave and stylish innings of 188 by the much-maligned captain himself. It may have been a final belated act of defiance in a meaningless dead runner at the end of a series that marked the rise of a brash new optimistic nation at the expense of their former imperial masters, but at least for a brief few days the Scot gained some respite from the unremitting hostility and derision that came with captaining a team of second-rate Poms.

Mike Denness continued as England captain until July 1975, but another crushing defeat at the hands of Lillee and Thomson at Birmingham in the First Test finally saw Denness fall on his sword and resign, with this time no possibility of another return.

The overall legacy of Mike Denness can be seen in two ways. He was the only Scot to date to have captained a Test nation and would lead England on nineteen occasions, with an overall record of a respectable enough six wins and only five defeats. However, it was for the five defeats and the fateful decision to drop himself in the middle of a Test series that he would ultimately be remembered, a historical reputation that the man himself dealt with in the same gracious manner that marked his entire cricketing career.

Curiously, for all the opprobrium that had come the way of Mike Denness for being a Scot who had the temerity to be captain of England, he was replaced as captain by another non-Englishman, the South African-born Tony Greig. And in 2010, with the victorious English Ashes-winning team having four non-English-born players on their side (Strauss, Trott, Pieterson and Prior) and with the twenty-first century having already seen two Scots (Blair and Brown) residing at No. 10 Downing Street, it could be said that Denness was actually well ahead of his time. And Denness would no doubt understand better than most what it is like being a Scot in charge south of the border when everything is collapsing all around you.

For Mike Denness and the other Scots who were good enough to play international cricket, England was the only realistic outlet for their ambitions. Since 1994 and Scotland's belated admission to become a separate cricketing nation, there is now the opportunity for young Scottish cricketers to gain experience of representing their home country in international cricket, and on two occasions, in 1999 and 2007, Scotland have qualified for the Cricket World Cup.

Unfortunately for the Scots, both of those appearances amongst the leading cricketing nations of the world would result in a clean sweep of comprehensive defeats, and with recent results seeing Ireland overtake Scotland as the leading Associate nation and next in line for promotion to the cricketing elite (despite the fact that the cricketing elite seem completely disinclined for any newcomers to join their lucrative party), the prospects of Scotland playing Test cricket seem as remote as at any time in the last 130 years.

However, for all Scotland's disappointments so far at the showcase of international cricket, it can never be denied that it was Mike Denness who was the captain of the host nation at the inaugural Cricket World Cup in 1975 and led his side in the very first World Cup match to be played, against India at Lord's on 7th June, with England winning by an overwhelming 202 runs. Furthermore, in a tournament that would encapsulate Mike Denness's tenure as captain, England would comfortably win all their group games to qualify for the semi-final at Headingley in Leeds unbeaten, where they would once more be crushed by Australia, and almost as predictably, Denness would top score with a defiant if ultimately futile 27. Which only goes to show that brave Scottish resistence in a losing cause is not restricted to actually playing for Scotland.

# 6

## *The Olympians*

Olympic sprinter Allan Wells

Even before the financial and media juggernaut of the 2012 London Games, Scotland has always had an uneasy relationship with the modern Olympics movement. Being no more than perennial non-participants 2,000 years ago in the original games in Olympia in Greece due to a chronic lack of disci, Scotland and Scots have played no more than a peripheral role in the history of the Olympics since its reinvention in Athens in 1896.

It can be argued that Scotland's relative lack of success and engagement in Olympic history (which stands in contrast to Scotland's integral role in so many other international sports) is that for a country that from the very early years of sport becoming organised and codified in the nineteenth century and its subsequent history of producing generations of individuals prepared and able to successfully lead, captain, coach and manage teams and organisations – no matter how disparate – the Olympic reality of being submerged in the ideal and cause of what would become Team GB has never truly been embraced by sporting Scots.

However, political and national sensibilities aside, there is perhaps another more obvious reason for Scottish indifference to the Olympic dream, and that can be found in the purely amateur ethos of participants that existed as the fundamental cornerstone of the Games for a century, from 1896 to the eventual acceptance of professional athletes in 1992. For Scotland, sport had been from the beginning a serious business, and as far from the principal founder of the modern Olympics, Baron Pierre de Coubertin's template of 'not winning that was important, but the taking part' as it was possible to be. Winning has always been very important to Scots, as demonstrated from an early age by your less obviously athletic children always chosen last and always put in goals. For what is the point of competition without proving victorious and what conceivable enjoyment could one possibly ever find in defeat? And let's not even get started on all of your post-ironic, self-deprecating celebration of glorious failure.

Yet, arguably even more important than winning has been sporting Scots' absolute determination that sport is, above all, their livelihood and that win, lose or draw, as with any other occupation or vocation, they should be honestly reimbursed and rewarded for their labours. Scots have been at the forefront of professionalism in sport since the nineteenth century, and this drive and necessity to make a living from their sporting talent would see them travel to England, America and beyond, in exactly the same manner as the millions of non-sporting Scots who left Scotland to find fame and fortune around the globe.

It is therefore not all that surprising that in the history of sporting Scots the noble amateur who merely wished to take part lies a distant second to the hard-nosed professional with myriad financial motives for desiring victory rather than mere competitive spirit. Yet amongst all the prize-money, contracts and sponsorship deals of professional sport, there have still been Scots who, through choice or lack of opportunity, have excelled in international and Olympic competition with no award on offer other than pride and glory.

It may not be particularly Scottish to compete without the incentive of financial gain, and in truth, there may indeed be a curious displacement in the sight of Scottish athletes decked out in the colours of the Union Jack; however, in one crucial regard these illustrious amateur Scots may in fact hold the true sporting spirit of Scotland, as for them winning was not the most important point, but it was the only point. As for sporting Scots, what could possibly be worse than a scenario of both coming second and also not getting paid!

## Rocket to Russia

Any trip to the capital of Russia would not be complete without a visit to the TSUM (or Central Universal Store), the prestigious, historic and fashionable six-storey department store in the very heart of central Moscow, which was founded in 1857 by two entrepreneurial Scottish traders, Andrew Muir and Archibald Mirrielees. They named their store after themselves, Muir and Mirrielees, and the name survived through to the 1917 Revolution, when the comrades preferred something a little more proletarian and a little less Scottish, much to the disgruntlement of many well-to-do Muscovites who had to wait for seventy years and the fall of communism for the Royal Stewart travel rug they had ordered to arrive.

This just goes to show that Scottish connections with Moscow began long before Glasgow-born winger Aiden McGeady left Celtic for Spartak Moscow in 2010 – although demonstrating how much times had changed in the former Soviet Union, McGeady was a left-winger who could also play on the right. However, as far as Scottish sporting history is concerned, Moscow is remembered as the location of the greatest achievement by a Scottish-born track and field athlete in Olympics history – and even though said achievement was just over thirty years ago, it is surprisingly forgotten today.

When one thinks of the epithet 'the Flying Scotsman' in association with athletics, for most people, Scots and non-Scots alike, the name that immediately springs to mind is Eric Liddell, in all his slow motion, no running on the Sabbath, *Chariots of Fire* glory along the sands of St Andrews. Liddell was born in China, the son of Scottish missionaries, and would commit his life to the land of his birth by himself returning to China in 1925 to work as a missionary and teacher. He remained there until he was captured and interned by the invading Japanese in 1943. Sadly, he died at the age of only forty-three, in camp in 1945, five months before the end of the war and liberation.

Although Liddell only lived in Scotland for the period when he studied at Edinburgh University, it was there he showed his prodigious sporting ability. He set a British 100 metres record that would stand for over thirty years, won seven Scottish caps at rugby union and in 1924 won an Olympic gold medal in the 400 metres (as well as a mostly neglected bronze medal in the 200 metres). Going into the Paris Olympics, it had been Liddell's preferred distance of the 100 metres that appeared to give him the best opportunity of success, but with a heat for the 100 metres being held on a Sunday and with Liddell's strongly-held religious beliefs preventing him from running on the Sabbath, it was a late switch to the longer distance of the 400 metres (rather than the 100 metres) that would bring unexpected glory and the legend that would live on over the decades. And it would be in fact another seventy-six years before a Scot would win the 100 metres and be crowned the fastest man in the world.

The Moscow Summer Olympics of 1980 was the first and so far only one to be held in a communist country; however, due to the Soviet Union's invasion of Afghanistan the previous year, the USA, West Germany and other countries boycotted the Games in protest. The pragmatic British, who knew from their own imperial past that invading Afghanistan was an occupational hazard for foreign powers that invariably ended in bloody disaster (a history lesson that sadly they would later seem to forget) unlike their American and German allies eventually agreed to send a team to Moscow, with the mitigating factor that they had a team of world-class athletes nothing more than a happy coincidence.

One of their medal prospects was a sprinter from Edinburgh by the name of Allan Wells. Wells' athletics career was a true fairytale story. He had been nothing more than an average long-jumper until turning to sprints as his main event at the belated age of twenty-four. Between 1978 and 1982 he won four Commonwealth gold medals, three European Cups at 100 metres and 200 metres, and in 1981 won the World Cup at 100 metres in Rome, where amongst others he defeated a certain up-and-coming sprinter by the name of Carl Lewis.

Wells never broke world records and never topped the fastest man of the year rankings, but when it came to the pressure of major events he was the supreme competitor. For the 1980 Olympics Wells travelled to Moscow as one of the favourites, his prospects enhanced by the fact that the top American sprinters were not there, but with the disadvantage that he would be forced to use, for the first time, starting blocks, which he had previously eschewed. Wells managed to qualify for the 100 metres final, but was given the unfavourable draw of lane eight. However, nothing could distract Wells on 25th July 1980, and with his formidable wife (and coach) Margot exhorting, 'Come on, Allan!' from the sidelines so loudly that the entire stadium probably heard her, her husband powered through to cross the line in a photo finish – along with the Cuban sprinter Silvio Leonard all the way over in lane one. Timings could not split the two runners, but Wells' dip for the line had proven decisive and he had already set off on his lap of honour before official confirmation came through that he had become Olympic champion.

Wells followed up his success in the 100 metres with a silver in the 200 metres where he only lost by 0.02 to the Italian Pietro Mennea, but arguably his greatest achievement came two weeks later. Wells had nothing to prove after the Olympics and was suffering from injury, but he knew that as the top American sprinters all with times better than him that year had not been in Moscow, there would be many who saw their absence as devaluing his victory, and he was not the sort of man to duck a challenge. In August 1980 at Koblenz in Germany Allan Wells took on all the best sprinters from America and the rest of the world, and once more defeated the lot of them to prove that, while he may not be the fastest man in the world, he was indisputably the best competitive sprinter on the planet. Not bad for an obscure long-jumper from Liberton.

As far as Team GB were concerned, the Moscow Olympics was also the venue of the legendary duels between the two great British middle-distance runners Steve Ovett and Sebastian Coe. And the achievements of Allan Wells are often overlooked in comparison to the Coe–Ovett rivalry. However, Wells remains the only Scottish-born athlete to win an individual gold medal in the history of the modern Olympics, and his heroics in Moscow against the backdrop of political intrigue, the struggle against adversity, courage against the odds and the love story of a husband

and wife, would be an ideal subject for a cinematic Russian epic, with the 100 metres final and 'Margot's Theme' as the stirring and somewhat raucous finale.

## C'mon Harold!

For a man who was to have had such an undistinguished and short-lived tenure as British Prime Minister from 1902 to 1905 before being summarily dismissed by the electorate, Scottish politician Arthur Balfour from East Lothian was to have a disproportionate influence on the histories of both Britain and the world – not dissimilar to another Scottish prime minister of Britain over 100 years later who also only served as PM for three years.

Balfour may not have claimed to have saved the world's banking system, but he certainly had a long and remarkable political career. He served as a Cabinet Minister between 1886 and 1929, was the Foreign Secretary who represented Britain at the Treaty of Versailles in 1919, and in 1926 was the minister who paved the way for the Commonwealth of Nations by stating that all nations in the Commonwealth were of equal status. Most famously of all, he wrote the Balfour Declaration of 1917 that stated the British government's support for a Jewish homeland in Palestine – one of the most important and divisive documents of the twentieth century with repercussions and ramifications that can still be felt throughout the Middle East today.

For such a controversial and contentious figure Balfour was, in fact, a curiously dispassionate man. He was a Conservative politically and a conservative by nature, who once memorably said that 'nothing matters very much and few things matter at all'. However, if there was one thing that did matter to Balfour it was sport, and throughout his life he was both an enthusiastic participant in and supporter of the games that he followed.

As an East Lothian local, Balfour learned the game of golf in North Berwick and would later become the captain of the Royal and Ancient at St Andrews. Balfour liked to play two rounds of golf a day, and with his political career based in London, it was therefore a prerequisite that he could find golf courses in England to indulge his obsession.

Golf had been played in England ever since the court of James VI, which had decamped to London on the Scottish king's accession to the English throne in 1603, and had begun playing on nearby Blackheath. For the next two centuries, no other English course had been built south of the border until Westward Ho! in Devon was founded in 1864 – a course designed by the legendary Old Tom Morris – and by 1880 there were still no more than twelve golf courses in all of England. And Arthur Balfour had presumably played on them all.

Balfour was a passionate cheerleader for the Scottish game, writing books and articles on the game's many virtues, and can be said to be the person who would have the greatest influence on the expansion of golf throughout Britain and Ireland. As his political career progressed, golf would be taken up by tens of thousands of the predominantly middle classes, in contrast to Scotland, where class distinctions in golf were far less pronounced. By 1914 there were over 1,000 golf courses to be found in England, with the wee dram on the nineteenth hole replaced by the obligatory gin and tonic.

However, golf was not the only sport that Balfour would have an historic impact on. In 1873 a Welsh major, Walter Wingfield, invented a game on his estate in Wales that was to be played outdoors with racquets and was based on the indoor game of real tennis that had originated in France as far back as the sixteenth century (at least). It had become popular through the royal courts of Europe and had flourished up until the French Revolution when the 'sport of kings', along with kings in general, went into long-term decline.

News of Wingfield's game soon spread to the gardens and estates of the upper echelons of society, promoted as a novel and socially acceptable pastime for both men and women looking for a little light exercise outdoors whilst crucially remaining fully clothed at all times. Wingfield called his game *sphairistike* meaning 'ball game' in Greek, but it was the keen sportsman, Old Etonian and newly-elected MP for Hertford, Arthur Balfour, who suggested the name 'lawn tennis'. Balfour's reasoning was simple: the game was based on real tennis but played on a lawn, so why not 'lawn tennis' as a name, an idea so simple and so obvious that Wingfield immediately adopted it when he issued the first rules of the new sport in 1874. Balfour would remain an enthusiastic player of the game that he had helped name for the rest of his life. And along with his two rounds of golf a day it does make you wonder how he ever had time to pursue a political career, never mind run the country, but nevertheless gives credence to the comment made by his Cabinet colleague, Winston Churchill, that 'if you want nothing done, then Balfour is your man'.

In all the 135 years plus since Arthur Balfour first missed a constituency surgery to practise his backhand, the best Scottish tennis player of all time has unquestionably been Andy Murray from Dunblane. At the time of writing, Murray has won eight ATP Masters titles; has had a career ranking of No. 2 in the world and has reached (but lost) three Grand Slam Finals at the US Open at Flushing Meadows in 2008 and at the Australian Open in Melbourne in 2010 and 2011. Already one of the most recognisable figures in world sport, all that is missing currently from Murray's CV is that elusive Grand Slam title, but even if such a scenario is not meant to be, it can safely be said that Andy Murray has already proven himself to be one of Scotland's greatest sportsmen.

Murray's achievements could be said to be even more remarkable when you consider that, along with cricket, tennis is a sport that in Scotland has historically been derided and which nobody wants to play, except during the two weeks that Wimbledon is on, and then people quickly lose interest when they discover that there are no ball boys to retrieve their over-hit forehands.

For many in Scotland, tennis is too English and too middle-class and requires a more temperate climate, which does somewhat overlook the international tennis successes of those tropical paradises of Sweden, Russia and the Czech Republic. Perhaps, as with the sport of cricket, Scottish antipathy to tennis has had more to do with the fact that until the Murray family came along, Scotland has never been very good at it.

And of all the racquet sports in the world, it was the arguably slightly more socially acceptable game of squash, which was played indoors and involved the inherent principle of hitting a ball against a brick wall, that seemed to better suit the Scottish sporting psyche. Scotland's greatest exponent of squash was Peter Nicol from Inverurie in Aberdeenshire who won the British Open (one of the two major tournaments in the squash calendar) twice in 1998 and 2002, was three-times winner of squash's World Series between 1999 and 2001 and after twice being defeated in the final of squash's premier tournament (the World Open) in 1997 and 1998 finally became Scotland's first World Champion in Egypt in 1999.

However Peter Nicol's victory in 1999 was not, in fact, the first occasion that a Scot had won a major title at a racquet sport. And even more surprising, it was amongst the strawberries and cream of southwest London, over a hundred years before Andy Murray either wins an elusive Grand Slam or continues to be gallantly defeated in a five-set semi-final, that Scotland celebrated their first Grand Slam men's singles tennis champion.

To be fair, Scotland's claim to 1896 Wimbledon champion Harold Mahony is circumstantial at best. Mahony's father was one of the wealthiest landowners in Ireland in an era when Ireland was still politically, and as far as the establishment were concerned, socially wedded to Union with Britain. Harold spent most of his childhood in Kerry, and as an adult split his time between England, America, Europe and Ireland. However, the Mahonys also had some property in Scotland and for reasons that are not altogether obvious, it was in Edinburgh in 1867 that Harold Mahony came into this world, with no one suspecting that a future Wimbledon tennis champion had been born – for in 1867 neither the Wimbledon Championships nor for that matter tennis had been invented.

Mahony was a tall and powerful man and played championship tennis in the 1890s and 1900s. He had learned the game on the tennis court especially built on the family estate at Dromore Castle in County Kerry. Through practice, he developed a serve and volley playing style that made the most of his natural strength and build. Mahony won a silver medal in the men's singles at the 1900 Paris Olympics and played competitive tennis for the best part of fifteen years. His greatest moment, however, came in the 1896 Wimbledon men's singles championship when at the age of twenty-nine he reached the Final against the three-times champion Wilfred Baddeley of England. After three sets Mahony was 2–1 down and facing defeat, but in a tense fourth set Mahony edged out Baddely 8–6 and closed out the fifth and final set of an epic and hard-fought match 6–3 to win his one and only Wimbledon title. This match would set the record for the longest Wimbledon final until 1954.

By all accounts, Mahony did not have the all-round game of

his contemporaries and his inheritance of the Mahony estate and numerous business interests meant that he could not give his full commitment to tennis. But his determination, combined with his powerful serve and backhand, always made him a dangerous opponent. Mahony was a colourful character with a reputation as a man-about-town, or considering his regular trips to America and Europe, a man-about-many-towns, and his eventful and sometimes mysterious life was mirrored by an eventful and extremely mysterious death in 1905, when in circumstances that have never been fully explained, his body was discovered next to his bicycle at a foot of a hill, after he had gone out for a ride in the country. He was only thirty-eight years old.

A confident and handsome individual on the court as well as off, Harold Mahony, the first and at the time of writing only man born in Scotland to become champion of Wimbledon, would regularly talk and joke with spectators during matches, making him one of the most popular and sporting players of his day, regardless of whether he won or not. Although if you just happen to be one of the wealthiest men in Ireland and have a castle as your home, then it perhaps does not matter so much if your forehand is a little wayward.

## Bronze Medals are Forever

It was in 2005 under the premiership of the Edinburgh-born British Prime Minister Tony Blair that it was announced that the Summer Olympics would be returning to the United Kingdom for the third time. Granted it was as much, if not more, an acknowledgement of the pulling power of the world's most cosmopolitan city, London, rather than for the UK as a whole, but the awarding of the 2012 Olympics in 2005 to Team GB could well be seen as a curious footnote to the career of a politician who history may well portray as the last truly British prime minister.

Under the New Labour government of 1997–2007 the United Kingdom experienced the greatest constitutional changes since the Irish Free State's departure from the Union in 1922 with the creation and restoration of parliaments and assemblies in Scotland, Wales and Northern Ireland. Although few at the time understood what the long-term ramifications of devolution would be, by the time of the premiership of Tony Blair's successor and rival, Gordon Brown, in 2007, it had become painfully evident how much had changed in the decade since 1997. As while Blair had the political acumen to know that in the UK the question of patriotism – like religion – should be understated at best and avoided where possible, Brown's ill-judged attempt to promote 'Britishness', no matter how sincere, came across as a politician from Scotland attempting to downplay his Scottishness, which ironically had, as far as Middle England was concerned, exactly the opposite effect.

Sport has, of course, not been immune to the continuing constitutional revolution that has taken place in the twentieth-century, and in many regards sport can be said to be the precursor of the devolution/federalisation/break-up of the United Kingdom. England, Scotland, Wales and Ireland have been playing international association and rugby union football as separate entities since the nineteenth century. And from the 1990s onwards the Cross of St George began to replace the Union Jack as the flag of English choice in both football and rugby, and staying with rugby, the British Lions became the more politically correct and geographically accurate British & Irish Lions, as year by year and step by step the 'Britishness' of UK sport and the UK as a single political and social entity was slowly but surely eroded away.

The task of uniting what remains of the United Kingdom is

therefore left to royal weddings, *The X Factor* and in sport, the Summer Olympics, where every four years, the British public are expected to get behind Team GB for three long, arduous weeks (before collective amnesia sets in almost the second that the last final is won, the last national anthem is played and the last drug test is failed). But even in Team GB, cognisance must always be made to the new realpolitik of the UK constitution and sensibilities so thin-skinned that under no circumstances whatsoever should commentators describe Scottish athletes as anything other than Scottish, Welsh athletes as anything other than Welsh and English athletes as anything other than British, with the question of the nationality of Northern Irish athletes avoided at all costs.

The twenty-first century (and for the sake of argument we will include the 2000 Sydney Olympics, even though it is technically the century before) has brought considerable success to these Scottish athletes who represent Great Britain but are never referred to as British.

Pride of place goes to cyclist Chris Hoy from Edinburgh with his four gold medals and one silver medal at three consecutive Olympics, but following close behind is Shirley Robertson from Dundee who won gold in sailing at both Sydney in 2000 and Athens in 2004, Stephanie Cook from Irvine who won the women's modern pentathlon in 2000 and also at Sydney, Andrew Lindsay from Portree on the Isle of Skye who was one-eighth of the victorious GB men's coxed eights in rowing.

Staying with rowing, the only Scottish woman to have won Olympic medals at three successive games is the Glasgow-born Katherine Grainger. Grainger won silver in the quadruple sculls in 2000 and 2008 and silver again in 2004 at Athens, but this time in the coxless pairs, and when combined with Grainger's six world championship victories between 2003 and 2011, this makes her the most successful Scottish female rower of all time.

Yet for all the recent success of Hoy, Grainger and other Scottish athletes, Scotland's most successful Olympics, to date, remains the 1912 Games that was held in the Swedish capital of Stockholm. Great Britain came third in the medal table of 1912, behind only the USA and the host nation, and out of Britain's ten gold medals, Scots contributed to six of them. Isabella Moore from Glasgow was one-quarter of the 4 x 100 metres freestyle swimming team; Robert Murray from Edinburgh was part of the British small-bore rifle 50 metres team; Henry Macintosh from Kelso, who would die six years later in 1918 at the Somme aged only twenty-six, was a member of the 4 x 100 metres athletics quartet; and George Cornet from Inverness won gold for the second time in Britain's water polo team after previous success at London in 1908.

Another Scot who in Stockholm would win gold for the second time was Aberdeen-born rower Angus Gillan. Angus Gillan had been part of the victorious coxless fours at London in 1908, but in Sweden he had moved to men's eights where he was joined in the boat by another Scot, Philip Fleming. Fleming was born in Newport-on-Tay and came from the Dundee-based Fleming merchant bank that had been founded by his father, Robert Fleming, who had made their international reputation and fortune through investing in American railroads in the reconstruction after the American Civil War. Philip Fleming was also the uncle of one Ian Fleming, the creator of James Bond, and in 1912, Philip Fleming rowed at stroke in the winning British team – although sadly this role as the most important rower on a boat meant that he had the rowing position of 008 rather than 007.

If Moore, Murray, Macintosh, Cornet, Gillan and Fleming had all won their gold medals as part of a team, then the final member of the seven Scottish gold medallists of Stockholm was very much his own man. William Kinnear from Laurencekirk in

Aberdeenshire had only taken up rowing in his twenties when he moved to a new job in London, and he was nearly thirty before he won his first major single sculling titles, the Diamond Challenge Sculls at the Henley Regatta and the Wingfield Sculls on the River Thames in 1910. Kinnear retained both titles in 1911, but his greatest achievement was to be the Stockholm Olympics.

William Kinnear would prove completely dominant in Sweden – winning all his heats by large margins before comfortably winning his final by more than eight seconds. And with Olympics gold to add to his other titles, Kinnear had conclusively proven that he was the greatest individual rower in the world, a remarkable performance made even more impressive when you consider that Laurencekirk is ten miles away from the sea.

Of course, it is perfectly true that, with the exception of Kinnear, all the Scottish successes of 1912 would not have been possible if they had not been representing Great Britain (and Kinnear himself did all his training in England), as the Scots involved were only but one member of teams that represented all parts of the United Kingdom – a reality that has continued to this day in the numerous Olympic team events. And for many it seems unthinkable that this sporting union that has been the cornerstone of British involvement in the modern Olympics since 1896 and brought so much collective success could ever come to an end. And furthermore, what is the problem with the concept of a UK football team, even if it does consist of ten Englishmen and Ryan Giggs?

Even the fact that, as far as the history of major international sports in the British Isles is concerned, Team GB has been more the exception than the rule does nothing to alter the fear and trepidation that the prospect of separate English, Scottish, Welsh and Northern Irish Olympics teams can often engender in sporting traditionalists. However, even here in this last bastion of sporting Britishness there is historical precedent for national independence. In the very same 1912 Stockholm Olympics where seven Scots won gold, a Scottish cycling team was entered alongside both an English and Irish team in the men's team time-trial, and just missed out on winning a medal by finishing fourth. But going one place better was the Scottish team that competed in the men's hockey tournament at the 1908 Olympics in London and won a bronze. Granted, only six nations entered teams at the 1908 Olympics hockey (and four of them were England, Ireland, Scotland and Wales) and Scotland only won one match in the tournament, but a medal is still a medal. And even though it was over a century ago, it is still one medal more than eighty current Olympic nations who inexplicably, considering their complete lack of sporting success, still find sovereign and political independence socially acceptable.

## Home and Away

It was at Melbourne in 1956, at the first Summer Olympics to be held in the southern hemisphere, that the home nation truly came of age as a major force in international swimming. Australia had always been good at swimming (well, they did have the weather and the golden beaches for it, after all) but in 1956 out of thirteen swimming events Australia would take gold in eight. And so a sporting legacy had begun.

Of all the Australian heroes, the most decorated was a seventeen-year-old by the name of Murray Rose from Sydney. However, it was not in the divine capital of New South Wales, but in the admittedly rather colder seaside town of Nairn in the Scottish Highlands that Murray Rose was born and although he was only one year old when the Rose family immigrated across the world to Australia, this still makes him, along with cyclist Chris Hoy on four gold medals, the equal most successful Scots-born Olympian of all time.

In 1956 Rose won gold in the 400 metres freestyle, the 1,500 metres freestyle (where he became the first man ever to break the eighteen minutes barrier) and the 4 x 200 metres relay to become the 'Golden Boy' of the Melbourne Olympics – which was a slightly more respectful nickname than the alternative of 'the Seaweed Streak' that had been given to Rose on account of his strictly adhered-to vegetarianism.

After his golden haul at Melbourne, Rose moved to the USA to continue his studies but continued to compete at the highest level. At the 1960 Olympics at Rome he won silver in the 1,500 metres, a bronze in the relay and a gold in the 400 metres (where he retained his 1956 Olympic title). Even then Rose was not finished, going on to break the 400 metres world record in 1962 and the 1,500 metres world record in 1964, where his time of seventeen minutes and one second was an incredible fifty-eight seconds faster than the world record he had set eight years earlier. Sadly, Murray Rose was denied the opportunity to almost certainly add to his medal haul at the 1964 Olympics in Tokyo when the Australian selectors took umbrage at the US-domiciled Rose missing the Australian trials. Yet despite this final Olympic disappointment, Murray Rose, with his revolutionary technique that fully utilised the power in his shoulders, combined with a broken kick to give him extra power in his stroke, was the premier distance swimmer of his generation and the first of only two men ever to retain his 400 metres Olympic title.

Murray Rose remained in America for thirty years but eventually returned home to the beaches and surf of Sydney of his childhood where he remains an Aussie sporting legend. And when you consider the story of the most important development in twentieth-century swimming, the Scottish origins of Murray Rose are perhaps more appropriate than one might first think.

\* \* \*

It was in 1910 that the twenty-two-year-old Alexander MacRae, accompanied by his young wife, left his home in Wester Ross over the not-especially-conducive-for-swimming sea from Skye to make a new life in Australia.

Hundreds of thousands of Scots had already made the long journey to the other side of the world. One of the most notable of those was an Ayrshire miner by the name of Andrew Fisher, who, in the same year that the MacRaes arrived in Sydney, was winning the 1910 Australian General Election to become Australian Prime Minister for the second time, and with an overall majority oversaw one of the most radical and important administrations in Australia's history.

MacRae himself first found work in Sydney as a milkman, but in 1914 founded the MacRae Hosiery Company in Bondi that would later become the MacRae Knitting Mills. His company concentrated on the manufacture of undergarments that they marketed under the brand name of 'Fortitude', which also being the motto of the Clan MacRae did demonstrate a markedly Scottish perspective when it came to the appreciation of underwear.

In 1914 Australia under Prime Minister Fisher entered the First World War in support of the British Empire, and while the conflict would become immortalised by the futility and loss of life that Australian and New Zealand forces suffered in Gallipoli, for MacRae Knitting the conflict brought the lucrative commission to produce socks for the Australian army.

After the war had ended, MacRae now turned his attentions to swimwear and the increasing popularity of swimming as a socially acceptable pastime in the less conservative post-war era. And in 1927 his company came up with a revolutionary figure-hugging costume that gave the swimmer more freedom of movement and allowed them to swim faster, and as an added bonus it was aesthetically more pleasing on the eye (not that the censorious inspectors who patrolled Sydney's beaches for any lapses in decorum were liable to agree).

MacRae soon gained a huge publicity coup when leading Swedish swimmer Arne Borg broke the 1,500 metres world record wearing the new design. However, the major breakthrough came during the 1932 Olympics in Los Angeles when Australian swimmer Clare Dennis, dressed in MacRae's costume, won the 200 metres breaststroke gold medal and broke the world record. By this time MacRae's design for competitive swimming was known as the 'racerback', and in 1928 the company had come up with a name and a slogan: 'Speed on in your Speedos'. And so, one of the most iconic sporting brands of modern times was born.

The Speedo that Dennis wore in 1932 caused a sensation, with disconcerted officials almost disqualifying the young Australian on the basis of showing too much exposed shoulder. But by 1936 and the Berlin Olympics, the entire Australian men's team was wearing Speedos and causing a further diplomatic incident by not only exposing the back and shoulders, but the front torso as well. Needless to say, this did not go down at all well with the hosts, although granted back in 1936 it did not take all that much to offend the sensibilities of the Third Reich.

After the Second World War, the success of the 1956 Australian team and the expansion later that decade of the company into America and Europe saw Speedos become the undisputed global leader in swimwear, so much so that by the 1970s there was a near universal wearing of the Speedo brand at international competitions. And Australia has also retained its position as one of the leading nations in the history of swimming with fifty-six gold medals up to and including the 2008 Olympics in Beijing, placing them second after the USA on the all-time medal list.

As for Alexander MacRae, the Scot from the Scottish Highlands who had left as a young man to make a new life on the other side of the world, he lived to see the first global success of the innovation that would permanently transform international sport before his death in 1938, appropriately on 30th November, St Andrew's Day.

Alexander MacRae remained throughout a dapper entrepreneur who had ventured into swimwear, as he had done previously with underwear and hosiery, primarily as an opportunity to advance his family business, and it seems highly unlikely that he was a regular wearer on Bondi Beach of his most famous invention, or at any point was involved in the illicit trade of budgerigars. However, as a MacRae and a true Highlander he would undoubtedly have shown great 'fortitude' if he had.

## Swimming in Sarks

When one thinks about the phrase *bon accord* (French for 'good agreement') in a Scottish context the city that comes to mind is Aberdeen. *Bon Accord* has been the civic motto of the city for centuries, and the Bon Accord Shopping Centre in the city centre has been the location for many retail 'good agreements' in recent years on the rare occasions when Aberdonians have been persuaded to open their wallets. And when it comes to Scottish sport *Bon Accord* also has a dubious claim to fame, when on 1st September 1885 a team called Bon Accord from Aberdeen travelled south to play a Scottish Cup First Round match versus Arbroath.

It has been speculated in the years since the 1885 match that the Bon Accord side in question were in fact a cricket, rather than an association football, club and had been asked to compete in the Scottish Cup in error when the invitation should have gone to a more established football team in Aberdeen. Whatever the truth concerning their football credentials, Bon Accord would go on to lose the match by the small matter of 36–0, still the worst defeat in the history of recognised competitive football anywhere in the world. And to make matters worse, apparently several additional Arbroath 'goals' were ruled out for various infringements, or one assumes, because the referee lost count. Which means that if it takes around thirty seconds for the game to restart after each goal, then Arbroath were scoring at an average of one goal every two minutes, and presumably had a fairly impressive possession percentage. Although, if you consider the match in a different way, and if Bon Accord were, as has been alleged, a cricket team rather than a football team, then to only concede thirty-six was a quite decent performance after all.

However, the name of Bon Accord also has a less well-known but more successful legacy to impart on the history of international sport, in the form of the unrelated Bon Accord Swimming Club, also from 'The Granite City'. In 1877 (although there is debate about whether the date might have been earlier) Bon Accord Swimming Club would play the first recognised game of water polo anywhere in the world on the banks of the River Dee. The game was not yet called 'water polo' but was known as 'aquatic football', and had far more in common with rugby football than the association variety, as it was in truth not much more than an all-in wrestling match that took place in the water, with the ball and scoring goals an optional extra. However, what differentiated the game from previous similar pastimes and brawls in rivers that had taken place over the years was the introduction of goals in the form of two flags around ten feet apart on both banks of the river and a rudimentary set of rules provided by a London-born swimming enthusiast residing in Glasgow.

A great deal of the development of 'aquatic football' into what we know as 'water polo' would take place in Glasgow, where William Wilson was manager of Arlington Baths in Charing Cross, Glasgow, one of the oldest-surviving swimming clubs anywhere in the world that opened in 1871.

The first water polo international was held in 1890 in London, with Scotland defeating England 4–0, and when water polo was introduced to the Summer Olympics in Paris as the first Olympic team sport, it was Great Britain, the originators of the game, who would prove the dominant nation in the early years, with George Cornet from Inverness winning Olympic gold medals in the British team of 1908 and 1912.

In the twentieth century, water polo was enthusiastically taken up around Europe in climates perhaps more conducive than its birthplace next to the North Sea and is now a global sport with World and European Championships and an annual World Cup between the leading nations. Since 1920 Great Britain has not won an Olympic medal of any colour as Hungary, Italy, Russia and Serbia have dominated the medal tables and major championships as the leading nations in the world. In Scotland, the country where the sport was born, you will sadly see few examples of water polo today, but when you change your name from 'aquatic football' and re-brand yourself after, of all sports, 'polo', it is perhaps not so surprising that it does not have a mass appeal.

The Victorians, as we have seen, were increasingly obsessed with the importance of sport and exercise as a means of promoting physical and mental well-being, demonstrating the benefits of competition from an early age and instilling discipline and moral values by following the rules and regulations of the sport in question. And there were few places more receptive to this belief in the power of sport than in that most Victorian of cities and self-proclaimed Second City of the Empire – Glasgow.

In 1851 there were 330,000 residents living in the city's boundaries; sixty years later the population had topped one million. Shipbuilding, steel, locomotives and commerce had brought great wealth and prosperity to Glasgow, but with such rapid and dramatic growth and the associated massive influx of people there were also major social, economic and geographic problems that had to be overcome. The second half of the nineteenth century saw Glasgow's city fathers undertake major programmes of grand civic buildings, new residential areas, improvements in public sanitation, schools, hospitals and libraries and a public trams system that would connect the city (which controversially was built on time and under budget). And as part of their commitment to the betterment of their citizens and embracing the spirit of the age, there would be new public parks and gardens within the city boundaries and by 1914 the construction of twenty public swimming baths and washhouses (or steamies) for Glaswegians to learn to swim and wash their clothes, although preferably not at the same time.

And as part of this new, increasingly more emancipated era these public swimming baths and private clubs were not the exclusive reserve of the male half of the population, but girls were also encouraged to swim in the noble cause that, while women were not yet considered capable of voting, at least they would be less likely to drown.

In 1892, in what is considered the first national women's swimming championship anywhere in the world, Ellen Dobbie won the 200 yards breaststroke Scottish title at Townhead Baths in four minutes twenty-five seconds and became a sadly unheralded trailblazer in the history of women in sport – and still had time to get her washing done afterwards.

As the nineteenth turned into the twentieth century and the long-overdue struggle for the right to vote intensified, sport became a new battleground for female emancipation. The founder of the modern Olympics, Pierre de Coubertin, had stated that women competing at the Games would be 'impractical, uninteresting, un-aesthetic and incorrect', and the inaugural Olympics in Athens in 1896 were a male-only preserve. In 1900 at the second Games in

Paris, women were allowed to take part, but only in the sports of tennis and, in a decision that would have made sporting pioneer Mary, Queen of Scots proud, golf. However, progress for female athletes, as in society as a whole, remained painfully slow, and taking track and field athletics as an example, it would not be until 1928 that the Olympics would belatedly deign to have women's events. And it would be another thirty-six years and the 1964 Olympics in Tokyo before it was deemed possible for the fragile little things to be able to run any distance longer than 200 metres.

It was therefore a major breakthrough for women's sport back in 1912, when after concerted campaigning, the Olympics in Stockholm became the first to have women's swimming. There were to be two events – the 100 metres freestyle and the 4 x 100 metres freestyle relay. Twenty-seven women competed, although the prudish Americans declined to send any competitors as they still were of the opinion that women should remain fully clothed at all times. The British, by contrast, were much more liberal and sent a strong team that would wear one-piece swimming costumes (that ended well above the knee and left the arms bare). And one of the women making up this team was Scottish national champion Isabella Mary Moore from Glasgow, who was better known as 'Belle'.

Belle Moore had been taught to swim when she was at school and would regularly walk miles to her nearest swimming baths to continue her training. At Stockholm she was entered in the 100 metres and won her heat, the very first in Olympics history, but was narrowly eliminated in the semi-finals. Moore was a strong swimmer better suited to longer distances, but 100 metres was as far as women were allowed to go in 1912. However, she had one more opportunity in the 4 x 100 metres relay where she would lead off the team. In a time of five minutes fifty-two seconds that broke the world record and set, of course, a new Olympic record, Great Britain stormed to a comfortable win. At the age of seventeen years and 226 days, Belle Moore remains Britain's youngest woman ever to win a gold medal at a Summer Olympics, and Scotland's only female swimming Olympic gold medallist. Belle Moore and the rest of the relay team would receive their gold medals and laurel wreaths from no less a personage than King Gustav V of Sweden himself, a royal seal of approval for the introduction of women's swimming to the Olympics and for the pioneering and courageous women who had demonstrated such strength of character and strength in the water to make sporting history. It was a great tribute to Belle and the British team that the king should deem it appropriate to present the medals in person, although it cannot be denied that the daring British swimming costume that they were wearing and the fact that said costume had gone almost completely transparent in the water might also have been a factor in Gustav's keenness to meet the victorious young women.

Isabella 'Belle' Moore later married and immigrated to Maryland in the USA where she lived for the next fifty years of her life. She may have left the public baths and 'steamies' of her home city and the glory of Stockholm in 1912 far behind, but Belle continued to swim, and more importantly, taught generations of young boys and girls just as she had been taught herself when she was a child. As, after all, for a city that had been founded on the banks of a river and had grown and prospered through its proximity to the sea, it was the Glasgow way.

# 7
## *The Europeans*

Football legends Denis Law (left) and
Sir Matt Busby (right)

It could be argued that when it comes to all things European there has always been a subtle but distinct difference between Scotland and England. While England has spent the best part of a millennium either ignoring or alternatively trying to invade the continent of Europe, Scotland has historically always been slightly more interactive. From the Auld Alliance with France that lasted from 1295 to 1560, through its relationship with the medieval Hanseatic League (which was not, as one might expect, a precursor to football's Europa League, but a Northern European trading alliance) and on to the establishment of substantial Scottish communities in Poland and Sweden in the seventeenth and eighteenth centuries, there has been a long-standing and enduring political, economic and cultural engagement with the continent of Europe that is above and beyond a preference for Stella Artois as your lager of choice.

The centuries that followed the Act of Union in 1707 did however see a temporary tactical retreat from Scotland's European love affair and a near terminal decline in Scots' ability to learn any foreign languages, as Scotland turned to the riches on offer from entry to the burgeoning British Empire. However, with the end of the Second World War and the slow decline of one form of British colonial imperialism, Scots once more began to look one time zone ahead.

Unlikely as it may now seem today, it was a British Conservative politician, one David Maxwell Fyffe from Edinburgh, who would play the leading role in the 1950 European Convention of Human Rights that was agreed by the newly-formed Council of Europe and demonstrated an early example of the democratic nations of Europe coming together to promote closer cooperation for the greater good of a continent slowly recovering from the ravages and horrors of war. This movement for greater political, economic and cultural integration to prevent such a conflict ever happening again would lead to the formation of the European Community in 1952 and the European Economic Community or Common Market in 1958, and the introduction in sport of European-wide championships for both national and individual clubs. While the English remained at first inherently cautious and at times openly hostile to these new developments, the Scots, after decades of isolationism, re-found their long-lost *esprit de corps* and enthusiastically embraced the brave new world of mid-week fixtures under floodlights, international airport terminals and cultural exploration and intermingling in the great capitals and cities of Europe – so as long as nobody actually expected you to speak the language and you always had enough loose change in case you had to pay off the local police.

For the last sixty years, Scottish sporting aspirations have undergone a geographical transformation. Where in the first half of the twentieth century Hampden and Murrayfield, Wembley and Twickenham were the sporting citadels to which players and supporters alike would dream, in the second half of the twentieth century (as sport is, as you all know, a game of two halves) it would increasingly be to Paris and Rome, Milan and Madrid and Barcelona and Lisbon that new legends would be created and true sporting greatness would be attained. And as always, wherever there is sporting glory to be obtained you will find sporting Scots either under their own flag, or as we have come to expect more often, under someone else's, ready and willing to grasp their disproportionate share and so continue the centuries-old history and tradition of Scots abroad and on the make. Why, Scotland in Europe? You could even turn it into a political ideology. Or as they say in the Camp Nou, the home of the current best football club on the planet and where Scotland's finest, Dundee United, twice defeated the pride of Catalunya in their own stadium in 1966 and 1987, 'Visca Escocia! Visca els Tangerine Terrors!'

## 1967 and All That

Of all the golden ages of Scottish football (and there have been several) it is the 1960s that can be said to shine the brightest. True, the world then was black and white rather than high-definition colour, and the national team had no World Cup Finals or European Championships to unite the country in heady optimism and gut-wrenching despair (which seems quite inexplicable now when you consider the talent that was at their disposal). However, as far as Scottish football was concerned, the 1960s saw the first, and so far only, occasion when a Scottish team won the premier club tournament in Europe; the first, and so far only, occasion that a Scottish footballer was voted European Footballer of the Year; and truly was the decade that began the tradition that Scotland makes from girders the best football managers in the world.

The arrival in 1955–56 of a Cup competition between the respective league champions to find the best club team in Europe had been a long time coming and did have some mostly forgotten Scottish heritage in the form of the Thomas Lipton Trophy that was named after the famous Glasgow tea magnate, and for older readers, the owner of a 300-strong chain of Lipton's supermarkets.

The Thomas Lipton Trophy was held twice in 1909 and 1911 in Turin, Italy. And for the first time ever club teams from Italy, Germany, Switzerland and England met in a knockout tournament. Local team Juventus were one of the favourites for the Trophy, but to the great embarrassment of them and the other leading sides from Europe it was a non-league English team, West Auckland, who won the Trophy on both occasions, results that no doubt contributed to English (and Scottish) notions of natural superiority towards football on the Continent and their reluctance to involve themselves in all things international for the next forty years.

And when the inaugural European Cup tournament was held in 1955–56, no English side agreed to participate, and for once it was the traditionally equally isolationist Scots who were the pioneers of Britain in Europe in the shape of the mighty Hibernian FC, who in an even earlier international competition than the Thomas Lipton Trophy had defeated England's finest, Preston North End in a challenge match in 1875.

The sun truly was shining on Leith in the decade after the Second World War, even if their pathological aversion to the Scottish Cup, which they had not won since 1902, had already lasted for over fifty years. Hibs won three League Championships between

1948 and 1952 and boasted in their 'Famous Five' of Gordon Smith, Lawrie Reilly, Bobby Johnstone, Eddie Turnbull and Willie Ormond, one of the most famous forward lines in Scottish football history. However, despite Hibernian's reputation as an acknowledged suntrap it was ironically the fact that Easter Road, Hibs' stadium, was one of the first clubs in Scotland to have floodlights, which saw Hibernian entered into the first European Cup in 1955–56, rather than the actual reigning Scottish League Champions, Aberdeen.

Hibernian performed admirably in the first European Cup, defeating the German champions Rot-Weiss Essen and Djurgardens of Sweden before losing in the semi-finals to Stade Reims of France. It would be another four years before the next Scottish side would reach the last four, when in 1960 Rangers would eventually be overwhelmed in the semi-finals by Eintracht Frankfurt 12–4 on aggregate. However, this would not be the last time that the Germans would appear in Glasgow that year.

On 8th May 1960, 135,000 Scottish football fans packed into Hampden Park in what would be the largest crowd ever to attend a European Cup Final, and coincidentally went some way to prove that the neutral Scottish football supporter (a species that had been previously thought long extinct) did actually still exist in the Deep South of Glasgow. And for those who were fortunate enough to be at Hampden Park in May 1960 they would witness the greatest-ever match in European club football history with the *primero galacticos* of Real Madrid, including the legendary Alfredo di Stefano and Ferenc Puskas, defeating (as Rangers had discovered to their cost in the semi-final) the not-at-all-bad-in-their-own-right Eintracht Frankfurt 7–3 to win their fifth European Cup in succession and set a benchmark for club football that has still never been surpassed.

In 1963 the third Scottish club to reach the European Cup semi-finals was Dundee FC from Dens Park. In Tayside in the

1960s the future may have been bright and the future tangerine, but in 1963 the present was most definitely dark blue. Dundee had won their one and only League Championship in 1962 under the management of Bob Shankly from Glenbuck in Ayrshire, the elder brother of a certain Bill, who at the time was frankly the more successful of the Shankly boys. Dundee's forward line consisted of Alan Gilzean from Coupar Angus who would go on to have an illustrious career in England with Tottenham Hotspur and the veteran Gordon Smith, who was the same Gordon Smith who had been one of Hibernian's 'Famous Five' and had reached the semi-finals in 1956. Smith was approaching thirty-nine when he played for Dundee in the European Cup of 1962–63 and is one of the greatest of Scotland's post-war footballers, having the unique honour of winning League Championships with Hibs, Hearts and finally Dundee to become the only player in Scottish football history to have won three League Championships with three different clubs, an extraordinary achievement that is often overlooked and made even more remarkable by the fact that none of the three clubs concerned were either Rangers or Celtic.

In the 1962–63 campaign, Dundee defeated the champions of Germany, Portugal and Belgium (Koln, Sporting Lisbon and Anderlecht) before finally succumbing 4–2 on aggregate to the mighty Milan, the eventual Cup winners. And between 1956 and 1966, such was the strength in depth in Scottish football at the time that five separate Scottish clubs had represented Scotland with distinction in the European Cup, demonstrating a level of competition in Scotland that seems almost unthinkable today. It would, however, be none of the previous five Scottish clubs who had participated in the European Cup (Hibs, Hearts, Rangers, Dundee or Kilmarnock) that would become Scotland's and Britain's first European champions, but the sixth Scottish side to play in the European Cup, who made their debut in 1966–67.

\* \* \*

When Jock Stein from Burnbank in South Lanarkshire was appointed manager of Celtic Football Club in 1965, he was joining a club that had been in truth in decline for at least two decades and had won only one League Championship since the end of the Second World War, despite all their historic dominance (along with Rangers) of Scottish football since the first Scottish League Championship of 1890.

Jock Stein had been the captain in 1954 when Celtic had won their last League title, but it was as a forward-thinking, innovative and inspirational manager of Dunfermline Athletic and Hibernian between 1960 and 1965 that he made his reputation. In 1966, during Stein's first full season in charge, Celtic won the League for the first time in twelve years, and their first-ever European Cup campaign saw victories over Zurich from Switzerland, Nantes from France, Vojvodina from the country formerly known as Yugoslavia and Dukla Prague from the country formerly known as Czechoslovakia, to reach the final on 25th May 1967 at the Estadio Nacional in Lisbon. Their opponents: Internazionale of Milan.

Inter were the overwhelming favourites, two-times winners of the European Cup and one of only four teams (Real Madrid, Benfica and Milan being the others) who had ever lifted the trophy. Around 7,000 Celtic supporters made the long trek from Glasgow to Portugal, more in hope than expectation, and after only seven minutes they fell 1–0 to an early Inter penalty.

The Inter team were renowned, even notoriously so, for a defensive style of play known as *catenaccio* (meaning 'door-bolt'), that meant as soon as Inter went ahead, this lead should be protected at all costs with a mass defence and men behind the ball. Having scored so early in the game, Inter now went into ultra-defensive mode and for the next eighty-three minutes in the heat of the Portuguese sun they were hit by wave after wave of incessant Celtic attacks.

In hindsight, Inter's early goal and their retreat into their defensive shell gave Jock Stein and Celtic the opportunity to release their attacking full-backs of Craig and Gemmell down the wings and allowed Bobby Murdoch and Bertie Auld to run the midfield, and much like the Pictish warriors versus the Roman centurions of nearly 2,000 years ago, they searched for a route through the Italian wall in front of them.

The Celtic team that day was: Ronnie Simpson, Jim Craig, Tommy Gemmell, Bobby Murdoch, Billy McNeill, John Clark, Jimmy Johnstone, Willie Wallace, Stevie Chalmers, Bertie Auld and Bobby Lennox, and famously all of the eleven had been born within thirty miles of Celtic Park in Glasgow. Of the eleven Celtic players that played, Billy McNeill from Bellshill was the imperious captain, leading Celtic to all of their nine League Championships in a row from 1966 to 1974 and holder of the record of the most appearances ever for Celtic; Ronnie Simpson from Glasgow was, at thirty-six, the experienced and unflappable goalkeeper who had won two FA Cup Winners' medals with Newcastle United more than a decade earlier; Bobby Murdoch from Bothwell in Lanarkshire was the midfield general and one of Scotland's most under-rated great footballers; Jimmy Johnstone from Viewpark in Lanarkshire was the jinking genius who terrorised defenders, and the archetypal wee Scottish wing wizard who was voted one of the top three European Footballers of the Year in 1967; Tommy Gemmell from Motherwell was the marauding attacking full-back with the thunderous shot who equalised in the sixty-second minute in Lisbon and would also score in the 1970 European Cup Final against Feyenoord and Stevie Chalmers from Glasgow was Celtic's centre-forward who deflected in Murdoch's eighty-fifth minute shot to score the winning goal.

Liverpool manager Bill Shankly had been watching the match in Lisbon, and for all his legendary success in England, like his older brother Bob at Dundee, he was never to manage a team in a European Cup Final. After the game Shankly greeted Stein in the Celtic dressing room with the words, 'John, you're immortal now,' in recognition of his team's achievement. The team were given the soubriquet of the Lisbon Lions, for reasons more to do with simple alliteration rather than any historic connection with big cats in Africa, and while it may be too early to say that immortality beckons, the 1967 Celtic team remains almost universally recognised as the most successful and most famous club side that Scotland has ever produced – with the notable exception of Leith. As supporters of Scotland's first entrants into the European Cup, Hibernian FC, point out, while Celtic became Champions of Europe in 1967, the Hibs team that beat Preston in 1875 were 'Champions of the World'.

## Win Some, Lose Some

It cannot be denied that Scotland's capital has a notable sporting history. The Gentlemen Golfers of Edinburgh published the first Rules of Golf in 1744; Raeburn Place was the venue of the first rugby international in the world in 1871; Murrayfield, built in 1925, is now the largest sporting stadium in Scotland, and Edinburgh has twice been the host city of the Commonwealth Games, in 1970 and 1986 – though the least said about the political and financial shambles of the latter event the better. However, it is truly curious that amidst this impressive sporting heritage, out of 114 Scottish League Championships that have taken place between 1891 to 2011, the two Edinburgh clubs of Heart of Midlothian and Hibernian have only won a grand total of eight between them, and not once since 1960. Statistically for a city that has a similar population to both Liverpool and Manchester it is an underwhelming return for 120 years in the top flight of Scottish football, and it is certainly true that of the millions of tourists who visit Edinburgh every year, the only ones who go to Tynecastle and Easter Road have undoubtedly got on the wrong bus.

Yet for the loyal Hibees and Jambos who have followed their teams through thin and thinner, hope, and the possibility of a first Hibs Scottish Cup victory since 1902, does spring eternal, and in the era immediately following the Second World War it was the Edinburgh teams, and not the Glasgow ones, that were briefly the top Greyfriars Bobby of Scottish football.

Between 1948 and 1960, Hibs with their 'Famous Five' forward line won three League titles in 1948, 1951 and 1952, and Hearts would win two League titles in 1958 and 1960. Furthermore, the Hearts side that won the League in 1958 would do so having lost only one out of thirty-four games and in an incredible season scored an extraordinary 132 goals against only twenty-nine conceded, unquestionably one of the greatest teams in Scottish football history. However, as has always been the history of Scottish football outside of Glasgow, domestic success would inevitably lead to Heartbreak as Tynecastle's two brightest stars would soon depart and the status quo where west was best and east was a cold, foreign land where they inexplicably put sauce on their chips inexorably returned.

Dave Mackay from Edinburgh was the captain of the 1958 Hearts team. A dynamic, all-action left-sided midfielder, Mackay was the most highly-prized player in Scotland when he joined Tottenham Hotspur in 1959. Mackay would soon be joined in the Spurs side by two other Scots, goalkeeper Bill Brown from Arbroath and attacking midfielder John White from Musselburgh. With this Scottish trio in place, Tottenham began the greatest era in their history, winning the FA Cup in 1962 and 1967, the European Cup Winners' Cup in 1963 (the first British side to lift an official

European trophy) and in 1961 became the first side since George Ramsay's Aston Villa in 1897 to win the League and FA Cup double.

John White was one of the goal scorers in their 5–1 demolition of Atlético Madrid in Rotterdam in the Cup Winners' Cup Final of 1963 and was known as 'The Ghost' on account of his unerring habit to find space anywhere on the pitch and to 'ghost' into the penalty box undetected and unmarked. White had already proven himself one of the greatest players to play for Tottenham and was at the peak of his career when, in a horrific freak accident, he died after being struck by lightning while playing golf in 1964. He was only twenty-seven years old.

Dave Mackay was the driving force of this great Tottenham team, combining consummate skill and reading of the game with a hard-as-nails will to win, and after twice fighting back from serious injuries that would have finished the career of lesser men, captained Spurs to another FA Cup victory in 1967. In 1968, Dave Mackay was thirty-four years old, but unlike most of his contemporaries who were considering retirement, he was persuaded by a young, ambitious manager by the name of Brian Clough to join Derby County in the Second Division. As sweeper and captain Mackay turned back the years and inspired Derby to first promotion and then established them as the new coming force in English football. And when Clough resigned from Derby in 1973, it was Mackay (who had finally retired from playing in 1971) who accepted the seemingly impossible task of becoming his replacement and defied the odds once again by leading Derby to their second League title in 1975 – with a certain Archie Gemmill from Paisley as his captain.

While Dave Mackay was becoming a legend first in North London and then the East Midlands, his former teammate Alex Young, who left Hearts after the 1960 League title victory, was gaining cult status on Merseyside. Young had joined Everton, a club that for seventy years had benefited from strong Scottish connections. Their first League title in 1891 had been based on a core of talented Scots, including captain Andrew Hannah. Jimmy Galt from Saltcoats in Ayrshire, who had already won three Scottish League titles with Rangers, was captain in 1915 when Everton won their second title, and continuing the unenviable record of being the only club to win championships immediately before a world war, Jock Thomson from Fife was Everton captain when they won the League in 1939. Furthermore, Alex Young's namesake, Alexander 'Sandy' Young from Falkirk, had scored over 100 goals for Everton in the 1900s, including the only goal in the club's first FA Cup victory in 1906. And with all that history to live up to, it is perhaps not so surprising that the young forward from Loanhead in Midlothian took time to settle in at Goodison.

In the 1962–63 season it all came together for both Alex Young and an Everton side that would become arguably the best-loved in the club's long and distinguished history. In that glorious season, Young would score twenty-two goals and create countless others as Everton won their first League title since 1939. And three years later in 1966 they won their first FA Cup since the 1933 side that featured 'Wembley Wizard' Jimmy Dunn.

The Everton team of the 1960s (that would also win the FA Cup in 1966) would be given the name of 'The School of Science' on account of their entertaining and innovative style of play, and featured many of the leading English internationals of the time, but it was the mercurial, fair-haired Scottish centre-forward Alex Young who was most adored by the Goodison faithful, and in recognition of his unique talent he was given the title of 'The Golden Vision' – a more cerebral nickname than you normally find in English and Scottish football, but then this was 'The School of Science' after all.

\*     \*     \*

When Alex Young moved to Goodison Park in 1960 the club's captain and five-foot-four midfield general was Glaswegian Bobby Collins who had joined Everton from Celtic in 1958. He was without question the most influential player at the club, and it was a major shock when he was transferred in 1962 – not that it did Everton any harm, as they won the League the following season. Collins was thirty-one when he left Everton, and it seemed that his time at the top was over, but as would be the case with Dave Mackay five years later when he moved to Derby County, Collins also agreed to join a Second Division side with an up-and-coming and highly ambitious manager. Collins became captain of Don Revie's Leeds United and led them into the First Division in 1964, where in their first season they made an immediate impact by finishing second in both the League and FA Cup, where they lost 2–1 in extra-time to Bill Shankly's Liverpool.

In 1966 a horrific broken leg would see Collins' career at Leeds brought to a premature end, and as at Everton he would miss the titles and the glory that came to the team-mates who had been inspired by his leadership. His replacement as captain was his midfield partner, another tenacious and talented Scot, who was only one inch taller than Collins, but like Collins and so many diminutive Scottish midfield generals before him never for one second did he let this genetic twist of fate get in the way of becoming the most commanding figure on the pitch.

There is a famous photograph taken in 1966 at a match between Tottenham Hotspur and Leeds United that shows the experienced Spurs captain Dave Mackay, who had just returned to playing after suffering a serious leg injury, remonstrating with and angrily grabbing the shirt of the younger and smaller opponent who had tackled him. The younger player in question was Stirling-born Billy Bremner, and while Mackay had been the hard-as-nails king of the midfield in Britain in the early 1960s, it was Bremner, who was once described as 'ten stone of barbed wire', who would go on to assume that role for the best part of a decade.

Bremner made his debut for Leeds in 1959 at the age of seventeen. He would captain Leeds to their first League title in 1969, their first FA Cup in 1972 and a second League title in 1974. In the late 1960s and early 1970s, Leeds United were clearly the strongest team in England, a talented, powerful and uncompromising win-at-all-costs side who were as loathed as they were loved for their style of play – not that Leeds cared what anybody else thought.

What Leeds did care about was their unenviable ability to lose trophies at the final hurdle – terrible bad luck as far as their fans were concerned, karma according to everybody else. Three times Leeds would lose the League on the final day of the season and three times they would lose in the FA Cup Final. And in the 1969–70 season in their first European Cup campaign as English champions they would lose out in the Semi-Finals to their Scottish counterparts, Celtic, in what was billed as 'the Battle of Britain'.

As far as the English press were concerned, Leeds were the overwhelming favourites to go through to the Final, but it was the 1967 European Cup winners, Celtic, who under Jock Stein's astute management tactically out-thought and out-played the English side to win both legs, home and away, and go through 3–1 on aggregate, with the second leg played at Hampden Park attracting a massive crowd of 136,000 (still the largest attendance for any European Cup or Champions' League match).

It was therefore Celtic who went through to the Final in Milan on 6th May, where they would meet Dutch champions Feyenoord. And unlike in 1967 in Lisbon, where Celtic had been unquestionably the how-you-say underdogs, in 1970 in Milan they were the overwhelming favourites – never a position that any Scottish side likes to find themselves in.

Seven of the Lisbon Lions were still present in the Celtic line-up: Tommy Gemmell, Bobby Murdoch, captain Billy McNeill, Jimmy Johnstone, Willie Wallace, Bertie Auld and Bobby Lennox and when full-back Tommy Gemmell repeated his heroics of 1967 with another trademark long-range effort to put Celtic 1–0 ahead, Scottish journalists began to ponder which other animal beginning with 'M' would sound best with Milan to commemorate a second victory. However, this was the beginning of the Golden Age of Dutch Total Football, and within two minutes Feyenoord had equalised and as the game wore on it was the side from Rotterdam that gained control over an under-performing and over-confident opposition.

At the end of ninety minutes the score was still 1–1, however with only four minutes remaining in extra-time Feyenoord's Swedish forward Ove Kindvall scored the winner, and Celtic had lost their opportunity to become the first Scottish, and British, club to win two European Cups. For Celtic there may have been the consolation of proving, with their victory over Leeds United, that they were indeed the Best of British, and under Jock Stein's management Celtic would continue to dominate Scottish football until 1974, but as far as Europe was concerned, Lions would remain the only animals that would be celebrated in the Jungle.

Five years later in 1975, Billy Bremner and Leeds United would themselves have one more chance to achieve what only Celtic and Manchester United had previously done before in Britain. The year 1975 would be the last hurrah for the team that Don Revie had been building since 1961, and in the 1974 English season they had finally seemed to slip their self-imposed shackles to win their second League title in imperious form. Revie had immediately afterwards left Leeds to take up the position of England manager, but the core of the side that had been together for years remained in place.

Ever since his key signing of Bobby Collins, Scots had played an integral role in the rise of Leeds United and by 1975 the long-serving Scottish trio of captain Bremner, fellow midfielder Peter Lorimer from Dundee, who was reputed to have the hardest shot in football, and winger Eddie Gray from Glasgow, who had all won League titles in both 1969 and 1974, had been joined by centre-forward Joe Jordan from Cleland in Lanarkshire, goalkeeper David Stewart from Glasgow, and Frank Gray, the younger brother of Eddie, at left-back.

In the League, Leeds United had struggled in the first post-Revie season of 1974–75, with his successor and former arch-rival Brian Clough only lasting a tumultuous forty-four days before being sacked. But in the European Cup Leeds United found their form and in the semi-finals defeated Barcelona 3–2 on aggregate, with both Bremner and Lorimer on the score sheet, to reach the European Cup Final for the first time in their history. In defeating Barcelona, Leeds United had overcome one of the two best players in the world, Johan Cruyff, and now all that stood between them and ultimate glory was the small matter of the team that was captained by the second of the two best players in the world, Franz Beckenbauer's Bayern Munich.

The European Cup Final between Bayern Munich and Leeds United was held at the Parc des Princes in Paris on 28th May 1975. There were five Scots in the Leeds United starting line-up that evening (captain Bremner, Lorimer, Jordan, Stewart and Frank Gray, with brother Eddie on the subs bench) and from the kick-off Bremner and Co. rolled back the years to take control of the midfield, with Bayern, the reigning champions, being pressed back inside their own half.

Two years earlier, Leeds had lost the 1973 European Cup Winners' Cup Final in Athens 1–0 to Milan, in a highly controversial game after which the referee was later suspended for his performance. Now in 1975 in Paris Leeds had already had a clear penalty claim waved away when, in the sixty-fifth minute, 'hotshot' Peter Lorimer unleashed one of his trademark thunderbolts to put the Yorkshire side ahead – only for an extremely belated decision by the officials to disallow the goal, after the Bayern team protested that Billy Bremner had been standing in an offside position when Lorimer had hit his shot (although clearly not interfering with play). And while all old football pros will tell you, 'If you were not interfering with play, what the **** were you doing on the pitch?', it was still a highly contentious and controversial decision.

For the second time in three years in a major European final it seemed to Leeds that they were not only playing against the eleven men in the opposing team, but the three officials as well. And with disturbances beginning to break out amongst their supporters in the Paris stadium, on the pitch Leeds fatally lost their concentration and within ten minutes conceded two breakaway goals to a Bayern side that had barely ventured into the opposing half in the entire game.

For Bremner and Leeds it was the end of this particular story. The great side was broken up, and Bremner left the club in 1976. Despite their two League titles and one FA Cup, the contentious and bitter defeat in Paris prevented them from joining the pantheon of British clubs who had won the ultimate club prize and prevented Bremner from becoming the second Scot (after Billy McNeill) to lift the European Cup.

The career of Billy Bremner would span the golden age of Scottish football, from when Jimmy Johnstone, Jim Baxter, Dave Mackay, Denis Law, Ian St John and Alex Young lit up the black and white 60s, to the Technicolor world of the 1970s where the red-haired Bremner became the talisman for the next generation of diminutive and not-so-diminutive Scottish giants.

For Leeds United the decades post-1975 would be turbulent in the extreme, combining both a League Championship victory in 1992 under the captaincy of Edinburgh-born Gordon Strachan alongside administration and relegation to the third tier of English football. However, despite their many travails, Leeds United remain one of the best supported clubs in British football, and thanks to the large number of their countrymen who played for them in their glory years of the 1970s, retain a considerable fan base amongst Scots of a certain age whose only other connection with Yorkshire is intermittent viewing of *Emmerdale*. But as they proudly still say in Stirling, Edinburgh and many other parts of Scotland, regardless of the official result of the 1975 European Cup Final – 'We are Leeds, Champions of Europe.'

## Can We Have Our Ball Back, Amigo?

The 2010 Football World Cup Finals in South Africa was a curious affair for the Scottish football fan. With Scotland comfortably failing to qualify for the third Finals in succession, the Tartan Army were once more excluded from the opportunity to converse with bikini-clad Brazilian beauties and of course the inevitable, melancholy return home after the first round (which, as the years went on, increasingly began to take on the nostalgic sheen of halcyon, happier times). There was, of course, always the clear and present danger of England actually managing to string three or four fortuitous results together and emulating the class of 1966, but once that dreaded scenario had been averted when the English were finally put out of their misery at the Last Sixteen stage, Scots could settle down to a stress-free and neutrally objective remainder of the tournament.

Under normal circumstances, watching sport where one has no strategic or sentimental leanings can be a strangely dissatisfying experience. However, anyone who was fortunate enough to be amongst the hundreds of Spanish congregated in the Three Sisters bar in Edinburgh watching the war of attrition that was the World Cup Final between España and the Netherlands could not fail to be swept up in the passion and fervour of witnessing a nation win the ultimate prize in world football for the very first time – even if one did have more than a pang of sympathy for the handful of unfortunate Dutch fans who had clearly found themselves in the wrong pub.

For Spain, who became the eighth country to win a World Cup, it finally put to rest all those jibes (almost exclusively from the English media) that they were the great under-performers of international football, who for whatever political or sporting reasons had never managed to replicate the success they had achieved in club football when it came to the major tournaments. This over-worked stereotype was comprehensively challenged in 2008 when Spain had won the European Championships and was now completely demolished by victory in South Africa, with it becoming painfully self-evident to the English that the tag of 'serial under-achievers' was now one that they themselves were clearly stuck with. And if this English discomfort was in itself not enough of a reason for Scots to join in the celebrations for the Spanish success of 2008 and 2010, then the higher-minded amongst them can also point to the crucial role that Scots had played in the origins of Spanish football.

In 1984, after ten years of La Liga failure since the glory days of Johan Cruyff, the despondency amongst the support of the Catalan giants Barcelona had only deepened with the departure to Napoli of the most exciting talent in world football, one Diego Armando Maradona. It was therefore imperative that a major international star would have to be found as a replacement to attempt to placate the Barca faithful, but few would have expected that man chosen to take on such an impossible mission would be a gallus Glaswegian who began his career as a midfielder for Clyde.

Steve Archibald had first come to prominence when he was converted into a predatory striker in Alex Ferguson's first League title win as a manager (the 1980 Scottish League Championship with Aberdeen). Archibald then immediately moved to Tottenham Hotspur where he won both FA Cup and UEFA Cup Winners' medals and became established, if not universally appreciated, as a regular in the Scottish national side. For all his success, it was still somewhat of a shock, however, when in 1984 Archibald was transferred to the Catalan giants of Barcelona, but would remain at the Camp Nou for three successful years. Above all, it was his debut season of 1984–85 where he truly made his name, snaffling fifteen goals to make him top scorer in a Barcelona side who won their first La Liga since 1974 by a comprehensive ten points.

The following season Archibald would feature in the Barcelona side that would reach the European Cup Final and crucially would score the vital away goal in their 2–1 aggregate semi-final win over the holders Juventus. For Barcelona in 1986, for all their history and all the club's glorious achievements, the European Cup remained the ultimate prize, and the sancta sanctorum, for while their Castilian arch-enemies, Real Madrid, had won the Cup on six occasions, Barca to their continuing pain and purgatory had still never won.

With the European Cup Final of 1986 being held in the Spanish city of Sevilla and with the opposition the unfashionable and un-fancied Steaua Bucharest from Romania, it seemed that the Catalans would never have a better opportunity to join the pantheon of European champions. However, in one of the worst finals in European Cup history (and there have been many to choose from), Barcelona could not break down the Steaua defence and crashed out on penalties. It would be another six years (and five years after Archibald had departed) before Barcelona could finally join the elite of Europe and add their name to the list of teams to be crowned Champions of Europe, and while by 1992 it would be fair to say that Diego Maradona (the man whom Steve Archibald had replaced at Barcelona) may indeed have eclipsed the Scot as the greater player on the international world stage, it was still the former Clyde player who of the two was more deserving of a homage in Catalonia.

If Barcelona had lifted the Cup six years earlier in Sevilla in 1986 with Archibald leading their attack, it would indeed have been highly appropriate as it was in the Andalusian capital on 8th March 1890 where the first football match in Spain to follow association rules was ever played and as you have probably suspected it was primarily all down to another Scot. The 1890 match was contested by the home team of Sevilla and also from Andalusia, Huelva, and it was in the mining town of Huelva that football in Spain can be said to have truly begun.

The background to the beginnings of Spanish football was the decision in 1873 by the Spanish government to sell the potentially lucrative mines on the Rio Tinto in Andalusia to an international consortium headed by Edinburgh-born industrialist Hugh Matheson. Incidentally Hugh Matheson was the nephew of James Matheson from Sutherland who was one-half of the famous Jardine–Matheson partnership who through the lucrative trade of opium in the nineteenth century, helped establish the British colony of Hong Kong and remains one of the largest conglomerates in Asian business today. Back in Andalusia, Hugh Matheson's consortium established the Rio Tinto Company and became the major source of copper mining in the world, bringing in large numbers of workers – predominantly from England but from other parts of Britain as well – to work in Andalusia and in particular the mining town of Huelva.

It was British workers who brought football with them to Spain, but it was thanks to the enthusiasm and determination of Alexander Mackay, a Scottish doctor who hailed from the Highlands and was employed in Huelva by Rio Tinto as a medical officer, that Spain's first football club was founded.

Mackay was a great proponent of the benefits of organised sport, and on 23rd December 1889, under his auspices the Huelva Recreation Club was formed. Initially, the team was made up almost solely of British expatriates, and in the famous first game in 1890, the entire Sevilla team and nine of the Huelva side were British, with only the remaining two Huelva players representing the local Spanish population. However, from such modest beginnings the game of fútbol slowly spread from Andalusia in the south to the Basque country in the north and then on to the major metropolitan areas and finally the rest of the country, culminating in Spain becoming one of the leading and finally the *numero uno* football nation in the world, and leaving their original British teachers in their 'tiki-taka' wake.

Dr Mackay and the British footballers of Huelva would eventually leave and return home, but they would forever remember those sporting years in the Andalusian sun when back in Britain they tucked into their half-time oranges.

As for the Huelva Recreation Club, who would change their name to the more Spanish Recreativo de Huelva, they have remained a mainstay of Spanish League football for well over a century. And while never quite reaching the same heights as many of the clubs that followed them, as recently as 2006–2009 Huelva could be found in La Liga (the premier division of Spanish football) and in December 2006 shocked the mighty Real Madrid no less with a 3–0 victory in the Bernabeu.

In honour of their longevity and their position as the oldest club, Huelva are known as 'El Decano' or 'The Dean' of Spanish football, and while they may not have attained the acclaim and the trophies of the great Castilian, Catalan and Basque clubs that have dominated the history of Spanish football, it can never be denied that a fixture against the team that was founded by a Scottish doctor way back in 1889 is anything other than 'one Huelva game'.

## *Red Devils in Disguise*

In 2011 Manchester City defeated their closest rivals, Manchester United, on the way to winning the FA Cup, their first domestic trophy for thirty-five years. For the disappointed United fans, defeat was shrugged off as nothing more than a minor irritation as they went on to win their record nineteenth League title and an appearance in another Champions League Final. But for supporters of Manchester City, decades of pent-up hurt, resentment and self-deprecation about being perennially overlooked and overshadowed by their nearest and dearest were joyfully released in a Wembley wonder-wall of celebration. And for some City fans, thoughts began to wander to a future where they would not only become the richest and most successful football club in the world, but that, more importantly, they would become the richest and most successful football club in Manchester. It was a time of hope and optimism for the City faithful, but for those who truly knew their club's history; it was not the first occasion that the blue moon had threatened to light up the city of Manchester only to be submerged by an all-encompassing red dawn.

In 1904, Manchester City won their first major trophy, the FA Cup, and came second in the League, and would have gone one better the following year if they had not lost in the final game of the season.

Manchester City were the rising force in English football in the beginning of the twentieth century and included in their team the greatest player of the generation, 'the Welsh Wizard' Billy Meredith, and heading their attack was one Sandy Turnbull from Hurlford in Ayrshire. It only seemed a matter of time before City won the League and began a period of dominance in English football; however, in 1905 City's dreams were in tatters when they were found guilty of illegally paying their players above the minimum wage and their entire first team was suspended. For City this was a disaster, but for Manchester's second side, Manchester United, who had only changed their name from the previous Newton Heath in 1902 and were at the time playing in the Second Division, this was an opportunity not to be missed. And on 1st January 1907, four of the best City players, including Turnbull and the great Meredith, were signed by United and the balance of power in Manchester irrevocably shifted.

With Turnbull top scorer with twenty-five goals, United were runaway winners of the 1908 League title, the first in United's history, and crucially had succeeded where City had previously failed – and to make matters worse, it was the former City players who had ultimately made all the difference. In 1910 United won their first FA Cup, with Turnbull scoring the only goal in a 1–0 victory over Bristol City at Crystal Palace, and in 1911 they won their second League title.

Turnbull remained with Manchester United until 1915, a colourful and strong-minded character willing to take on opposing defenders and the football authorities in equal measure. But his career was once more brought to a shuddering halt, with this time no hope for a second chance, when he received a suspension for life after being implicated in a betting scandal. With his football career over, Sandy Turnbull joined up to fight in the First World War where in 1917 he would sadly die in France at the age of thirty-two. Turnbull's body was never found and his principal role in the first great Manchester United team is little remembered today, but of all the legendary Scots who left a legacy at the club, it was the man from Ayrshire who was the first.

In Edwardian Britain football was booming, having well and truly crossed over from its public school beginnings to become the working man's enthusiasm of choice. And in order to cater for this newfound public demand, new giant sporting citadels had to be constructed. A prime example of this was Manchester United, who in 1902 under their previous name of Newton Heath were on the brink of financial ruin, but only eight years later with new owners and new success they were rich enough to build the largest club football ground in the land, and there was only one man to go to when you wanted a new football stadium built.

Archibald Leitch was a Glasgow architect who made his reputation when he designed Ibrox Stadium and Hampden Park in his native city in 1899 and 1903, respectively.

Over a forty-year period, Leitch was the football architect *par excellence* and was involved in the design and redevelopment of over thirty sporting stadia throughout Britain and Ireland and had more landmark buildings to his name than those other famous Scottish architects, Charles Rennie Mackintosh and Robert Adam, put together.

Millions of football fans knew by heart the names of those Saturday afternoon crucibles where their heroes performed, but very few knew the name of the unassuming Glaswegian who built these stages where dreams were made. It was in the era before the First World War that Leitch was at his most influential, moving from Ibrox and Hampden in Glasgow to the development of Stamford Bridge in 1905, Goodison Park and White Hart Lane in 1909, Highbury Stadium in 1913 and in February 1910 a brand new home for Manchester United, that with a capacity of

80,000 would make Old Trafford the largest club football ground in England.

In October 1945, thirty-five years later, the Theatre of Dreams was in ruins, having been severely bombed in the Second World War, and would not be reopened until 1949. Between 1945 and 1949 Manchester United would temporarily play their games at Maine Road, the home ground of their magnanimous City neighbours. In the year between the two World Wars the Mancunian axis had shifted once more. City had won both the League and the FA Cup, but United had not won anything since their last League title of 1911, and following the precedent of history it was to a former City player that United now turned, and so entered the next legendary Scottish Red Devil.

As with his contemporaries Hughie Gallacher and Alex James, Matt Busby hailed from Bellshill in Lanarkshire and had moved to England at the age of seventeen to sign for Manchester City in 1928. He remained at Maine Road until 1936, winning an FA Cup Winners' medal in 1934 in the process, before moving to Liverpool where he became club captain.

Busby's playing career would end by the Second World War, and when the war was over in 1945 the thirty-six-year-old Scot was appointed the new manager of Manchester United in his first managerial position.

Busby was one of the first of a new breed of modern football managers, taking training, wearing a tracksuit, having complete control over team selection and crucially deciding on who should be transferred in and out of the club. As with another Scottish manager forty years later, it would take Busby seven years to win a League title, but in the interim a string of second places, an FA Cup victory in 1948 and the return to Old Trafford in 1949 had strengthened and established the Busby revolution.

The first League title victory of 1952 would see the beginning of an era where Busby and his Welsh assistant Jimmy Murphy would assemble the best young talent in the country. Nurtured and developed by Busby, these players became known as 'the Busby Babes', the like of which English football had never before seen. United won the League in 1956 and 1957, and when Busby defied the English football authorities to become the first English champions to enter the European Cup in 1956–57, it was only the great Real Madrid team of Alfredo di Stefano that defeated them in the semi-finals.

On 5th February 1958 Manchester United once more qualified for the European Cup Semi-Finals after a hard-fought draw in Yugoslavia against Red Star Belgrade. The following day, the Manchester United party chartered a plane from Belgrade to fly back to England (and so enable them to fulfil their weekend league fixture that the English FA insisted must be played as scheduled), with the plane stopping off in Munich for refuelling. Of the forty-four people on the plane that attempted to take off that afternoon, twenty would lose their lives in the snow of the Munich airfield and another three – including the colossus of the team, twenty-one-year-old English international Duncan Edwards, who despite his age was already one of the greatest players in the world – would die in hospital from their injuries. Eight of the Busby Babes died in Munich and another two would never play again. Busby himself would remain in hospital for nine weeks, his injuries so severe that he would be administered the Last Rites, so minimal were his chances of surviving.

Matt Busby returned to manage Manchester United the following season and began the painful transition of rebuilding a completely new team. There had been no Scots in the precocious Busby Babes, but now Busby began to look to his native land. Hamilton-born forward David Herd (the son of Alec Herd from Fife who won a Winners' medal in Manchester City's first League title in 1937) was signed from Arsenal; midfielder Pat Crerand joined from Celtic; and most crucially of all, the greatest Scottish striker of his (or arguably any) generation joined in 1962.

Denis Law was born in Aberdeen but never played club football in Scotland. He made his debut for Huddersfield Town in 1956 as a sixteen-year-old, made his international debut in 1958 at the age of eighteen and had already demonstrated that he was an exceptional talent by the time he joined Manchester City in 1960. It was with City in January 1961 that Law once scored six goals in an FA Cup tie versus Luton, only for the game to be abandoned with twenty minutes to go because the pitch was waterlogged. Law also scored in the rescheduled match, but on that occasion Luton would end up victorious, meaning that the Scot had scored seven goals in one match and still ended up on the losing side.

Law only spent one season at City before another big-money transfer to Torino in Italy, the first Scottish football international ever to play for a club outside Britain and the first British player to be transferred for £100,000, but he failed to settle in Italy and within a year was back in Manchester for another British transfer fee record, however, not to return to Maine City but to join his fellow Scots at Old Trafford and become yet another former City star who had gone over to the red side.

With Law in place to lead the attack of a Manchester United side that included Bobby Charlton and an emerging young Irishman by the name of George Best, United won first the FA Cup in 1963 (with Herd scoring twice and Law once) in a 3–1 win over Leicester and then two League titles in 1965 and 1967. Even in such exalted company, it was the Aberdonian Law who was nicknamed 'The King' by the United faithful, scoring over 200 goals with his trademark outstretched right arm celebration between 1962 and 1973, scoring forty-six goals alone in the 1963–64 season that still remains a club record and in 1964 was voted the first, and so far only, Scottish winner of the European Footballer of the Year.

After their English League title in 1967, the 1967–68 European Cup campaign would be Matt Busby's fourth attempt to lift Europe's premier club trophy, a trophy that since Munich 1958 had become both to him and the club a personal Holy Grail. And while Celtic under Jock Stein had become the first British club to lift the European Cup the previous year, the honour of being the first English club was still on offer.

In their three previous attempts Busby's United had gone each time at the Semi-Final stage, but in 1968 they would finally reach the European Cup Final that would be conveniently held at Wembley Stadium in London (where even then it was alleged that there were more United supporters in the capital than there were in Manchester itself).

On 29th May 1968, Manchester United defeated the former Champions, Benfica, 4–1 after extra-time to become European Champions for the first time. They would do so without the great Denis Law, who in the biggest disappointment of his sporting career would watch the Final from a hospital bed after suffering a serious knee injury. The middle of the park, however, would still have the Glaswegian Pat Crerard, the 'heartbeat' of the United team, and he would join the eleven Lisbon Lions of 1967 in the list of Scots to win a European Cup Winners' medal.

However, above all, the triumph belonged to Matt Busby, now Sir Matt Busby, the revolutionary, inspirational and autocratic man from Bellshill who, twenty-three years after he first walked into war-torn Old Trafford and ten years after surviving the tragedy that had ripped apart his greatest team, had finally won the European Cup, so enshrining the mythology and legend of Manchester United as Britain's favourite football team, revered by their supporters, admired by neutrals and hated by everyone else. And it is a mythology that would never have happened without Matt Busby and Denis Law, and before them Sandy Turnbull, all of them Scots, and all of them former Manchester City players, but as the song says, 'Don't look back in anger', as there is always an oasis in the oil-rich desert.

## Take the Long and Winding High Road

The 2010–11 season was yet another campaign of thwarted ambition and expectations frustrated for all the devoted fans around the world of Liverpool Football Club. They still held the record of more European Cup/Champions League victories than any other British team and they may have finally seen the back of one set of unpopular American owners to be replaced by Americans of hopefully a more benign nature, but never mind not winning the League title for a twenty-first season in succession, they finally had to stomach the bitter pill that, with Manchester United's nineteenth League Championship putting them one ahead of Liverpool's eighteen, it was now their northwest rivals who could claim the honour of being the most successful club in the history of domestic English football. And as for retaining their European advantage by five to three, even the most hard-core of Barca-supporting Liverpool fans had to admit that, while it was all quite amusing seeing United and Fergie once more humbled in Europe by Lionel Messi and friends, this *schadenfreude* was somewhat tempered by the inconvenient truth that Liverpool had failed to qualify for the Champions League for the second year in a row.

Yet Scousers are by nature a resilient and optimistic people and have suffered far worse in the past and survived, and Liverpool Football Club – who (with apologies to all the eternally overlooked Evertonians out there) have, along with The Beatles, come to represent the city around the world – responded in the face of adversity by re-appointing as manager, after a twenty-year interregnum, their greatest-ever player and someone who was not just a sporting living legend, but Merseyside football royalty itself.

Only time will tell whether the second coming will have the same success as the glory days of the first, but if you know your history of Liverpool FC – that most Scottish of all the major English clubs who were christened 'the team of the Macs' on their formation in 1892 – then you will realise that sanctioning the return of King Kenny was the only appropriate and logical step that the new board, or any board, could have taken when faced with adversity – for although Liverpool may cherish their hard-won and deserved European and global reputation, none of it would have been possible without the influence of Scots.

Since the days of the dashing Alex Raisbeck from Polmont, who became Liverpool's first Championship-winning captain in 1901 and 1906, every time that the club has been successful there has always been a Scot at the forefront. Donald McKinlay from Glasgow was captain of their third and fourth League titles in 1922 and 1923, and in 1947 he would be followed by Willie Fagan from Musselburgh. Fagan played for Liverpool for fifteen years in a career interrupted by the Second World War, and in the post-war years it would be two more Scottish Williams who would become became the club's dominant figures.

Billy Liddell was born outside Dunfermline in Fife and joined Liverpool as a sixteen-year-old in 1938. Like Willie Fagan he would lose six years of his career to the war and did not make his League debut until 1946, but from then until 1960, twenty-two years after he had first travelled to Anfield, Liddell was a constant presence in the Liverpool forward line, making over 500 appearances and scoring 215 League goals, and long before the advent of the discount supermarket Liverpool was re-christened 'Liddellpool' in his honour.

For all Billy Liddell's unstinting efforts, the 1950s marked a period of deep decline for Liverpool and they were relegated in 1954. Five years later, with little sign of progress or promotion, they made the fateful decision to appoint the second William from Scotland who in the ten years of his varied managerial career to 1959 had never managed a club in the top division.

Bill Shankly came from the small East Ayrshire mining village of Glenbuck and was the youngest of five brothers who all escaped a life in the pits by playing professional football. Bill Shankly moved to England at the age of eighteen and made his name at Preston North End where, as with most footballers of his generation, a promising career never reached its full potential due to the outbreak of war.

In 1949, at the age of thirty-five, Bill Shankly was appointed manager of Carlisle United, and so began a decade at the metaphorical coalface of lower-league management that would take in the cultural hotspots of Grimsby, Workington and Huddersfield before Shankly's arrival as manager of Liverpool in December 1959. Shankly was determined to resurrect the fallen giants of English football, but his revolution would take time, and it was not until 1962, the same year that older brother Bob managed Dundee to their first and only Scottish League title, that Liverpool were finally promoted back to the top division.

As part of his transformation of the club, Shankly had seen a complete overhaul of the playing staff, with Billy Liddell finally retiring in 1961. However, as one legendary Merseyside Scot left it would be the arrival of two others in the very same year who would take Liverpool to the next level. Ian St John from Motherwell, who had already established himself as a prolific forward for his home club, and defender Aberdonian Ron Yeats, who played for Dundee United, were both signed in 1961 and proved the pivotal new figures on the pitch, with St John leading the attack and Yeats, the appointed captain, leading the defence.

With another Ayrshire man in goals, Tommy Lawrence, who was affectionately christened 'The Flying Pig' on account of both his agility and his stocky build, Liverpool won the League twice in 1964 and 1966 and the FA Cup in 1965. And Ron Yeats, who was known as 'The Colossus', became the fourth Scot after Raisbeck, MacKinlay and Fagan to lift the League Championship trophy.

But it was Shankly who was the driving force behind the new Liverpool, a highly intelligent and passionate man who never forgot his Ayrshire upbringing or his socialist principles, and his musings on life, death and football became as much a part of Merseyside folklore as The Beatles. It was Shankly who introduced the world-famous all-red Liverpool strip in 1964, and acquainted the world with the cult of 'The Boot Room'. This small room (where the boots were kept) was where Shankly and his coaching staff, which included future Liverpool managers Bob Paisley and Joe Fagan and fellow Scot Reuben Bennett from Aberdeen, would meet and discuss players, opponents, tactics, football in general and anything else that came to mind. Above all, though, Shankly was responsible for the Liverpool Way, where football was played simply and on the ground, pass and move, pass and move, pass and move until you had passed and moved your opponents off the park. Fitness was essential, and even more important was the unbreakable spirit that Shankly inspired and demanded from his team and his unquestionable devotion to the success for Liverpool Football Club that was in turn reciprocated by the fans. Shankly loved Liverpool and The Kop loved Shankly. And at the end of the 60s when The Beatles split up and the team of Yeats and St John started to decline and football was no longer a funny old game, Bill Shankly began the process of building a second great team that won the League and UEFA Cup in 1973 and the FA Cup in 1974 before he shocked the football world by announcing his retirement.

Shankly was sixty years old, in his prime by today's managerial standards, but after fifteen years at Anfield he felt it time to walk away, a decision he would quickly come to regret. Unlike the other members of the legendary Scottish triumvirate (Matt Busby and Jock Stein), Bill Shankly had never succeeded in lifting the ultimate trophy, the European Cup, but with his longstanding assistant Bob Paisley and with a team consisting of players, often previously unheralded, that he had signed and moulded into world-beaters, Liverpool became the third British side to win the European Cup in 1977. It was Paisley who was manager and Kevin Keegan who was the star player for the triumph in Rome, but to paraphrase one of his most famous quotes, it was the man from Glenbuck in Ayrshire who was more important than that.

There had been no Scots in the 1977 Liverpool European Cup team, but when Keegan departed immediately afterwards for the hair salons of Hamburg, Bob Paisley once more followed the tried and tested formula of venturing north of the border to find his replacement. In fact, Paisley signed three Scots in the next six months, all of whom, hard as it was to imagine in 1977, became even more influential figures than the sainted Keegan, in what would become the most successful era in Liverpool's history.

Defender Alan Hansen from near Alloa in Clackmannanshire was signed from Partick Thistle; midfielder Graeme Souness from Edinburgh arrived mid-season from Middlesbrough and above all, Kenny Dalglish from Glasgow, four-times Scottish League winner, captain of Celtic and the best player in Scotland, was bought for a British record transfer fee. All three Scots were in the Liverpool side that won the European Cup Final at Wembley in 1978 against Bruges, and they repeated this achievement in 1981 against Real Madrid at Paris, and again in 1984 against Roma in the Italian club's home stadium. Only the great Real Madrid side of the 1950s and 1960s had won the European Cup more times.

\* \* \*

In the era of Dalglish, Souness and Hansen between 1977 and 1991 Liverpool would win the European Cup three times and the English League title eight times. Kenny Dalglish scored the winner in the 1–0 victory over Bruges and became the first Scot to score in a European Cup Final since Tommy Gemmell in 1970. Graeme Souness captained the side to three League titles in succession from 1982 to 1984 and lifted the European Cup in Rome in 1984, and as Liverpool's moustachioed and menacing midfield general, he was the latest in a long line of Scottish playmakers from Alex James to Dave Mackay to Billy Bremner, who ensured that nothing or no one would prevent them from bossing the middle of the park, and left a trail of mayhem across the fields of Europe in the process.

Souness departed Liverpool after the European Cup Final of 1984, but both Dalglish and Hansen remained, with King Kenny having established one of the greatest striking partnerships in British history with Welshman Ian Rush. Continued success seemed ensured; Liverpool were the dominant club in England and English clubs had won the European Cup in seven of the previous eight years, but this particular era would come to a horrific end with the Heysel Stadium disaster and the tragic death of thirty-nine Juventus fans during the 1985 Liverpool–Juventus European Cup Final. As a result, all English clubs were thrown out of Europe and a shattered Liverpool appointed the thirty-four-year-old Dalglish as their new player-manager.

It was a brave appointment of an untried manager who furthermore still had a vital role to perform on the pitch and it could have gone horribly wrong, but in his very first season of 1985–86, Dalglish managed a Liverpool side that won both the League and the FA Cup. This was the first and only time that they had won the double. Alan Hansen became the second Scot (after Frank McLintock with Arsenal in 1971) to captain an English double-winning side, and Dalglish became the second Scot (after George Ramsay in 1897 with Aston Villa) to manage an English double-winning side, with Dalglish himself scoring the winning goal against Chelsea at Stamford Bridge, and so clinching the League title. Under Dalglish Liverpool would win two more League titles, in 1988 and 1990. Alan Hansen would take his total number of English League Winners' medals to eight – a then-record haul for a player – and they would be joined in the Liverpool side (still as good as any of its predecessors but without the opportunity to demonstrate this in European competition) by the versatile defender/midfielder Steve Nicol from Irvine, who won five League titles between 1983 and 1990, and Glasgow-born midfielder Ray Houghton who won League titles in 1988 and 1990.

Despite being born in Glasgow, Houghton would elect to play international football for the Republic of Ireland and in 1990 became the first Scot to reach the last eight of the World Cup Finals since the Scottish-Americans who played for the USA in the World Cup of 1930. The Irish team of Italia 1990 would finally be knocked out of the tournament by the host nation, but would gain some semblance of revenge four years later in 1994 when Houghton scored the only goal in a famous 1–0 group match victory in New York. Houghton won seventy-three caps in a ten-year career for the Republic and is arguably the most successful Scots-born export in the history of international football with any Scottish disgruntlement at his decision to commit to the country of his father somewhat lessened by the fact that Houghton also scored the only goal in Ireland's win over England at Stuttgart in Euro 1988.

Alan Hansen finally hung up his boots in 1991, and his retirement would signal a marked rise in 'terrible defending' across the country, but while Hansen's departure was not unsurprising, it would be a shock on the same level as the exit of Shankly in

1974 when Kenny Dalglish suddenly announced his resignation in February 1991. He had been manager for less than six years and was not yet forty years old, but in a tenure that had seen both triumph and the terrible tragedies of Heysel and the Hillsborough disaster of 1989 where ninety-six Liverpool fans lost their lives, those six years must have felt like a lifetime.

Twenty years later, Liverpool's and arguably Scotland's greatest-ever player returned to Anfield. Ironically, he was now the same age Bill Shankly was when he retired, and there were no guarantees whatsoever that the restoration of King Kenny would succeed when all of his successors in the past two decades had tried but failed to add to Liverpool's eighteenth league title that Dalglish himself had won in 1990.

But as we have seen from their very formation and throughout their history, Liverpool's success has almost exclusively been based on Scottish foundations, and appropriately one of Dalglish's first signings in the summer of 2011 was midfield playmaker Charlie Adam. So, will the Dundee-born Adam help return Liverpool FC to the pinnacle of English and European football and become the latest Scot to join the roll call of Liverpool legends that has included Raisbeck, MacKinlay, McQueen, Fagan, Liddell, Shankly, Yeats, St John, Souness, Hansen and above them all, Kenny Dalglish himself? As the King himself might say, 'Mebbes aye, mebbes naw.'

## *Sir Alex and the Merrie Men*

As we have seen, historically it is golf that can truly lay claim to the honour of being considered Scotland's national game. And furthermore horse racing, motor-sport, boxing and in certain strata of society even rugby union, also all have their diehard adherents and aficionados, but when it comes to column inches, internet chatter, cable sports subscriptions and the sports and pastimes section of the few endangered bookstores that remain, it is 'the beautiful game' that still reigns supreme. And even though we watch *Match of the Day* rather than *Sportscene*, would rather go to B & Q at the weekend than see our nearest SPL club and struggle to name, never mind picture, a single footballer in Scotland who does not play for Celtic or Rangers, it is still football that stirs the soul, captures the imagination and breaks your heart when you forget to change your Fantasy Football team by the Saturday morning deadline.

It is difficult what to make of the state of Scottish football in the twenty-first century so far. Both Celtic and Rangers have reached the final of a major European tournament, the UEFA Cup (now the Europa League) in 2003 and 2008, respectively, and regularly attract 60,000 and 50,000 supporters, respectively, to Celtic Park and Ibrox. Yet while the Old Firm remain two of the best known and best supported clubs in the world, both have found themselves inexorably dropping out of the list of the world's richest football clubs and struggle to compete financially even with the second tier in England. And that was even before the administrators were called in.

As for the national team, hope springs eternal (or at least until the fifth game of the qualifying rounds when that 0–0 draw away to Moldova is not quite as good a result as we initially thought), and the Tartan Army are always enthusiastically welcomed as they come down the road in downtown Amsterdam, Prague and Tallinn, but Scotland have not qualified for any major finals since 1998, a situation that is unlikely to alter any time soon, especially when you consider that in the first-ever international of 1872, Scotland played six forwards (which compared to England's seven was even then deemed somewhat conservative), but in 2010 when they played the Czech Republic away, six had been reduced to zero.

Yet as pragmatists and realists point out, when it comes to international football you can only choose from the players at your disposal, and we are a long way from the golden age when all Scottish sides were almost universally made up of Scots and all the leading English clubs had at least three Scots in their first team, and even then Scotland regularly missed out on major finals. And as for Scottish football optimists (if such a rare breed actually exist), they will claim that sport is cyclical, that clubs and countries go through peaks and troughs that can last decades and with the appropriate financial investment and nurturing of talent, there will be new generations of Scots every bit as good as the Celtic team who won the European Cup in 1967, the Rangers and Aberdeen sides who won the European Cup Winners' Cup in 1972 and 1983, the Dundee United side who reached the UEFA Cup Final of 1987 and the various national sides who got knocked out in the first round of the World Cup Finals.

And furthermore, despite all the despondency and resignation concerning Scottish football in 2011 and all the nostalgia and deserved recognition of the legendary Celtic and Rangers players and teams of the past, the triumphant European nights that took place at Pittodrie and Tanna-dee-chee, and those bygone, carefree days when Scottish football was truly competitive and the rivalry between the various clubs' casuals even more so, there is still one regard where Scots in football have never been more influential.

The five most successful clubs in the history of English football are, on the basis of League titles won: Manchester United, Liverpool, Arsenal, Everton and Aston Villa (in that order) and at the beginning of the 2011–12 season four out of five of them were managed by Scottish managers. Even more remarkably, at a time when there will be weekends when no more than four Scots will actually manage to get a game in the whole of the English Premier League and there will be less than four in both the first teams of Celtic and Rangers, seven out of the twenty clubs in the Premier League will be managed by Scots, and all from a radius even smaller than that of the Lisbon Lions.

The players that they recruit may be multi-lingual multi-millionaires from all over Europe, Latin America, Africa and the rest of the world, but the men who decide which of these superstars starts and which gets sent on loan to QPR all talk with the same defiantly uncompromising West of Scotland accent that has served Scottish managers in England for more than a century.

The magnificent Scottish seven that began the English Premier League 2011–12 season (and curiously a far greater number than actually managed in the SPL at the same time) and all hailing from within a twenty-mile radius were Alex Ferguson of Manchester United (born Glasgow), Kenny Dalglish of Liverpool (born Glasgow), David Moyes of Everton (born Glasgow), Alex McLeish of Aston Villa (born Barrhead), Owen Coyle of Bolton (born Paisley), Steve Kean of Blackburn (born Glasgow) and the youngest of the septet Paul Lambert of Norwich (born Paisley).

Paul Lambert had joined Celtic in 1997 and as an accomplished defensive midfielder he had been captain of the Celtic team that had lost the UEFA Cup Final in extra-time to Jose Mourinho's Porto in 2003 in Sevilla. This game became famous for the 50,000 to 80,000 Celtic fans that travelled to Andalusia, so continuing the long-standing relationship between Scotland and the Spanish city that hosted the first football match in Spain in 1890 – although that Scots–Spanish relationship can, in fact, go back even further to 1797, when a consignment of Sevilla oranges arrived in Dundee and Dundonian Janet Keillor turned them into marmalade.

For the exemplary behaviour of their unprecedented travelling support, Celtic fans were awarded the FIFA Fair Play Award of 2003, the second time that Scottish supporters had won this award after fans of Dundee United won in 1987 for the sporting reception the Tannadice crowd gave to IFK Gothenburg, who had just defeated them 2–1 on aggregate to win the UEFA Cup Final. The United fans were the inaugural winners of the Fair Play Award, a highly prestigious accolade given to the best example of outstanding sporting behaviour in football in the world for that year, although one can but only suspect where long-serving and long-suffering United manager Jim McLean would have ideally liked to have stuck it.

Lambert went on to have a distinguished career for both the Glasgow club and for Scotland, but he had actually made his international reputation in 1996, one year before joining Celtic, when he made the unlikely switch from Motherwell to German giants Borussia Dortmund. Lambert only played for one year in the Bundesliga, but swiftly became a regular in the side and a fan's favourite, and after Dortmund had knocked out Manchester United in the semi-finals of the Champions League, he played a starring role in the Final against Juventus in Munich on 28th May 1997 by setting up one goal and marking a certain Zinedine Zidane out of the match as Dortmund won a famous 3–1 victory. 1997 remains the only year that Dortmund have won the European Cup or Champions League, and Lambert was the first Scot to win a Winners' medal for a club on the European continent and remains to date the last Scot to play in a winning Champions League side. Which only goes to show the talent you can find if you keep going to Fir Park long enough.

Juventus had been the pre-match favourites for the final in 1997 and the Turin giants have long been the most successful club in Italian football with more Serie A titles than any of their rivals. What is less known, however, is that when the first national Serie A Championship was held in 1929–30 it was an unheralded Scot from Edinburgh, George Aitken, who was managing the *bianconeri* or 'the black and whites'. Aitken, a dignified and respected figure in Juve history, managed Juventus from 1928 to 1930 and led them to a third-place finish in the very first Serie A season, but would leave the club immediately before the glory years of their five titles in succession between 1931 and 1935, and retired into obscurity, another all but forgotten Scottish football pioneer on the continent of Europe.

When it comes to Scottish managers winning the ultimate club prize in Europe, three Scots have won the European Cup or Champions League – Jock Stein with Celtic in 1967; Matt Busby with Manchester United and Alex Ferguson, also with Manchester United in 1999 and 2008, in two of the most dramatic nights in European football history at the Camp Nou in Barcelona versus Bayern Munich, and the Luzhniki Stadium in Moscow against Chelsea.

The statistics of Alex Ferguson's managerial career are phenomenal. Alongside his two Champions League victories, he also twice reached the Final in 2009 and 2011, won the 2008 FIFA World Club Cup and the Intercontinental Cup in 1998 (the only British side to win either trophy), and at the beginning of the 2011–12 season Alex Ferguson had won twelve English League titles between 1993 and 2011, six more than Bob Paisley of Liverpool and Scot George Ramsay of Aston Villa a century before. In fact, of the eleven managers who have won three or more League titles since 1988, six have been Scottish – Ferguson, Ramsay, Busby, Kenny Dalglish, Frank Watt (with Newcastle United between 1905 and 1927) and Bill Shankly. So perhaps it is no wonder English chairmen remain so keen to appoint managers from north of the border. Furthermore, Ferguson's three League and FA Cup doubles of 1994, 1996 and 1999 are the most won by any manager, and when you add in his three Scottish League titles with Aberdeen between 1980 and 1985, it gives him to date a grand total of fifteen League titles in Britain, leaving him only three behind the eighteen won by legendary Rangers manager Bill Struth between 1920 and 1954 – and who is to say that even at the age of seventy Ferguson is not going to surpass even that extraordinary achievement?

When one thinks of the Ferguson era at Manchester United, the great teams that he has built and re-built over the twenty-five years and counting since he arrived in 1986 and the legendary names of Giggs, Scholes, Keane, Cantona, Schmeichel and Ronaldo that have turned the Old Trafford club into the greatest in the world, it is easy to forget that amongst all the international superstars Brian McClair from Bellshill and Darren Fletcher from Dalkeith have both been at different times integral players in United's midfield and both have four League Winners' medals to prove it. And furthermore, it was with the all-Scottish Aberdeen side of Miller, McLeish, Strachan et al, that Ferguson first made his international reputation. In May 1983, the Dandy Dons overcame the mightiest side in the history of European football, Real Madrid, with the great Alfredo di Stefano (who as a boy Ferguson had watched score a hat trick in the great 1960 Real Madrid–Eintracht Frankfurt European Cup Final at Hampden) as manager, to win the European Cup Winners' Cup. Aberdeen's victory in a rain-drenched Gothenburg remains the last time to date that a Scottish club has won a European trophy and saw the greatest Scottish invasion of the Swedish city since the substantial Scots community settled there in the seventeenth and eighteenth centuries, and the Aberdeen fans of 1983 felt so at home in the city that they briefly even forgot to complain about how expensive the drinks were.

The late 1970s and early 1980s saw an unprecedented run of success for Scots in Europe. The Liverpool trio of Dalglish, Souness and Hansen had won three European Cups in 1978, 1981 and 1984, but while the Anfield club's victories reinforced their position as the premier team in Europe, the era would also witness triumphs from some more unlikely locations.

In 1981 Aston Villa, who at the end of the nineteenth century had been the leading side in England under the stewardship of Glaswegian George Ramsay, won their first League title since Ramsay's last of 1910, seventy-one years before. Villa had been unexpected League Champions in 1981 and were not one of the favourites to do well in Europe, but they were to prove all the doubters wrong by progressing to the European Cup Final the following year, where they would meet Bayern Munich in Rotterdam in May 1982. Three Scots were at the heart of the Villa side – the all-Fife central defensive partnership of Allan Evans from Dunfermline and Ken McNaught from Kirkcaldy, and in front of them midfielder Des Bremner from Aberdeenshire. Bayern Munich were the pre-match favourites, but it would be the team who proudly display the Scottish lion rampant on their club crest that would take the European Cup back to Birmingham with a narrow 1–0 victory. In hindsight, no one should have been too surprised by Villa's victory. 1982 was the sixth year in succession that an English club had won the European Cup, and if Aston Villa were an unexpected addition to the list of elite European clubs that had lifted the trophy, then they could be considered football nobility when compared to the team that had twice won in 1979 and 1980.

Despite being founded way back in 1865, Nottingham Forest only had two FA Cups to their name when Brian Clough came to the Second Division club in 1975. Scots had already played a prominent role in Forest's history, with John McPherson the captain and goal-scorer in their 1898 3–1 FA Cup Final victory over arch-rivals Derby County. Clough, who had of course first found managerial success at the aforementioned Derby where he signed the legendary Scot Dave Mackay (who was actually one year Clough's senior) to lead his team into the First Division, wasted no time in bringing a coterie of Scots to begin his latest football revolution.

Midfielder Archie Gemmill from Paisley and forward John O'Hare from Renton in Dunbartonshire had both featured in Derby County's shock 1972 League title race, when the outsiders ended up one point ahead of three other clubs on the last day of the season to win their first League title, and were recruited along with tempestuous Glasgow-born striker Kenny Burns and one final member of the 1972 Derby side, Montrose-born defensive midfielder John McGovern. McGovern had been signed by Clough at lowly Hartlepool as a sixteen-year-old schoolboy at the start of Clough's managerial career and followed his mentor for the best part of twenty years, first to Derby County then the brief and ill-fated disaster that was Leeds United of 1974, before finally moving on to Nottingham Forest where he was made captain.

In 1977, Forest were promoted to the First Division, and in their very first season took the English game by storm to win their first League title in the club's long history. McGovern was captain; Gemmill, who had been captain of Derby County's second League title in 1975 (when Dave Mackay had been Clough's managerial successor), was the driving force in midfield; Kenny Burns was converted into a disciplined (more or less), no-nonsense centre-half and John Robertson from Uddingston, the one Scot who Clough had inherited rather than signed, was transformed from being an unheralded, under-performing and unfit Second Division wide man into the most exciting and deadliest left-winger in the entire League.

To demonstrate that their League title had been no fluke, Forest then knocked defending champions and previously invincible Liverpool out of the European Cup the following season and went on to defeat Malmo 1–0 in the Final in Munich in May 1979.

Archie Gemmill, who had proven so integral to the rise of Forest, was, along with a certain Martin O'Neill, surprisingly omitted from the final eleven, but at least he would have the consolation of being the only player in the history of English football ever to have won three League titles whilst playing for teams in the East Midlands, a record that one imagines is unlikely to be broken anytime in the near future. However, McGovern, Burns and Robertson all played in Munich that evening in 1979, with Robertson setting up Forest's only goal and McGovern becoming the second Scot since Billy McNeill to lift the European Cup.

One year later, on 28th May 1980 at the Bernabeu in Madrid, Nottingham Forest returned to defend their title of European champions in the final against a Hamburg team that included the reigning European Footballer of the Year and England's finest, Kevin Keegan. McGovern, Burns and Robertson were all still in place and were joined by left-back Frank Gray – the first and so far only Scot to appear in European Cup Finals with two different clubs, having played in the debacle that was Leeds United's defeat in Paris in 1975. If Forest had been the favourites the previous year against Malmo they were very much the second favourites against the German champions and were out-played and battered for almost all of the game. But in the twenty-first minute John Robertson, the winger from Lanarkshire whose skill, craft, trickery and intelligence belied his stocky stature and perceived lack of pace in the same manner that Scots wingers, inside-forwards, strikers and midfield schemers had shown ever since football had first been played, received the ball wide left, dropped his shoulder to beat his man, moved inside, played a one-two, and from the edge of the box drilled the ball into the corner of the net.

Nottingham Forest held on to Robertson's moment of magic to retain the European Cup 1–0. Robertson joined Tommy Gemmell, Stevie Chalmers and Kenny Dalglish as the only Scots to have scored in a European Cup Final, and the unassuming John McGovern became the only Scot to lift the European Cup for a second time. It may seem incongruous in today's Champions League, where the richest clubs in Europe spend billions on maintaining their supremacy over the rest, that clubs such as Aberdeen, Aston Villa and Nottingham Forest could ever have defeated the biggest names and won the greatest trophies on such a regular basis, but it just goes to show what is possible in football with a genius manager and a handful of Scottish players, and preferably both together. A scenario that, as far as the manager part is concerned still remains to this day, even if having Scottish players in your team seems sadly to have been temporarily abandoned.

And as for the Scots who played for the Nottingham Forest team of 1978 to 1980, John McGovern, the most successful Scottish captain in European football, astonishingly would never win even one cap for his national team, although whether this was because there were so many great Scottish midfielders around at the time (and remember this was in an era when even Graeme Souness was not picked for over three years) or because he had been in England for so long that successive national managers actually forgot that he was Scottish has never been fully explained. John Robertson, Kenny Burns and Archie Gemmill would all go on to play for Scotland in the 1978 World Cup Finals, and Robertson and Frank Gray would also feature in the 1982 Finals in Spain.

On 11th June 1978 in Mendoza, Archie Gemmill would score twice in a 3–2 group stages victory over the Netherlands. Gemmill's first goal was a penalty, but it is for his second in the sixty-eighth minute where he beat three world-class Dutch defenders before coolly chipping the keeper to score that he will always be remembered. One of the greatest goals in World Cup history and the only moment in Scottish World Cup history that can in any way be considered enjoyable, Gemmill's goal has become the personification of all that is best about Scottish football. The wee, tough Scot leaving one of the best defences in the world on their backsides as he jinks and dribbles around them in an incredible demonstration of skill, nerve and undying defiance.

Yet for all that Gemmill and that goal is held up to the world as a personification of all that is great and magical about Scottish football, it is a memory that in truth sits uneasily with the history of the game in Scotland. For Gemmill, Dalglish, Souness (who all played in Mendoza that day) and all the other legendary Scots who have graced the game since 1872 in Scotland, in England and in Europe, they were professional sportsmen, and above all *winning* professional sportsmen, who, once they had tasted victory, wanted to taste it again and again, and defeat, no matter how glorious or how iconic, was still a defeat and nothing to be proud of.

# Post-Match Analysis

Sport matters. And to many, sport matters a great deal. It is the sage of Glenbuck, East Ayrshire, the legendary Liverpool manager Bill Shankly, who is attributed to have once said that 'while some people see football as a matter of life and death, it is more important than that', and Shankly's words, no matter how mischievous, have frankly over the centuries repeatedly found an echo in the pride and the passion, the pain and the ecstasy in what sport means to millions around the world. And as for that oft-repeated homily that sport and politics should not mix, the evidence of the past century of organised sport is that, rather than there having been some golden age of idealised and noble separation with sport existing as an expression of international competition and fair play at its purest, sport and politics have from the very beginning been intertwined through the social, economic, racial and political circumstances of the participants, clubs and countries involved. The post-war introduction of European sporting competitions, the advent of the Commonwealth Games, the Cold War rivalry between the USA and the USSR and the intermittent meetings between India and Pakistan on the cricket and hockey pitch are all examples of sport being seconded to promote political integration or help prevent the countries involved from bombing each other into obliteration.

And if there is any further doubt about the implicit relationship between sport and politics, then one need look no further than the machinations and the geo-political power struggle involved – not forgetting the billions invested and wasted in the bidding and hosting of sport's two greatest international showpieces – the Olympic Games and the Football World Cup Finals –

where sporting considerations and colossal debt are but nothing compared to the prestige and the power on offer to the political leaders who get to have their photo taken with David Beckham and Rihanna, and the financial benefits that can be attained by local businesses specialising in fireworks, transportation and vuvuzelas.

And as we have seen, wherever there are multi-million sports and sporting competitions around the world, attracting multi-millions in sponsorship and with multi-millions watching on television, we have found that there have been Scots throughout history at the forefront as players, managers, administrators and innovators – and was it not John Logie Baird from Helensburgh who was the inventor of television itself back in 1926?

The first football international in the world was played in Glasgow in 1872, and it was Scots who led the way in football's early development, first in England and then exported to Central Europe and South America. The first rugby international in the world was played a year earlier in 1871, and lost in the mists of time it was Scots who had invented the game of golf that in the twentieth century would take over America and then the rest of the world. For these achievements alone Scotland can rightly claim an undeniable place in the history of international sport, but when you add to this Scotland and Scots' involvement in the birth of such diverse sports as horse racing, cycling, ice hockey and water polo and the twentieth-century exploits of Scots in motor sport, boxing, baseball and athletics (to name but a few), you begin to realise the extent of Scotland's contribution to the sporting world that we know today.

The history of Scottish sport can best be differentiated into two parts (as I have already used the game of two halves analogy once, to do so again at this late stage when we are approaching the light at the end of the tunnel would just be a Gael Clichy too far), and those are: on one side the individual sporting Scot and on the other Scotland, the sporting nation. The history of the sporting Scot is one that mirrors the story of Scots for centuries who have travelled the globe for fame and fortune, and once established in their adopted home and given the Scots abroad tendency never to take orders from anybody, have wasted little time in acquiring as much control over the levers of powers and influence as possible – hence your tradition of Scots as authoritarian, disciplinarian, omnipotent managers, coaches and captains with West of Scotland accents remaining firmly intact no matter how many decades they have spent away (as scientific research has proven, nothing puts the fear of God into a group of sportsmen more than an incomprehensible Glaswegian with a glint in his eye and a bee in his tracksuit).

Without the sporting Scot, the English Premier League would never have become the dominant (or one of the leading two) football leagues in the world, and within that Premier League there would be very different clubs at the top, so influential have Scots been in the rise of so many of the leading sides. Without the sporting Scot, golf would never have been exported to America, would never have flourished across the Continent and without those pioneering Scottish golf course designers, Tom Bendelow and Donald Ross, and the hundreds of courses they built from the Atlantic to the Pacific, the world of golf may never have discovered the joy of beige. And without the sporting Scot's longstanding passion for speed and racing in all its forms, as exemplified by such greats as Jim Clark, Jackie Stewart and Chris Hoy, the very term 'the Flying Scotsman' that is recognised today as an internationally accepted alternative to the more traditional Dutch variation would have undoubtedly become as incongruous as the delayed 10:30 Express from King's Cross to Edinburgh Waverley.

In comparison, the story of Scotland as a sporting nation has followed its own very distinctive path and one that can be said to be one step ahead of its political destiny. While Scotland was prepared to share its greatest sporting invention, golf, and its greatest and oldest tournament, The Open, with its UK neighbours and for over a century they were more than happy to concede that any ambitions on the cricket pitch, although admittedly well-hidden, would be best satisfied under the English flag of St George, when it came to the twin sports of rugby and football the Scots would take a distinctly independent, or if you prefer (in the spirit of political balance), a distinctly separatist route.

As we have seen it was at Raeburn Place in Edinburgh in 1871 and at Hamilton Crescent in Glasgow in 1872 that, respectively, the first rugby football and association football internationals were held in the world. But what made those fledgling sporting encounters between what was after all two constituent parts of the same sovereign nation who shared the same parliament and the same head of state so important, was that if these matches between England and Scotland were to continue, then administrative bodies would have to be formed. And it was the fateful and far-reaching decisions by those pioneering sporting Scots to found within a few days of each other in 1873 first the Scottish Football Union (later the Scottish Rugby Union) and then the Scottish Football Association in order to protect the right of Scotland to play rugby and football under the name of Scotland, under its own national flag and under its own national colours, that truly established Scotland as sporting nation in its own right.

In many regards these events were perfectly logical. In the Victorian nineteenth century, only the British Isles actually played football and rugby, so without the division of the British Isles into its original kingdoms and principalities, international competition could not have existed. And perhaps more pertinently, as far as Scotland was concerned, in the years leading up to the turn of the century the Scots just happened to be very good at both of them, and in the case of football, exceedingly so. However, the determination to continue an independent Scottish sporting identity in the world of the twentieth-century, where international sport became increasingly synonymous with national political sovereignty and in a British political and constitutional environment where the Scottish National Party would not be founded until 1934 and would gain little electoral support until forty years later, does display a very Scottish 'thrawnness' ingrained by decades of sporting endeavour through adversity on the wind-lashed links courses of Fife and East Lothian and the boggy mud-heaps that pass for football pitches in Glasgow and South Lanarkshire.

It can even be argued that the true Scottish sporting identity of the past 140 years is, when all is said and done, not in fact particularly prescient to Scotland the nation, but to be honest, more a stubborn determination of when it came to sports we were actually quite good at never again being dictated to by anybody else. And all the saltires and lion rampants, and 'Flower of Scotland' and Tartan Armies that would follow were merely cultivated accessories added on for purely commercial reasons and to make the original premise slightly more positive. However, as with all mythology and as is especially true of a nation that bases a national tourist industry on a reclusive prehistoric sea creature living in a lake and the notion that all of its male population wear skirts, if you repeat this mantra for long enough, history can be rewritten and the legend does indeed become fact – especially, as in Scotland's case, when there is no television or Inter-web-net-tube-footage to show a time when Scottish sport had not been tartan.

Perhaps the final irony of the many contradictions of the Scottish sporting national identity is that while Scotland the political nation has slowly but inexorably become more nationalistic, Scotland the sporting nation has become slowly but as inexorably less successful when it comes to international sport. True, the SNP's breakthrough by-election in Hamilton in 1967 coincided with the same year that Scotland defeated the then World Champions, England, at Wembley and Celtic won the European Cup, and furthermore the disastrous Scottish campaign in Argentina in 1978 after months of patriotic fervour and interminable marching with Ally's Army did precious little for a nation's self-confidence when it came to the first Devolution Referendum the following year. However, when it comes to Scotland in the twenty-first century, there is little in the way of evidence to back up any theory that national sporting glory (or the lack of it) has an influence on how a country feels about itself and the people that govern them, as the newly devolved Scots appear to show a continued enthusiasm for ever greater powers no matter how often their football team fail to qualify for major tournaments, how often their club sides get knocked out of Europe before Christmas and how often their rugby side finishes bottom of the Six Nations. And who of us even ten years ago would ever have predicted a situation where Scotland would have a government with an absolute Nationalist majority and simultaneously tennis would be its most successful sport?

Yet if there is anything that encapsulates the Scottish sporting spirit over the centuries more than anything else, it is that very same 'thrawnness' that lies at the core of so many of our great sporting Scots and the ability to recover from innumerable setbacks, troughs of despondency that can last for decades and even a sporting public that has long since resigned itself to the acceptance of mediocrity and disappointment. For as long as Scotland continues to produce such sporting greats as Henry Cecil, Alex Ferguson, Dario Franchitti, Katherine Grainger, Chris Hoy and Andy Murray, then the great tradition of the sporting Scot can be sustained around the globe. And when, or in the case of Sir Alex if, these sporting superstars finally decide to bid their farewells and ride, drive, row, cycle and stride off into the sunset of life as a television pundit, a new generation of sporting Scots will emerge. And if history tells us anything these new sporting Scots who have graduated from their training on the Wii and have made the perilous journey beyond the sitting room will appear when least expected and in the most unlikely of places and sports.

In the meantime, Scottish sport will continue its long and winding odyssey at its historic national citadels of Hampden Park and Murrayfield, the crucibles of Celtic Park and Ibrox, and the great links courses of St Andrews, Muirfield, Troon, Carnoustie and Turnberry (that despite all the riches on offer in America, Europe and Asia make winning The Open in the country that will always be the 'home of golf' the ultimate and greatest prize in the sport).

And looking forward, in 2014 Scotland will host in the Perthshire setting of Gleneagles, the biennial Ryder Cup for the first time in thirty-one years, and will also see for the first time since 1986 the return of the Commonwealth Games, the largest sporting event ever to be held in Scotland with up to seventeen different sports and up to seventy-two national teams descending on Glasgow. All the city's famous sporting stadiums of Hampden Park, Celtic Park and Ibrox will feature prominently in the 2014 Commonwealth Games, with Hampden hosting the athletics and the Closing Ceremony, and so bringing full circle an illustrious and continuous history that first began when the world's most legendary sporting architect, Glasgow's Archibald Leitch, designed the stadium in 1903 as the new home for Queen's Park and Scotland, respectively the greatest football club side and national team of the nineteenth century.

Scotland may have long since lost their pre-eminent role in international football and all the other sports in which they were to prove so influential in the early years of their development, but what the history of sport also shows is that, despite a population of only five million, Scotland has consistently produced individuals and teams that have left their mark on international sport and become revered around the globe. And it is for this outstanding contribution over so many sports in so many countries and for so many years that Scotland can with some justification lay claim to not just being 'the home of golf', but 'the home of sport' itself – and even today, every now and again, we are still occasionally allowed to win.

# 50 Great Sporting Scots

Everyone likes a list, and of no sector of the population is this truer than the sports-obsessed male (and occasionally, if far less frequently, the sports-obsessed female) who from their formative years have immersed themselves in sporting statistics, dates, averages and the eternal debate of discussing given the data accrued and memorised over years of study who were the best, who were the most successful, who were the most talented and who in the ultimate poll of polls were the greatest. For that is who we are and that is what we do.

Compiling a list of the greatest sporting Scots is a thankless task, which even with a total of fifty to play with results in debatable choices, painful exclusions and glaring omissions. It is difficult enough trying to compare the achievements of sportsmen and sportswomen from different generations who have actually played the same game – so much have their sports evolved and radically changed over the decades and centuries, never mind then extrapolating this inherently unscientific, purely subjective and many would say totally pointless exercise to compare and contrast sports as diverse as rugby and motor racing, swimming and baseball before finally coming up with a final list of fifty.

To make matters slightly easier, I have followed the long-lasting, but now obsolete, rule of the Scottish Football Association that no matter what the circumstances and no matter how long the bloodline, only players who were actually born in Scotland could ever play for Scotland – an unbending policy that lasted for the best part of a century, and incidentally completely at odds with the policy of the Scottish Rugby Union which since the very beginning has seemed to be to select as many players not from

Scotland as humanly possible. Therefore, sporting luminaries such as the inventor of basketball, James A. Naismith; Scottish rugby's record-breaking winger Ian Smith; US Masters winner Sandy Lyle; legendary Olympic champions Eric 'Chariots of Fire' Liddell and swimmer David Wilkie; one of rugby's greatest coaches, Ian McGeechan, and what seems like half of the current Scottish football team, are all regrettably excluded from consideration. Not that this makes finalising the selection of the final fifty any easier, but such difficulties and self-imposed restrictions are to the dedicated list-compiler merely conundrums that must be overcome. For that is who we are and that is what we do.

The final list of fifty covers four centuries of sporting excellence and innovation. As one would expect, football and golf, the two sports that can lay claim to be Scotland's national game, are well-represented, but despite this bias towards the tried and tested, twenty-one sports in total are featured in the final list – a demonstration (if one was needed) of how Scotland and Scots have taken sport in all its many varieties to their hearts, or perhaps more realistically to their wallets, as if you can't make a living out of one then there are plenty more to choose from.

You will also see that in the final fifty there are precious few female sporting greats. This can, of course, be partly explained by the history of sport across the world, where despite the laudable exploits of the fishwives of Musselburgh in the early nineteenth century, the Victorian lady golfers of St Andrews and the pioneering performances of Glasgow swimmer and Olympic gold medallist Belle Moore in Stockholm in 1912, sport has been and arguably remains a social and cultural male preserve with sportswomen and women's sport perennially struggling to gain the recognition, media coverage and financial rewards of their male equivalents. And when you combine this with Scotland's long tradition of being a male-dominated society, that unlike England's seemingly historical preference of being ruled by someone wielding a handbag, has seen no female leader or national figurehead as Scottish head of state since Mary, Queen of Scots 450 years ago (and that did not exactly turn out very well), it is perhaps not so surprising that so few Scottish sportswomen have made the final selection. But when all is said and done, the three women chosen on the list are still three more than the short-list for the 2011 BBC Sports Personality of the Year.

So we are left, for good or for ill, with a final list of fifty great sporting Scots. Many of these Scots were chosen because they were the best in their particular field, world-beaters without peer. Others were innovators and inspirational figures who changed the history of their sports forever. And others again featured and were responsible for some of the most legendary and iconic moments in global sporting history. No attempt has been made to rank the final fifty in any order of merit or achievement, as even for the most dedicated of list-compilers there are some commissions that just hurt the brain too much.

However, to the question of who of all the numerous sporting Scots was the greatest of them all – I give you one name. A sporting Scot who was unquestionably the best of his generation – not just in Britain and Europe but also throughout the entire world. And a sporting Scot who during his career and in the decades that have followed has become a legendary and revered figure, with a reputation for humility and grace to complement an incomparable talent, genius and passion for his sport and a list of achievements that have never been surpassed. Our greatest sporting Scot – it can only be Jim Clark. But then again, as you can see, there are plenty of other deserving contenders.

JOHN RATTRAY, born Perth & Kinross (1701–1771), golf. Captain of The Honourable Company of Golfers – the oldest surviving golf club in the world – and author of the 1744 *Rules of Golf* – the oldest surviving rules of golf in the world.

'OLD' TOM MORRIS, born Fife (1821–1908), golf. Four-time Open Champion and for fifty years greens-keeper and club professional at St Andrews – 'the home of golf'.

WILLIE PARK, born East Lothian (1833–1903), golf. Four-time Open Champion and in 1860 first-ever winner of a golf 'major'.

ANGUS BUCHANAN, born Argyll & Bute (1847–1927), rugby union. In 1871 the first player to score a try in international rugby.

'YOUNG' TOM MORRIS, born Fife (1851–1875), golf. Four-time Open Champion and youngest player ever to win a 'major'.

CHARLES CAMPBELL, born Perth & Kinross (1854–1927), football. Captain of Queen's Park and Scotland, in the 1870s and 1880s the greatest football club and country in the world.

GEORGE RAMSAY, born Glasgow (1855–1935), football. First captain and manager of Aston Villa, leading them to six English League titles in a fifty-year career with the club.

BILL MACLAGAN, born Edinburgh (1858–1926), rugby union. In 1891, winning captain of the first-ever Test series by the British Isles.

JAMES BRAID, born Fife (1870–1950), golf. Five-time Open Champion.

ALEX RAISBECK, born Falkirk (1878–1949), football. Captain of Liverpool's first two English League titles.

WILLIE ANDERSON, born East Lothian (1879–1910), golf. Four-time US Open Champion – equal most US Open titles ever won.

WILLIAM KINNEAR, born Aberdeenshire (1880–1974), rowing. Olympic gold medallist single sculls, 1912.

JOHN ('JUAN') HARLEY, born Glasgow (1886–1960), football. International player and coach with Uruguay and credited as the inspiration for introducing the style of play that would see Uruguay become football's first World Champions.

HAROLD MAHONY, born Edinburgh (1887–1905), tennis. Wimbledon Men's Singles Champion, 1896.

TOMMY ARMOUR, born Edinburgh (1894–1968), golf. Winner of all three 'majors' of his era – The Open, the US Open and the US PGA.

JIMMIE GUTHRIE, born Borders (1897–1937), motorcycling. Three-time European Champion and multiple Isle of Man TT winner – greatest motorbike racer in the world in the pre-WWII era.

ALEX JAMES, born North Lanarkshire (1901–1953), football. 'Wembley Wizard' of 1928 and midfield general in Arsenal's first four English League titles.

CHARLIE GARDINER, born Edinburgh (1904–1934), ice hockey. Stanley Cup-winning captain, 1934, and one of the greatest goaltenders of all time.

ARCHIE JACKSON, born South Lanarkshire (1909–1933), cricket. Youngest player ever to score a Test cricket century for Australia.

MATT BUSBY, born North Lanarkshire (1909–1994), football. Won five English League titles and one European Cup, 1968, with Manchester United.

BILL SHANKLY, born East Ayrshire (1913–1981), football. Liverpool's most famous and inspirational manager and winner of three English League titles.

BENNY LYNCH, born Glasgow (1913–1946), boxing. Undisputed Flyweight Champion of the World.

JOCK STEIN, born South Lanarkshire (1922–1985), football. Manager of Celtic's 'Lisbon Lions' – the 1967 European Cup-winning side.

BOBBY THOMSON, born Glasgow (1923–2010), baseball. Hit the homerun that won the 1951 National League pennant – 'The Shot Heard Around the World' and possibly the most iconic moment in the history of baseball.

DAVE VALENTINE, born Borders (1926–1976), rugby league. Dual-code rugby international and in 1954 first ever winning captain of the Rugby League World Cup.

JIM CLARK, born Fife (1936–1968), motor racing. Two-time Formula 1 World Champion and in 1965 became only driver to win Formula 1 Championship and Indy 500 in same year.

MURRAY ROSE, born Highlands (1939–), swimming. Won four Olympic gold medals for Australia in 1956 and 1960.

JACKIE STEWART, born West Dunbartonshire (1939–), motor racing. Three-time winner of Formula 1 Championship.

DENIS LAW, born Aberdeen (1940–), football. Won two English League titles with Manchester United and in 1964 European Footballer of the Year.

MIKE DENNESS, born North Lanarkshire (1940–), cricket. England Test cricket captain.

ALEX FERGUSON, born Glasgow (1941–), football. Managed Manchester United to two Champions League victories in 1999 and 2008, and with twelve English League titles has won more than any other manager.

WILLIE CARSON, born Stirling (1942–), horse racing. Five-time Champion Jockey and winner of fourteen British Classics, including four Derbys.

BILLY BREMNER, born Stirling (1942–1997), football. Captained Leeds United to two English Championships in 1969 and 1974

IAN MCLAUCHLAN, born South Ayrshire (1942–), rugby union. Ever-present in successive British Isles Test series victories in 1971 and 1974.

HENRY CECIL, born Aberdeen (1943–), horse racing. Six-time Champion Trainer and winner of twenty-five British Classics.

KEN BUCHANAN, born Edinburgh (1945–), boxing. Undisputed Lightweight Champion of the World.

JOHN MCGOVERN, born Angus (1949–), football. Captained Nottingham Forest to two European Cup wins in 1979 and 1980.

KENNY DALGLISH, born Glasgow (1951–), football. Liverpool's greatest-ever player, winning eight English League titles as player and manager and three European Cups.

ALLAN WELLS, born Edinburgh (1952–), athletics. Olympic gold medallist in the 100 metres in 1980.

FINLAY CALDER, born East Lothian (1957–), rugby union. Captain of the winning British & Irish Lions in 1989.

ROBERT MILLAR, born Glasgow (1958–), cycling. Winner of the 'King of the Mountains' in the 1984 Tour de France.

LIZ McCOLGAN (nee LYNCH), born Dundee (1964–), athletics. 10,000 metres World Champion at 1991 World Championships.

COLIN McRAE, born South Lanarkshire (1968–2007), rallying. Youngest-ever World Rally Champion in 1995.

STEPHANIE COOK, born North Ayrshire (1972–), modern pentathlon. First-ever women's Olympic modern pentathlon gold medallist in 2000.

PETER NICOL, born Aberdeenshire (1973–), squash. World Open Champion in 1999.

DARIO FRANCHITTI, born West Lothian (1973–), motor racing. Four-time winner of Indy Car series and twice winner of Indianapolis 500.

KATHERINE GRAINGER, born Glasgow (1975–), rowing. Six-time World Champion and silver medallist in three successive Olympics.

CHRIS HOY, born Edinburgh (1976–), cycling. Four-time gold medallist at 2004 and 2008 Olympic Games – equal most successful cyclist ever in Olympic history.

LAWRENCE TYNES, born Inverclyde (1978–), American football. Placekicker and two-time Super Bowl winner with New York Giants in 2008 and 2012.

ANDY MURRAY, born Glasgow (1987–), tennis. Three-time Grand Slam Singles finalist.